Jean-Étienne Liotard

French edition, 2002
Published on the occasion of the exhibition
*Jean-Étienne Liotard (1702–1789) dans les collections des
Musées d'art et d'histoire de Genève* at the Musée
d'Art et d'Histoire, Geneva,
from May 22 to October 27, 2002,
with the support of the Société des Amis des Musées
d'Art et d'Histoire de Genève.

Catalogue:
Claire Stoullig, former Curator of the Cabinet des
    Dessins at the Musées d'Art et d'Histoire,
    Chief Curator of the Musée d'Art et Archéologie
    of Besançon
Isabelle Félicité Bleeker, former Assistant Curator
    at the Beaux-Arts Department of the Musées
    d'Art et d'Histoire
Armelle Carreras, documentation
Cécile Roulet, rereading, corrections

New edition in English, 2006
Published on the occasion of the exhibition
Jean-Étienne Liotard (1702–1789): Swiss Master,
presented at The Frick Collection,
New York from June 13 to September 17, 2006.

Editorial coordination:
Colin B. Bailey, Chief Curator, The Frick Collection
Elaine Koss, Editor in Chief, The Frick Collection
Kristel Smentek, Andrew W. Mellon Curatorial
    Fellow
Hélène Meyer, Curator of the Cabinet des Dessins,
    Musées d'Art et d'Histoire
Caroline Guignard, Researcher at the Cabinet des
    Dessins, Musées d'Art et d'Histoire

Photographs
Bettina Jacot-Descombes
Flora Belivacqua
Atelier de Photographie, Musées d'Art et d'Histoire,
    Geneva

Edited and published by Somogy Éditions d'Art
Graphic design: Benoît Fleurance (French edition),
    ■ couleurrouge.com (English edition)
Translation from French: Charles Penwarden
Translation from German: Toby Alleyne-Gee
Editing: Cathy Lenihan
Fabrication: Michel Brousset, Béatrice Bourgerie
Coordinating editor: Isabelle Dartois
Assistant: Camille Aguignier

© Somogy Éditions d'Art, Paris, 2006
© Musées d'Art et d'Histoire, Geneva, 2006
© The Frick Collection, New York, 2006
© The authors, 2006
ISBN 2-85056-947-X
Photoengraving: Labogravure (Bordeaux), Quat'coul
(Toulouse), Color'Way (Arras)
Printed in Italy by RE.BUS srl
Legal registration: May 2006

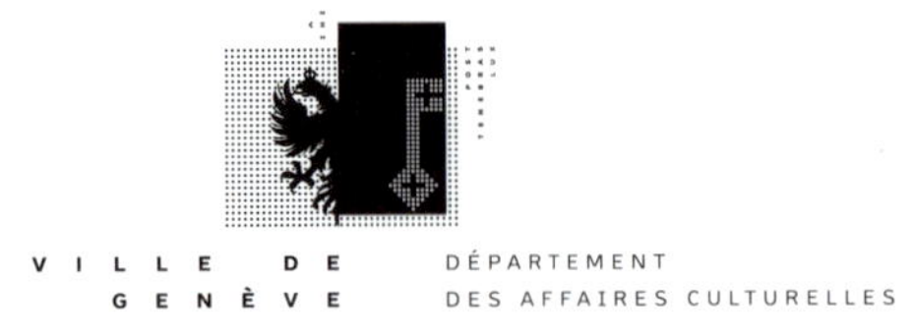

VILLE DE GENÈVE   DÉPARTEMENT
DES AFFAIRES CULTURELLES

Jean-Étienne Liotard

1702-1789

Masterpieces from the Musées d'Art et d'Histoire of Geneva and Swiss Private Collections

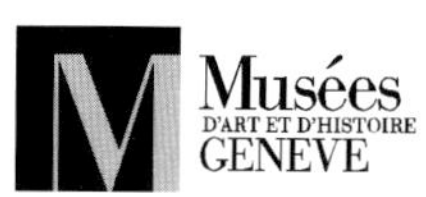

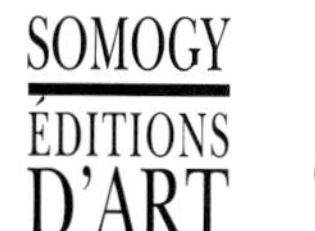

Musées d'Art et d'Histoire Genève

SOMOGY Éditions D'Art

The Frick Collection

Musées d'Art et d'Histoire, Geneva

Cäsar Menz
Director of the Musées d'Art et d'Histoire, Geneva

Danièle Fischer-Huelin
Administrator of the Musées d'Art et d'Histoire

Muriel Pavesi
Assistant Director

Christophe Cherix
Curator of the Cabinet des Estampes
assisted by Mayte Garcia-Julliard and Véronique Yersin

Estelle Fallet
Curator of the Musée de l'Horlogerie et de l'Émaillerie

Paul Lang
Curator in charge of the Beaux-Arts Department
assisted by Brigitte Monti and Laïla Tourki

Hélène Meyer
Curator of the Cabinet des Dessins
assisted by Caroline Guignard

Victor Lopes
Conservation and restoration of paintings

Valentine Greco and Gisèle Méroz
Restoration, mounting and framing of drawings

Véronique Strasser
Restoration, mounting and framing of engravings

Visual materials
Isabelle Brun-Ilunga and Marc-Antoine Claivaz
Atelier de Photographie, Musées d'Art et d'Histoire

Management of artworks and loans
Géraldine Quenet
Roberto Papis
assisted by Cinzia Ludovici
Nicolas Moro and the transportation service of the
Musées d'Art et d'Histoire

The Frick Collection, New York

Anne L. Poulet
Director

Colin B. Bailey
Chief Curator

Diane Farynyk
Registrar

Elaine Koss
Editor in Chief

Kristel Smentek
Andrew W. Mellon Curatorial Fellow

Mary Lydecker
Administrative Assistant to the Chief Curator

Acknowledgments

Our special thanks go to Renée Loche,
Marcel Roethlisberger, Estelle Fallet, and
William Eisler for their help in updating the
documentation for this catalogue and to Lisa Micara
for the restoration of the drawings.

Our warmest thanks, also, to Marianne Bervas,
Danielle Buyssens, Anne de Herdt, Elizabeth Fischer,
Michel Grillet, André Le Prat, Jean-François Méjanès
and Pierre Skira.
We are grateful to Charles Penwarden for his elegant
translation.

Presentation of the exhibition is made possible, in
part, through the generous support of Margot and
Jerry Bogert; Melvin R. Seiden in honor of Jean A.
Bonna and Inez and Yves Oltramare, with additional
support from Inez and Yves Oltramare; Jean A.
Bonna; Pro Helvetia, Arts Council of Switzerland;
The Helen Clay Frick Foundation; and the Fellows
of The Frick Collection. Transportation costs have
been generously underwritten by Swiss International
Air Lines. The catalogue is made possible, in part, by
Lawrence and Julie Salander.

Contents

Anne L. Poulet

Preface and Acknowledgments

An accomplished draftsman, painter, pastelist, miniaturist, and experimental printmaker, Jean-Étienne Liotard is one of the most fascinating and least familiar artists of the eighteenth century. The Frick Collection is pleased to present a monographic survey of the work of an artist who enjoyed an international reputation in his own time, yet is little known today, even among specialists. Inspired by Liotard's *Trompe l'œil* of 1771, bequeathed to The Frick Collection in 1997 by Lore Heinemann in memory of her husband, Dr. Rudolf J. Heinemann, this exhibition comprises paintings, drawings, miniatures, and prints from the Musées d'Art et d'Histoire of Geneva, the world's greatest repository of Liotard's œuvre, as well as pastels and other works from Swiss private collections. It provides a singular opportunity for the public to become better acquainted with the achievements of one of the most engaging artists of the Age of Enlightenment.

The project to bring Liotard to New York was the result of a friendly collaboration between the Chief Curators of the two institutions, and the selection of works from both the Musées d'Art et d'Histoire and from private collections has been made by Colin B. Bailey, a tireless advocate for the exhibition. We are immensely grateful to the Musées d'Art et d'Histoire in Geneva and to private lenders for so graciously agreeing to part, temporarily, with their remarkable Liotards. It is also a pleasure to acknowledge Professor Marcel Roethlisberger, doyen of Liotard studies, and Renée Loche who offered support and assistance throughout the project. More than three-quarters of the works in the exhibition have been lent by the Musées d'Art et d'Histoire. The museums' generous loans are admirably complemented by a selection of paintings, pastels, and miniatures from Swiss private collections, and we thank Jean A. Bonna, Walter Feilchenfeldt, Jan Krugier, Inez and Yves Oltramare, and those collectors who wish to remain anonymous. Most of the works in this exhibition have never been seen before in the United States, and we are grateful to our lenders for affording American viewers this chance to become more familiar with this highly original artist.

Our colleagues in Geneva have been enormously supportive of this project. Warmest thanks are due to Cäsar Menz, Director of the Musées d'Art et d'Histoire, Paul Lang, Chief Curator of the Art Department, Hélène Meyer, Curator of Drawings and her assistant Caroline Guignard at the Musées d'Art et d'Histoire in Geneva, for their unstinting help in coordinating the exhibition. It has been a pleasure to work with them. We are grateful as well to Estelle Fallet, Curator at the Musée de l'Horlogerie et de l'Émaillerie, Christophe Cherix, Curator of the Cabinet des Estampes and his assistant Véronique Yersin, as well as Nathalie Strasser and Rainer Michael Mason, former Curator of the Cabinet des Estampes.

At The Frick Collection we are grateful to Elaine Koss, Editor in Chief, who has coordinated the English edition of this book with Somogy, a dynamic publishing house with whom it has been a pleasure to collaborate, Nicolas Neumann, CEO, Jean-Louis Fraud, Isabelle Dartois, and Michel Brousset. We thank Diane Farynyk, Registrar and Exhibition Manager, Kristel Smentek, Andrew W. Mellon Fellow, who has worked with our Chief Curator in the installation and interpretation of the exhibition in New York, and Mary Lydecker, Administrative Assistant to the Curatorial Department.

Cäsar Menz

Surprising Liotard

Jean-Étienne Liotard, whose life, give or take a few years, spanned almost the entire eighteenth century and who died one month before the fall of the Bastille, was born on December 22, 1702, in Geneva. In 2002, the Musées d'Art et d'Histoire, which hold the richest and most important part of the artist's œuvre (four oil paintings, thirty-seven pastels, thirty-four drawings and seven miniatures and enamels), celebrated the tercentenary of Liotard's birth and published this book updated in this new edition.

A peripatetic, cosmopolitan painter who traveled through Europe and Asia Minor, an esteemed portraitist and prized and innovative pastelist, Liotard undoubtedly left a deep mark on the art of the eighteenth century. He was, alongside Jean-Baptiste Chardin, Rosalba Carriera, and Maurice Quentin de La Tour, one of the finest pastelists of his day. He was a portraitist to princes and to the bourgeoisie, to philosophers and artists. His art perfectly embodies the Enlightenment spirit of rationalism. Considered in his day as the "painter of truth," he met the requirements formulated by Roger de Piles in *The Principles of Painting* (1708): "Since in portraiture resemblance is paramount, it would seem that one must imitate defects as well as beauties, for then the imitation will be more complete." And, as Anne de Herdt, editor of the catalogue raisonné of Liotard's drawings, and curator of the exhibition held in 1992, observes: "The obsession with objective reality that so tormented Liotard was shared by the Genevan scientists of his day who, like the Enlightenment thinkers, saw the observation of reality as the first phase in an experimental process leading to knowledge." This experimental striving for truth, for reality, is magnificently expressed in the painter's many fascinating self-portraits, which touch us with their honesty and their profundity. But Liotard was more than just a portraitist or curious observer of everyday life when he sojourned in Asia Minor from 1738 to 1742. His penetrating gaze never failed and, in his final years, he made a series of still lifes that, in their simplicity, in the modesty of the means used, and in the clarity of their composition go beyond the art of the eighteenth century and possess a modernity that seems to prefigure the artistic experiments of Cézanne.

An eminently international painter, Liotard is still not very well known in North America, despite the presence of several of his masterpieces in Cleveland, at the Getty, and even in The Frick Collection. I am therefore deeply grateful to Colin Bailey, a most enlightened connoisseur of the eighteenth century, who, wanting to make this Swiss artist known beyond the frontiers of Europe, took the initiative for this exhibition based on the collections of the Musées of Geneva. I have no doubt that this outstanding event will be a real revelation for the public from New York and beyond, one that will greatly enrich their perception of the period and of its multifaceted art.

The original French edition of this book was published in 2002, to coincide with the exhibition at the museum in Geneva. It was edited by Claire Stoullig, then Curator of Drawings. She has since moved on to become Chief Curator of the Musée d'Art et Archéologie in Besançon. Her valuable work, and that of Fabienne Xavière Sturm, Isabelle Félicité Bleeker and Armelle Carreras, her collaborators at the time, remains highly germane, even if recent discoveries have clarified one or two dates, added new biographical data and led to the removal from the corpus of a pastel hitherto considered as a portrait of Liotard's son (inv. 1949–20), and a drawing of an unidentified woman (inv. 1993–51). For this new information we are indebted to Renée Loche and Marcel Roethlisberger, the dedicated compilers of the artist's upcoming catalogue raisonné. My warm thanks go to them for their cooperation and advice in preparing this new edition.

I would also like to express all my gratitude to the curators at the Musées of Geneva: Estelle Fallet, Hélène Meyer, Christophe Cherix, and Paul Lang, for their commitment to this undertaking and for the loans that they have generously granted to ensure that this fine exhibition in New York is a success.

Marcel Roethlisberger

Liotard and Europe

How does one pay homage? Liotard's public is familiar with him—as it is with most other painters regardless of category—via a few masterpieces made conveniently accessible by chance, exhibition, or design. In Liotard's case, in Geneva there is *Madame d'Épinay*, the *Self-Portrait, known as "Liotard with a Beard,"* the *Frankish Woman and Her Servant*, the *Portrait of a Young Woman in Turkish Dress Sitting on a Divan*; in Dresden, *La Belle Chocolatière*; at the Louvre, *Anne Tronchin*; in Amsterdam, *The Beautiful Reader*, and the *View from the Artist's Studio in Geneva*; in Cleveland, *François Tronchin*; at the Getty, *Maria Frederike van Reede-Athlone at Seven* and *Lord Mount Stuart*. Other paintings would join this parade of premium art, were they available for viewing: the two *Luncheon*s in England, the nine English royal children who adorn the queen's private salon, the royal portraits at the Weimar Museum (last on view in 1939), the case with eight miniatures of the French royal family, *The Tambourine* (pastel), the first version of the *Princess of Hesse*, of *Madame de Vermenoux*, and *Buttering a Piece of Bread*, among others.

The dominant selection criterion in this competition is the beauty of the sitter, over and above artistic beauty. The same happens throughout the history of art: painting is a trompe l'œil leading the viewer to take the mirage for the truth. The women in Turkish dress, the pretty young ladies, and the children depicted by Liotard please viewers more than his severe syndics and dignified officers. The large pastel of Maria Theresa of Austria at the age of forty-seven, without a doubt the most prestigious figure represented at the Musées of Geneva, has not found favor with critics. The counselor *François Tronchin* in Cleveland is accepted because his gaze, and ours, goes to Rembrandt's *Lady in Bed*, to which he is pointing. The *Self-Portrait, known as "Liotard with a Beard"* is impressive in both size and presence, and therefore "passes" the test, as Liotard himself did after his return from Constantinople (Istanbul), because of the oddness of his Turkish clothing (with which the painter himself managed to fascinate the empress, who was no bad judge of character), but is it beautiful?

Which Liotard should be presented? To represent the whole man—or, rather, all the objects and documents we have pertaining to him—we would need the catalogue raisonné (currently in preparation). But then, would we really want to see everything, including disparities in quality and in the state of conservation of his works? There are currently some four hundred and fifty paintings (oils and pastels), two hundred drawings, fifteen prints, an undefined number of enamels and miniatures (possibly less than a hundred), and a vast number of copies. Like porcelain, pastels are both extremely durable (they do not darken and require hardly any restoration) and fragile (volatile, vulnerable to dampness). And then there is the work of his youth: only four pictures survive from the years before his departure for Paris in 1723, seven from the dozen years he spent in the French capital (1723–35), eight from Italy (1736–37), and later, five from Holland (1771–72) and four from Vienna (1778). In other words, most is lost.

A selection, yes, but which selection? The dream exhibition, an unrestricted tour of highlights, cannot be realistically envisaged (too difficult to travel), and might also be too artificial, too idealized. It might be done as a set of color plates, but reproductions betray the originals. Rather than aim for a complete retrospective, whose chief determinants are limits on loans and capricious refusals, the Musées of Geneva chose to celebrate the tercentenary of the artist's birth by showing all of its Liotards (but not the prints) together for the first time: an excellent solution, for it conveys a historical reality that developed over two centuries of collecting, with the mixture of planning and chance that this implies.

The Musées of Geneva is the only institution with a collection capable of providing a genuinely representative survey of Liotard's œuvre (except for the 1720s and the work from his sojourns in Paris, Italy, and England). Ever since the *Self-Portrait, known as "with a New Beard"* was bequeathed to the Public and University Geneva Library (BPU), the public collection has grown harmoniously, decade after decade, more by luck (the five pastels donated by David Claparède in 1865, the permanent loan of the eleven drawings of the Austrian royal children in 1947) than by design. We shall not dwell here on the missed opportunities that no museum likes to mention. Works in long-standing local collections have left Geneva. Still, we should recognize that the twenty or so Liotard paintings acquired—and *exhibited*—by the big American museums do serve as eloquent ambassadors of Geneva.

Other groups of Liotard's works are the twenty-five pieces in Amsterdam, all but one of them donated by the artist's Dutch descendants in 1873 and 1885 (at a time when the Musées of Geneva had only nine Liotards); the two dozen formerly in the Salmanowitz Collection, most of them from the Tilanus-Liotard sale of 1934; eight in the Oskar Reinhart Museum at Winterthur, acquired between 1935 and 1957; twelve in the Royal Collection, England, ever since their execution; eight at Stupinigi; six in Weimar; and a score of drawings at the Louvre. Nothing in Zurich.

It is in the nature of any monographic exhibition or publication to glorify its subject and at the same time to isolate it from the historical, artistic, and economic context from which it emerged and in which it could not avoid acting. This is particularly true for Liotard who, throughout his life, and whether he was living in Geneva or beyond, was always an outsider, an individualist, with no students, a "soloist" (he had two collaborators in Vienna in 1744–45) who was imitated but had no followers, and formed no friendships like the one between Wolfgang-Adam Töpffer and Jacques-Laurent Agasse. The constant of his life was defined by his starting point: his apprenticeship in Geneva as a miniaturist and enameler, a discipline he perfected in Paris and would always pursue with matchless technical virtuosity as a second activity alongside pastel painting. His pictorial language is rooted in France, steeped in the atmosphere of the 1720s, just after Watteau's death. His Parisian master, Jean-Baptiste Massé, competent but little known, was probably more important to him than is thought. After his Turkish sojourn, Orientalism became another guiding thread through Liotard's work. It recurs throughout his life in different forms, in the costumes and the poses, or when he reprised earlier works. For Liotard, as for many European portraitists, from Holbein to Van Dyck and Élisabeth Vigée-Lebrun, travel was an economic necessity, as it was for many painters in his century, including Angelica Kauffmann, Sebastiano Ricci, Canaletto, and other Venetians who traveled beyond the Alps or across the Channel.

Not having been shaped by the constraints of any school or academy, Liotard belonged to none; he never fully belonged to any one local community and was hardly influenced by his contemporaries. In Paris, where he made three long sojourns totaling about eighteen years, he was refused the official recognition that he sought from the Royal Academy. He was never a threat to court painters. His famous Viennese portraits left no trace in the history of Austrian court portraiture. He did not become English, as Füssli (Henry Fuseli) or even Agasse did, or Saxon, like Anton Graff, nor did he become integrated in a school like Antoine Pesne did in Berlin. But it was precisely because of this lack of any kind of strict training in painting, coupled with his itinerant status, that he was sometimes able to overstep the boundaries. With the imperial couple, he was less bound by protocol than were other court painters. Chardin, in his portraits of humble servants and of children at the table, or in his still lifes, never relinquishes narrative embellishments or atmospheric effects the way Liotard does in *La Belle Chocolatière* and *Buttering a Piece of Bread.* Boucher endows his *Luncheon Party* with a much more bourgeois atmosphere than Liotard, whose treatment of the theme has a more incisive permanence. It was his refusal to conform that accounted for much of Liotard's success with a clientele eager for something different.

His register of types and themes is limited, but art and iconographic diversity are not the same thing. He made only three full-length portraits, and no group portraits. It is a pity that at the age of seventy-five he lacked the strength to execute the group portrait of his own family, with five or seven figures, for which he made preparatory drawings. In most of the half-length figure portraits the absence of arms and hands is cleverly hidden: no attributes, plain backgrounds. Among his finest works are a small number of Turkish and Western genre paintings, and two landscapes. From circa 1763 to 1771 he executed a few still lifes and trompe l'œil, in enamel, pastels, and oil, including the one in The Frick Collection.

Liotard's life spanned the entire eighteenth century, from Louis XIV to the French Revolution. The internal logic of his development hardly reflects the stylistic changes of the day, from Rococo to Neoclassical, terms that one would not instinctively apply to his art. He painted some of the great figures of his day: the pope (now lost), Austrian, French, English, and Dutch royalty, other princes and princesses, Voltaire and Rousseau (both lost), the marshal of Saxony, Count Kaunitz, English earls, Genevan syndics, "cameriere… contessine, baronesse." As at any other moment in history, the stratification of generations was complex: Hyacinthe Rigaud lived to 1741, Nicolas de Largillière to 1746. Liotard was also the contemporary of Pompeo Batoni, Joseph-Marie Vien, and then of Fuseli, Vigée-Lebrun, Anton Raphael Mengs, Goya's tapestries, David's *Oath of the Horatii*, and in Geneva of Jean-Pierre Saint-Ours, Pierre-Louis De la Rive, and the Hubers. To acknowledge the merits of other portraitists of the day is not to belittle Liotard. The recent Jean-Marc Nattier exhibition in Versailles revealed the splendor of his portraits, whose settings are nearly always more elaborate than Liotard's bust-length figures. Although in the shadow of Maurice Quentin de La Tour, the full-length figures in the pastels of Jean-Baptiste Perronneau have a dazzling elegance and richness that Liotard could never claim. Seeing such works—and those of La Tour, François-Hubert Drouais, and others— one can understand the reticence of French patrons and critics toward Liotard. One can also understand his bitterness as an old man seeing the success of Alexandre Roslin's magisterial portraits in Vienna.

Liotard's early progress in Geneva and, as of 1723, in Paris, seems to have been slow, but this merely reflects our almost total ignorance about it. He was thirty when he did his first "good" portraits. And while Rome was still the inspiration for all academically trained artists, Liotard was hardly affected by the two years he spent in Naples, Rome, and Florence (from 1736 to 1738). He copied the antique *Three Graces* and Bernini's *Apollo and Daphne*, he painted the exiled Stuart court in Rome; he knew Pier Leone Ghezzi, but had no contact with the Italian portraitists. It was his four years in Constantinople that suddenly revealed him as a quite unique European draftsman and painter. There he made French-style drawings in two colors that are extraordinarily fine, delightful genre scenes in pastel, Turkish-style portraits of important Western merchants and diplomats, epitomized by the small Turkish double portrait in oils at the Louvre. In comparison, the Turkish images by Jean-Baptiste Vanmour (1671–1737) and Antoine de Favray (1706–circa 1792) seem merely folkloric, and the fantastical *Turqueries* of Jacob Van Loo look theatrical. Little remains from the short year Liotard spent in Moldavia (present-day Romania).

After his departure from Turkey, he emerged as that surprising and unlikely bearded eccentric at the court of Vienna, where he stayed for two years, painting almost exclusively the royal family. With no prior experience, but as an accomplished master of faithful portraiture, he immediately adapted his technique to the requirements of royalty, with its coats of arms, changing fabrics, ermine furs, and frothy drapery. He created the most human portraits of the royals, but he could not shake the supremacy of the grandiose full-length court portraits by Martin van Meytens, which are not well known in this part of the world but are vital to understanding the context of Liotard's portraits. He repeated a few Turkish genre scenes and, perhaps as relief from the constraints of portraiture, painted the elegant chambermaid of *La Belle Chocolatière*, which he took with him at once to Venice, where it was admired by Rosalba Carriera and all the other painters. His probable encounter there with Pietro Longhi would inspire his works in the style of the *Princess of Hesse*. There followed a small number of German commissions: the Margravine of Bayreuth and her daughter, and the young Prince of Gotha, painted when the prince was traveling through Geneva.

Liotard's second Parisian sojourn, from 1748 to 1753, was richly productive, culminating in the series of royal portraits (without the queen) painted in a more compact, controlled style than in Vienna. These portraits went to Parma by inheritance and then, by an administrative quirk, to Stupinigi.

From this period we date the *Reclining Reader à la Turque* and the *Seated Woman à la Turque*, which he repeated on request in either oils or pastel.

England had always offered a receptive environment for painters from the continent. During Liotard's first sojourn, from 1753 to 1755, London proved more promising and stimulating than Paris, allowing him to renew his acquaintance with the aristocrats he had met and painted in Constantinople. Reynolds and Gainsborough, his juniors by a generation, were just starting their careers. The Royal Academy had yet to be founded. The charming portraits of Philippe Mercier, Francis Hayman, and Arthur Devis were less ambitious, but Allan Ramsay's portraits must have impressed Liotard. With its formal simplicity and tight composition, his portrait of the nine young children of the Princess of Wales is as fine as anything else in the history of child portraiture.

After his Parisian experience came the Dutch sojourn, during which he produced his most homogenous group of portraits and half-length figures, and the marriage to his young Franco-Dutch wife, with whom he settled in Geneva, where he made the unforgettable character head portraits of the aged women of the Tronchin family. In 1762 he made his second trip to Vienna, resulting in the large portraits of the sovereigns, including the portrait of the imperial couple at the Albertina, where he competes brilliantly with the courtly style, and *Maria Theresa of Austria* (Geneva), whose monumentality and heightened realism signal an artistic maturity corresponding with the stylistic developments of the day. About a decade later, the artist went to Paris to paint Dauphine Marie-Antoinette (the portrait has not survived), and made new trips to Holland and London, where his sitters included Earl Clanbrassill in a pose inspired by Joseph Wright of Derby, and members of the family of the Earl of Bessborough, his most loyal patron. In Geneva, Liotard received a number of illustrious visitors, such as the young Lord Mount Stuart in 1763, of whom he painted a very English full-length pastel with a final echo of Watteau in the pose, and, in 1777, Emperor Joseph II, who encouraged him to make his third trip to Vienna. This he undertook the following year, making a final series of imperial portraits (all but two of which are now lost). From now on, Liotard was isolated, wealthy, and had virtually no commissions. The European capitals were dominated by the august styles of Batoni, David, Vigée-Lebrun, Gainsborough, and Goya. Liotard never did produce a supreme masterpiece. Around him, there were no other portraitists in Geneva, except Jean-François Guillibaud, Jean Preudhomme, Huber in the Vaud; Saint-Ours was in Rome. He had no contact with Johann Caspar Füssli, Emanuel Handmann, or Jean-Melchior Wyrsch in Germanic Switzerland. His visit to Johann Caspar Lavater in Zurich in 1777 was cut short because of mutual ignorance. Liotard wrote his treatise not as an Enlightenment man of letters, as Hogarth or Reynolds did, but as a zealous technician. He took up mezzotint engraving and the minor genres of transparencies and still life. Removed from the context of his genre scenes, where they are prefigured, the fifteen or so still lifes of fruits and flowers painted from 1783 to 1786 are even more stripped down than those of Chardin, Anne Vallayer-Coster, and Roland de La Porte. Independent of the established conventions of still-life painting, these works of his seem timeless.

What does Liotard mean to us today? Museums and art historians can, in the space of an exhibition, bring back any historical epoch. Some artists from centuries past may connect with the present by virtue of a theme, a stylistic analogy, or a biographical detail (El Greco, Artemisia Gentileschi, Goya). Discoveries, too, can lead to exhibitions. There is no such imperative in Liotard's case. And yet he continues to interest us as a living heritage, especially in Geneva. He interests us as a man for his wanderlust, for the eccentricity of his person and his ideas (which do not pay homage to the spirit of the Enlightenment), for his individualism and, artistically, for the authenticity of his response to Turkey, his uncompromising realism as a portraitist, his clear colors, the modesty of his late still lifes, and the general non-conformism of his art. His divergence from the academic norms of a Perronneau or a Drouais is now seen as an advantage. His art lives on through the beauty and freshness of his technique and his artistic sensibility. It lives by virtue of the fascinating human encounter that it offers us, through his portraits, with his subjects and, through them, with the artist. This double dialogue brings the past right into the present and is a source of constant wonder to any receptive viewer.

Claire Stoullig

Liotard in the Musées of Geneva:
the History of a Collection

In 2002, three centuries after the birth of Liotard and the creation of Geneva's first public collection,[1] the Musées d'Art et d'Histoire exhibited eighty-seven works by the painter, including thirty-seven pastels and thirty-five drawings, four oils and eleven enamels and miniatures. There are also five other works whose attribution is contested. The forthcoming publication of the catalogue raisonné edited by Renée Loche and Marcel Roethlisberger will cast new documentary light on these points of contention that are part of the natural life of the living discipline of art history.[2]

To the Public and University Geneva Library (BPU), Geneva's first museum, Liotard bequeathed his very fine *Self-Portrait, known as "Liotard with a Beard,"* circa 1749. This gift to the city of Geneva warrants some remarks. In his concern that his art should live on after his death, the artist seems to have understood that a work donated in his lifetime could be the beginning of what is today the jewel in Geneva's artistic patrimony. This capital painting is a fine example of the art of pastel in the eighteenth century, and of the originality and unique personality of the artist. Liotard's gesture succeeded that of Jacques-Antoine Arlaud, who, a few years earlier, had donated his portrait painted by Nicolas de Largillière, and was, similarly, a way of contributing to the growth of the portrait gallery constituted by the Geneva Library's collection of paintings.[3] Both men wanted to perpetuate a very positive and spectacular image of themselves. These portraits perfectly illustrate their desire to be part of the illustrious assembly of doctors and wise men that already lined the walls of what in those days was considered the city's showcase.

Nearly a century later, at the creation of the Musée Rath, an exchange was made and the *Self-Portrait, known as "in a Red Cap"* (1767–68, inv. 1827–20), bequeathed by the Odier-Lecointe family in 1827, was placed in the library on permanent loan. This substitution appears to have resulted from the concern, at the time, to dissociate art from history. However, it may be inferred that the second self-portrait was better suited to the library's gallery of prestigious figures, not least in terms of its format. At the same time, for the museum, the portrait of Liotard as a Turkish painter made it easy to identify the most original painter of the eighteenth century.

Before this exchange, the Société des Arts, which was founded in 1776, and whose collections became the cornerstone of the Musée Rath, owned a portrait of Madame d'Épinay executed circa 1759 (inv. 1826–7). It was donated by the Tronchin family. When the museum was nationalized, this pastel was the first notable contribution to its collections, one whose quality was as high as its subject was prestigious. This pastel, together with the self-portrait from the library, was clearly vital for the creation of the nascent Liotard collection.

It should be noted that the high patrimonial value of these works was an important factor in the enrichment of the collection. The interest they attracted was both public and private, with the city's political authorities and museums, alongside individual collectors, supporting and encouraging this purchase. Consequently, the first acquisitions were donations, bequests, or permanent loans.

With the donation of seventeen drawings and pastels by the Société Auxiliaire du Musée de Genève[4]— the museum's first society of friends—1934 was clearly a most auspicious year. The Société acted

1. As mentioned elsewhere in the book, the Bibliothèque Académique of Geneva, founded in 1559, was given institutional status in 1702. The Bibliothèque Publique et Universitaire of the city immediately received numerous portraits and gathered historical and archaeological items from the city's history, notably the altarpiece by Konrad Witz. See Claude Lapaire, "Le musée, reflet de la cité," *Cinq siècles de peinture au Musées d'art et d'histoire de Genève*, Geneva, 1983.

2. Since the edition of 2002, a number of works have been excluded from the artist's corpus while others have been rehabilitated. Not including prints, the collection of the Musées d'Art et d'Histoire now numbers eighty-two works by Liotard: four oils, thirty-seven pastels, thirty-four drawings, and seven miniatures (four others having been stolen during the break-in at the Musée de l'Horlogerie et de l'Émaillerie in 2002).

3. My special thanks to Danielle Buyssens for all the information she provided concerning the formation of the collections in Geneva. See Danielle Buyssens (ed.), 1702: "*. . . La Bibliothèque étant un ornement public,*" Geneva: Bibliothèque Publique et Universitaire/Georg Editeur, 2002.

4. Created in 1897, it was the ancestor of the museum's Société des Amis. See Claude Lapaire, "De la Société auxiliaire à la Société des amis, 1897–1997," *Genava*, XLV, 1997, pp. 163–72.

5. Jean Lullin, Société Auxiliaire du Musée de Genève, "Rapport du président pour l'exercice 1934," *Genava*, XIII, 1935, pp. 27–35.

6. "Rapport du président sur l'exercice 1935," *Genava*, XIV, 1936, pp. 17–24.

7. *Journal de Genève, La Suisse*, February 19, 1935. *Courrier de Genève*, January 30, 1935.

8. Auguste Bouvier, "La Société des Amis du Musée d'art et d'histoire (ancienne Société auxiliaire) de 1923 à 1959," *Genava*, VIII, 1960, pp. 25–43.

9. The Fondation Gottfried Keller continues to acquire works of art, which it then places with Swiss museums and public institutions in accordance with their requests.

10. Claude Lapaire, "Peintures et sculptures genevoises de la Fondation Gottfried Keller aux Musées d'art et d'histoire," *Musées de Genève*, June 1990, no. 304, pp. 2–5.

11. The Fondation Jean-Louis Prevost, named after the eminent psychologist at the University of Geneva (1838–1927), gathered collections of paintings, sculpture, drawings, engravings, and art objects. These have been on permanent loan to the museum since 1973. The museum has continued to develop its collections using its own capital.

12. *Self-Portrait, known as "in a Red Cap,"* 1767–68 (inv. 1827–20).

13. *Maria Theresa of Austria (1717–1780)*, 1762 (inv. 1839–10).

productively and effectively on the museum's behalf in acquiring this collection offered by the Tilanus family, who were descendants of the Dutch branch of the painter's family. The Société Auxiliaire played an exemplary role at the time, one continued by the friends of major museums today: that of supporting institutions by raising funds to help enrich the collections. This policy is all the more useful in light of the excessive prices fetched by certain artworks. The acquisition process implemented by the Société more than sixty years ago was very astute:[5] by soliciting a number of generous subscribers, it bought the entire portfolio of drawings, sketches, and red chalk drawings from Amsterdam (thirty-four in all), then sold off a sizable number, keeping only the most interesting pieces—seventeen drawings and pastels— for the museum. The president's report, made the following year, mentions the efforts made by the society to secure this acquisition,[6] an event also noted in the press.[7] An earlier acquisition, a pastel entitled *Frankish Woman from Pera, Constantinople*, made in 1930, was the first work from Liotard's Turkish period to find its way into the collections. A financial statement details the sums provided by the society to help the museum complete its purchases.[8]

On several occasions, foundations, too, have been a significant source of donations, in the form of permanent loans. The Fondation Gottfried Keller has made many of these.[9] In 1930 it donated what was then thought to be the portrait of the Countess of Coventry, and other works followed in 1940, 1947 (an outstanding year, when the Fondation donated eleven works by Liotard, not least the portraits of the children of Empress Maria Theresa, acquired with the museum in mind), and 1948. Through this support, "The Fondation Gottfried Keller has succeeded in securing these masterpieces for the artist's home town."[10] The Fondation Jean-Louis Prevost[11] also helped to enrich the Liotard collection by buying two pastels and one drawing, in 1975, 1985, and 1997, respectively.

The constant attention on the part of the Société des Amis and other institutions convinced the museum that it was vitally important to enhance the Liotard collection. In the period from 1893 to 1998, it made twenty-nine acquisitions and received donations from private collectors. And it is with the latter that we will end this journey through the years, in order to give an idea of how this rich collection was developed. Whatever the period, it has always been the passion and the generosity of one art lover that initiates and guides the very conception of a collection. Except for the donations by Monsieur Odier-Lecointe of a self-portrait to the Musée Rath (listed in 1827)[12] and by Mademoiselle Salles-Pallard of a portrait of the empress in 1839,[13] the first really significant donation was the David Claparède bequest in 1865. This was of primary importance in terms of both quantity and aesthetic value, comprising as it did portraits of the artist's family (notably his nephews and nieces, who by then were rich bourgeois in Geneva), executed at various times and reflecting the different styles employed by the painter in the course of his career.

These donations, thanks to the generosity of a wide variety of individuals, span the two centuries from the painter's death to the present. The most recent was the magnificent portrait of Liotard's daughter, *Marie-Jeanne, known as Mariette, de Bassompierre* (inv. 1998–501), an unusual combination of the portrait and still-life genres, bequeathed by the Baron de Rothschild. Some donors willingly repeated their acts of generosity. Monsieur and Madame Grégoire Salmanowitz, for example, did so with miniatures. They were well aware of the patrimonial value of these pieces, and of the importance to the town of holding and building up the collection of work by the great eighteenth-century Genevan painter. May this short account stand as a tribute to these private initiatives.

Isabelle Félicité Bleeker

Pastel, Liotard's Preferred Technique

Jean-Étienne Liotard tried out every technique: miniatures on ivory and vellum, small- and large-format enamels painted on porcelain and glass, oil painting, gouaches, printmaking, three-crayon drawing, and so on. However, most of his works were done in pastel. Before considering the Genevan artist's highly personal and original use of this technique, however, I think it important to summarize briefly its history up to the eighteenth century.

The oldest mention of this form of dry color comes from Leonardo da Vinci, who attributes its origin to France. It seems that he was shown the technique at the end of the fifteenth century by one Jean Perréal, who came to Milan with Louis XII in 1499.[1] Leonardo later noted it down in the *Codex Atlanticus*. Throughout the sixteenth century, pastel was used to add colored highlights to drawn portraits. In the seventeenth century, its use spread more widely and was established as an independent technique, perfectly adapted to the art of portraiture. The period of greatest production was the eighteenth century, when there was an extraordinary vogue for pastel portraits. The technique reached its apogee in the French School, where it was perfected by Jean-Marc Nattier, Jean-Baptiste Perronneau, and Maurice Quentin de La Tour. A genre of solemn, majestic likenesses now emerged with the production of full-length, life-size portraits. The opportunity to make a rapid sketch of a facial expression, without demanding long hours of sitting from the model, the ease of reworking, and the handiness of the support all constituted clear advantages in the execution of portrait commissions. The artist could simply draw the sitter's head on a small sheet at the scene, and then expand this fragment with the full portrait when back in the studio.[2] Because of these characteristics, then, the technique was particularly well suited to portraits.

Pastel comes in sticks made of ground pigment that is either pure or mixed with white clay, the quantity of which varies depending on the intensity of color required. The pigments are blended also with glue, lead or talc, gum arabic or sometimes honey or milk, and shaped into small cylinders that are then set out to dry. Pastel is rubbed on colored paper or cardboard (usually gray-blue, gray-beige, buff) with a certain degree of graininess. It can also be applied to parchment or to sized canvas. The support is usually glued onto canvas on a stretcher, and then placed under glass to protect the pastel from abrasion. Unlike oil paint, pastel does not darken; the color remains unchanged, which explains the freshness of most of the works we have today. Pastel does not flake, either; it does, however, get covered in mold and become blotchy as a result of dampness. Because of its ephemeral, volatile nature, artists have always been confronted with the problem of fixing it on the support. The deterioration of the material and, with it, of the image are a constant concern. To solve this problem, a procedure was developed that consists in spraying over the entire surface a "fixative," made once using gum arabic and now with alcohol and a transparent resin (gum-lacquer).[3]

The main qualities of pastel are flexibility, speed of execution, variety of finish, and the possibility of reworking, with fine or thick hatching, crisscrossing, or completely blurred strokes. This matte, opaque material makes it possible to build up several layers without having to erase. The technique permits endless nuance and surprising textural effects; it allows stumping, erasure, and reworking; and it is superb at creating the effects and variations of light and the shimmering of fabrics. Silk, satin, velvet,

1. Patrice Georges Rufino, *Le Pastel: or bleu du pays de Cocagne. L'épopée de la couleur de l'Antiquité à nos jours*, Paris, 1990.
2. Jean Leymarie, Geneviève Monnier, Bernice Rose, *Le Dessin*, Geneva, 1979, p. 67.
3. Ibid., p. 66.

and lace can be rendered to perfection. The faithful evocation of skin that is made possible through the overlayering and juxtaposition of cold and warm tones helped to make pastel an outstanding technique for portraiture. Like drawing, it immediately transcribes an emotion or idea through line, to which it also adds color. Since it is not diluted by brush, it does not cover the surface in the same way as paint: the underlying color will be more or less evident, depending on the heaviness or lightness of the touch.

As support for his pastels, Liotard, like his colleagues, used vellum, parchment rubbed with pumice stone, or gray or blue paper. In the last quarter of the fifteenth century and throughout the sixteenth, blue paper was used primarily by the artists of the Veneto, where it was produced and known as *carta azzurra* or *carta turchina*. Later, it was used by French and Dutch artists.[4] Because of the limited paper sizes available then, when Liotard wanted to paint large-scale pastels he had to join several pieces together or add strips of paper.[5] This assemblage is very much evident in *Ami-Jean De la Rive*. There, the joins, which had originally been invisible, now stand out clearly against the ground because the pastel has subsided somewhat over the years. Whether the paper was gray or blue, sized or left in reserve, Liotard made skillful use of its effects to add relief and modeling.

Pastel is a colored powder with infinitely varied shades and gradations.[6] Liotard knew how to get the most out of the medium, to use it for vaporous, blurred effects, stumping and *gommage* and vigorous hatching. He used and experimented with all the possibilities afforded by this technique, taking it as far as it would go. He worked both dry and with watercolor or gouache. The finish of pastel, allowing for extraordinary diversity, at once lively and colorful, made up of supple or taut straight lines, stippling and parallel or tangled hatching, serves the artist's purpose. He frequently layers or crisscrosses lines to create relief and a sense of light. This play of lines, which might appear rather random, is in fact deliberate and controlled. The different stylistic effects, ranging from precise, meticulous, and even illusionistic rendering to a free, broad, and expressive graphic system, combine, complement, and cohabit with one another but never disrupt the unity of the composition.[7]

Liotard's independence is also evident in his way of using pastel. Unlike La Tour or Perronneau, who use their pictorial language to express grace, finesse, and psychological insights, Liotard used the medium in a graphic way, contenting himself with the scrupulous and totally objective representation of the outward appearance and features of his models, respecting their individuality. La Tour's portraits, for example, are characterized by modeling that is at once supple, firm, and light. Going beyond resemblance, he seizes on the psychological truth behind the sitter's expression or smile, further highlighting this by touches of light and shadow. His chromatic range is generally dominated by blues and pearl grays; he makes frequent use of pink, but rarely of red or yellow. The accessories, scrupulously denoted but not rendered in great detail, define the character. The backgrounds are delicately nuanced in a gentle half-light.

Liotard's technique derives from his training as a miniaturist and enameler. We must remember that he came from the watchmaking and enameling workshops that were the sources of Geneva's prosperity in the seventeenth and eighteenth centuries, and he made the most of this training in his use of pastel. The precision of his line, the clarity and translucency of his colors, and the layering of tones and materials all come from his craft background.[8]

One characteristic of his art, particularly in his pastels, is the combination of techniques—pastel, gouache, and watercolor—within a single work. Close examination of his portraits reveals countless layers of different types of materials. Thus, in his *Self-Portrait, known as "with His Hand on His Chin,"* executed between 1770 and 1773, Liotard uses not only pastel but also liquid color, gouache, and watercolor, whose thickness heightens the effect of relief. He was also consummately skilled at rendering the satiny appearance of a fabric or the brightness of a silk ribbon with a few touches of white gouache artfully applied to the chalk. The sumptuous *Ami-Jean De la Rive* typifies this talent. Note, here, the very fine quality of execution, the sureness of touch, and the intense presence conveyed by the magistrate's face. The smooth, soft gray satin of his outfit contrasts with the fur of the muff, so realistically rendered

4. Geneviève Monnier, *Le Pastel*, Geneva, 1983, p. 16.
5. Numa S. Trivas, "Jean-Étienne Liotard, Peintures, pastels et dessins," manuscript, 1936, p. 77.
6. As many as six hundred and fifty shades can be obtained, across the spectrum.
7. Anne de Herdt, *Dessins de Liotard*, ex. cat., Paris, Geneva, 1992, no. 111, p. 8.
8. Renée Loche, "Jean-Étienne Liotard dans les collections genevoises," *Le Livre du Richemond IV*, 1990, p. 16.

that one could almost count the hairs. There are also bold contrasts between the red of the ribbon and the rose highlights of the coat. Liotard's use of color here is perfectly free from convention.

He usually represents his models against a neutral ground, without props. The plain, gray, or brown backgrounds, which are often darker on one side and lighter on the other, allow the subject's gaze, smile, or other expressions to stand out all the more effectively, thus conveying a striking sense of life and truthfulness.

The successive layers of pastel that can be observed in many of the artist's works suggest that he built up layers of material as he worked toward perfection of structure, tone, and texture. The quantity of matter applied to the canvas is sometimes evident on the edge of the parchment that is folded over the stretcher, as has been observed in the case of *Marc Liotard de la Servette*. There the thick blue-mauve pastel has indeed overflowed onto the edge of the stretcher.

The fine, precise, and assured strokes of pastel, left visible on the surface, heighten the subject's presence and, when seen from a distance, blend in with the ensemble. The technique seems smooth, giving a velvety effect of unity and perfection. The artist underlines the eyes, nose, and lips with a few spare touches. He rubs the surface the better to evoke the skin of the face. He uses hatching to suggest shadow. *Madame Sarasin* is one admirable example of this, with those green and yellow lines rendering the shadow on the face. Liotard's precision is meticulous, his attention and execution served by a precise technique. The drawing is clear, the touch free and devoid of dryness. The contours are never blurred but always assured, as they structure the composition and heighten the presence and reality of the model. The lines are highlighted with color. The difference of treatment between the very detailed faces and the almost expressionistic freedom with which the clothes are rendered is so masterfully managed that unity is never lost. A single portrait may contain every pastel technique. Thus in the *Presumed Portrait of Jean-Michel Liotard*, the vigor, vivacity, and freedom with which the coat is rendered strongly contrast with the precise drawing of the face, a treatment surprising to find in one of the artist's early works, for it occurs mainly in his second period. It may be that Liotard felt freer when portraying himself or his close circle.

Liotard's use of pastel is unique. He developed a prodigious technique that gave a perfect illusion of relief and conveyed with virtuosity the shimmer of material, the texture and density of each fabric. With an extraordinary economy of means that makes him seem a century ahead of his time, his taste for truth triumphs in the exact rendering of each expression and each feature, even the most unflattering. The subtle play of light, the highlights in the shadows, the chromatic relationships, and the spontaneity of touch all bespeak a bold and unrestrained approach. Liotard does not try to make his models more handsome. He scrupulously renders each line of a face with total objectivity. A sensitive colorist and draftsman of genius, he seems to have found in pastel the medium most suited to transcribing reality and achieving truth of representation. Liotard exploited its possibilities to felicitous effect. The technique served his purposes well. It was perfectly responsive to his need to experiment, to his constant searching for the truth, his constant striving to get as close as he could to reality and reveal the human soul in all its depth. It was the favorite tool for conveying his vision of the world.

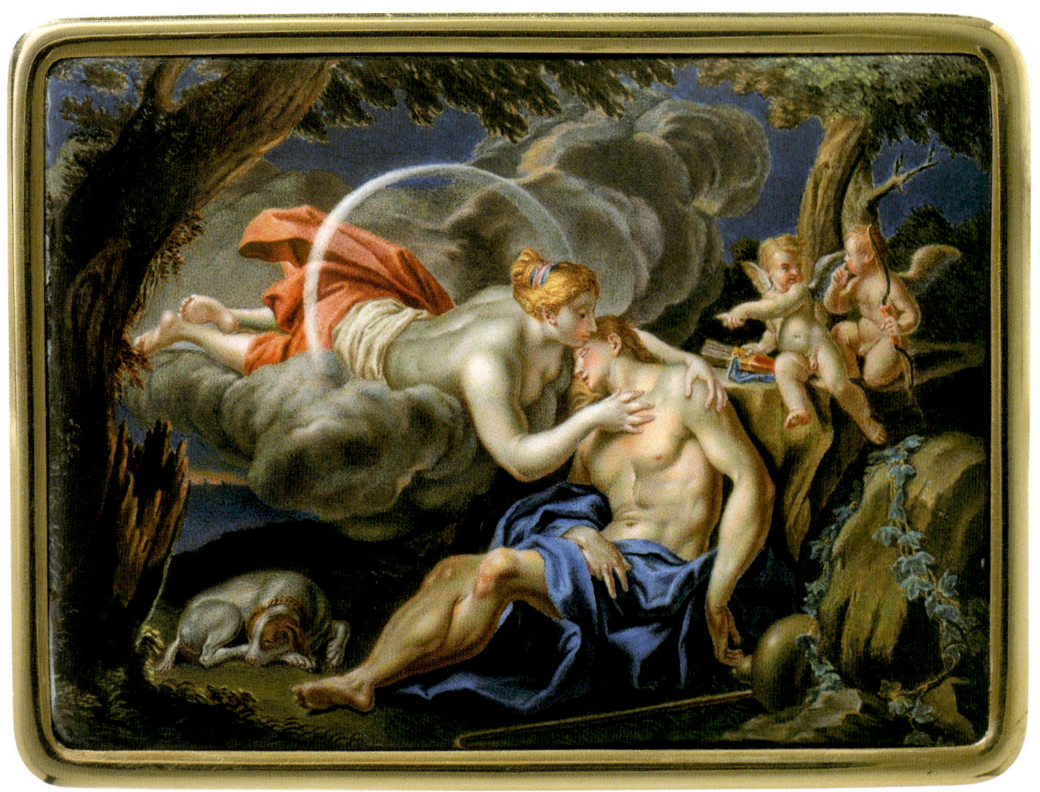

Selene and Endymion

1722
Signed and dated
Painted enamel on copper
5.10 x 7.15 cm
Bequest of Madame Philippe
Plantamour, 1899
Inv. E 137

Fabienne Xavière Sturm

Liotard the Miniaturist

Whether painted on enamel, in gouache and watercolor on vellum or ivory, or drawn in pencil and red chalk on paper, parchment, or board primed with chalk, there is nothing secondary about the miniature in Liotard's œuvre. On the contrary, the severely reduced format of these portraits provided the painter with a concentrated, dense space that seemed to give him—and him in particular—a kind of freedom of expression that drew power and vivacity from the very modesty of the spaces in which it was deployed. It is surely no coincidence that Liotard, who came to Paris in 1723, worked in the studio of Jean-Baptiste Massé, one of the finest French miniaturists of the day. A tireless explorer of the faces and personalities of his models, throughout his long career as a painter of miniatures Liotard combined innovative procedures with spectacular results. He always made the pressure of his hand—often tender, always exact, sometimes ironic—coincide with the message he intended to convey. And it did so in the tone that he wished to impart to what, for him, was not simply an image, but the strikingly manifest truth of a being: neither objective nor subjective, but simply pure truth.

Selene and Endymion

Jean-Étienne was twenty when he painted this enamel plaque on copper, in a shape that suggests it may have been intended as the lid of a snuff box. The son of a goldsmith, and therefore familiar from a young age with the precious crafts of the Genevan jewelers and watchmakers, and a student of the miniaturist Daniel Gardelle—a painter who worked not on enamel but on vellum—Liotard no doubt served an apprenticeship as an enameler with one of the city's numerous masters. The skill of this small painting certainly indicates as much.[1] Endymion, sitting against the thick trunk of a felled tree, with blue drapery about him, is being chastely kissed in his sleep by the moon goddess, whose drapery is red and white. She lies, stomach down, on a cushion of dark clouds and puts her arms round Endymion's shoulders, bending her head with its chignon of burnished red hair down to the sleeper's peaceful face. The blue-black night sky is partly hidden by the oak that reaches across from the left and, together with the ivy tumbling like a garland down the rock on the right, forms a tight frame around the scene. Endymion's stick in the foreground, his sleeping dog off to the left and, sitting on the trunk, two watching cupids all bring a little gossipy animation to this theater of love. Liotard uses strong, contrasting colors and enriches his flesh tones with black, green, and yellow, heightening the developed musculature and opulent bodies of the two protagonists. Already, this work evinces a bold use of color and successfully negotiates the dangerous move from Francesco Trevisani's big painted canvas to a minuscule enamel.

Empress and Friend

"Attempt by Liotard" were the words Liotard wrote on the counter-enamel of the large and irregular plaque that he used as a draft for the definitive portrait kept at the Rijksmuseum in Amsterdam.[2]

1. The iconographic source of this enamel is *Selene and Endymion*, a canvas painted by Francesco Trevisani (1656–1746). It was identified and comprehensively studied by Dr. Hans Boeckh in "Remarques sur l'origine et la place de la peinture en émail dans l'œuvre de Liotard," *Genava*, n.s., XXXVII, 1989, pp. 117–28.
2. Ibid.

Liotard was less concerned with the firing here than with the success of the portrait. He was working in what was an unusual format for him, on a flat plaque that was thickly coated in glass paste front and back so as to protect it from the stress from the heat—which, however, could not be avoided, since the queen's face is striated with "hairs" and the rest of the surface pocked with little craters made by air bubbles. In this draft he creates a gentleness in the sovereign's lips and eyes. He brought a similar degree of personal feeling to the miniature of the *Presumed Portrait of Maria Theresa of Austria in Turkish Costume (1717–1780)*.[3] He was adept at blending the necessarily official quality of these portraits with his own respectful affection for the Austrian royal family.

English Aristocrats

Liotard made several visits to England between 1753 and 1774, and his reputation as a matchless painter brought him some very select patrons. Among them were John and Georgina, Viscount and Viscountess Spencer of Althorp. The miniature of the viscountess was stolen from the Musée de l'Horlogerie et de l'Émaillerie of Geneva in 2002.[4]

Georgina Poyntz wears a saffron yellow dress with large pearls for buttons and a lace wimple to which Liotard's frothy touch imparts a truly creamy consistency. A coat in a bold violet color covers her shoulders. A double row of matched pearls worn as a choker seems to float on the surface of the enamel in a succession of barely separated white disks. Yet more pearls are entwined along the light black ribbon of her chignon with its perky little aigrette.

This was in 1754. Georgina was to marry the first Count Spencer in 1755. She was very beautiful, with regular features, full lips, an English rose complexion, small ears, and fine chestnut hair in harmony with the very light, almost transparent brown of her eyes. Liotard applied coal black enamel to the eyebrows and lashes, as if seeking to emphasize the absence of a smile, which here does not reveal disdain but the seriousness of a wise child, the future wife of an important aristocrat.[5]

The portrait of the very young Henry Benedict Marie Clement Stuart, which Liotard painted during his Roman sojourn in the winter of 1737–38, is another remarkable work, unfortunately also stolen in 2002.[6] Astonishingly enough, Henry Benedict's elongated face almost equals his bust in length. This imbalance in the composition may well be deliberate rather than the result of any awkwardness on the painter's part. Is not this, and the slight shoulders and narrow neck, his way of indicating the youth and fragility of this child who is just twelve years old? He will grow up to be a great prelate, and his destiny can already be read in the unusual distinction of his expression and posture. The soft gray of the coat, bisected by the blue ribbon of the Order of the Holy Spirit, is broken up by three areas of pink and one of olive green suggesting an embroidered waistcoat. The stippling of the face is calm; the painter gives a hint of the hair's natural color underneath the wig, while a fine, precise red line in the hollow of the eyelids and along the lashes accompanies the form of the eye and gives the expression a delicate coldness that is confirmed in the slightly pinched mouth.

The Genevan Bourgeoisie

In 1733 Liotard painted his first oil portrait of Andrienne Cannac, née Huber-Calandrini. She was thirty-one and had just settled in Lyons with her husband, the banker Pierre-Philippe Cannac. Thirteen years later, in 1746, he made another one in enamel, this stolen in 2002 as well.[7] Andrienne had a big nose, and Liotard registers this without nastiness. He makes this uncomely feature central to a physiognomy that exudes intelligence and self-assurance. Possessed of a simple elegance, the sitter seems to be sharing something with the painter, as if she were listening to his stories, and it looks as if the superbly depicted

3. *L'Âge d'or du petit portrait*, catalogue of miniatures at the Musée de l'Horlogerie et de l'Émaillerie of Geneva, Fabienne Xavière Sturm, Paris: Réunion des Musées Nationaux, 1995, p. 162.
4. Anne Baezner, Cäsar Menz, Fabienne Xavière Sturm, Laurent Chenu, "Musée de l'Horlogerie et de l'Émaillerie. Catalogue raisonné des pièces dérobées le 24 novembre 2002," *Genava*, 2003, pp. 45–48, and pp. 87–88, ill.
5. See Liotard's 1755 portrait of John, first Count Spencer, *The Gilbert Collection, Portrait Miniatures in Enamel*, by Sarah Coffin and Bodo Hofstetter, London: Philip Wilson Publishers Limited, 2000.
6. Hans Boeckh, "Henri-Benedict-Marie-Clement Stuart, futur Cardinal d'York (1725–1807) et Jean-Étienne Liotard par lui-même en costume turc: deux miniatures sur émail dans leur rapport aux pastels du maître," *Genava*, n.s., XLI, 1993, pp. 147–54.
7. Hans Boeckh, "'Mᶜ Cannac': une miniature sur émail de Jean-Étienne Liotard," *Genava*, n.s., XXXVII, 1989, p. 129.

irony in her expression is addressed more to Liotard than to the viewer. In contrast, Liotard's painting of Madame Charles Bonnet, née Jeanne-Marie De la Rive-Franconis,[8] painted around 1760, dwells on sartorial details and shows the young woman holding a miniature portrait of a man, probably her learned husband. The insistent details of the outfit and jewelry seem to attest to the painter's desire to show that a miniature can be as rich as a pastel. Finally, in his portrait of an unknown man,[9] Liotard uses the unique resources of drawing in miniature and, in a sumptuous, tiny composition in grays and pinks, renders all the virility of this man of quality. The same technique can be found in the miniature representing the young woman with a letter.[10] She is totally absorbed in musing on what she has just read, and her gaze eludes us. Liotard leaves her alone, so to speak, immersed in the thoughts aroused by the missive. Here too, in the rigorous choice of composition, Liotard seems to be telling us with his adroit line that what she has just read is her business alone.

Himself

In 1748, at the age of forty-six, in his self-portrait painted in enamel on golden copper, which was stolen in 2002 as well, Liotard makes a kind of vibrant declaration of love to the material, enamel, whose expressive qualities he exploited with exceptional power.[11] The face is an accumulation of juxtaposed or overlayered dots, a mix of white, red, and gray. The long beard is a battlefield in which the hairs are like lively black commas that mix, on the ground and in the white paste, with carmine, yellow, and green. The sensual lips are painted in the same red as the Turkish hat. He makes daring use of subtly orchestrated contrasts, with zones of darkness played off against highlights in the fur, the shadows and lights in the background and in the face. Just as the beard and long, curly, gray hair reflect the painter's age, so the bright complexion, the firm mouth, and the gaze directed at us poor mortals endow him with eternal youth of stunning precision and presence, set for eternity by the firing.

A Collection That Was Exemplary

Thanks to the great generosity of Madame and Monsieur Grégoire Salmanowitz, who donated the artist's famous *Self-Portrait, known as "Liotard with a Beard"* as well as the portraits of Andrienne Huber and Henry Benedict Marie Clement Stuart, and who also supported the acquisition of the Jean-Baptiste Massé self-portrait, the museum collection featured, up until fall 2002, ten exemplary pieces fully illustrating the importance of the miniature to Liotard's art. I would encourage admirers of his work to read the studies published in *Genava* by Dr. Hans Boeckh, whose dogged and fruitful research sheds interesting light on a number of the mysteries still surrounding the master.
[FXS]

The Loss of Four Miniatures by J.-É. Liotard (by Estelle Fallet)

In fall 2002, a bold burglary at the Musée de l'Horlogerie et de l'Émaillerie in Geneva resulted in the loss of one hundred and seventy-four very valuable works.[12] In addition to historic watches (dating from the seventeenth to the twentieth century) and five very fine snuff boxes, four miniatures painted on enamel by Liotard were also lost. These were the three works from the Salmanowitz Collection and the portrait of Georgina Poyntz, acquired in 1979. The delicate colors, combined with the great mastery acquired by the painter in the delicate techniques of enamel work, made these modestly sized works true masterpieces.

8. Ibid., p. 245, note 3.
9. Ibid.; see Anne de Herdt, *Dessins de Liotard*, ex. cat., Paris, Geneva, 1992, p. 166, no. 90, p. 167, repr. p. 284, no. 103.
10. Ibid., pp. 244–45, note 3; see Fabienne Xavière Sturm, "L'Art du petit portrait," *Genava*, n.s., XLI, 1993; see Anne de Herdt, p. 166, no. 91, p. 167, repr. p. 284, no. 104.
11. See note 5.
12. Anne Baezner, "Musée de l'Horlogerie et de l'Émaillerie. Catalogue raisonné des pièces dérobées le 24 novembre 2002." Offprint of the journal *Genava*, 2003, 133 p. ill.

These miniatures were executed in 1737–38, 1746, 1748, and 1754, respectively, and three of them, including the very fine *Self-Portrait*, came from the same collection in Geneva, whose owner donated them in 1988 and 1993. Their maker and their subjects, as well as their presence over the years in British, French, and Swiss collections, gives them a special connection with our institution.

We have decided to keep the pieces stolen in 2002 in this catalogue: they remain part of our public heritage, and we hope that they will one day return to the city of Liotard's birth in optimal conditions of conservation, back among the admirers of this Genevan artist.

The articles are based on information culled from the books by Anne de Herdt (1992), Danielle Buyssens (1988), and Marcel Roethlisberger and Renée Loche (1978). The biographies of the archduchesses and archdukes of Austria were taken directly from the catalogue by Anne de Herdt (1992). We are very grateful to these authors for the remarkable quality of the information they assembled. Most of the quotations also come from Anne de Herdt's catalogue; when this is not the case, the source is specified. We have also referred to a number of articles published in the journal of the Musées d'Art et d'Histoire, *Genava*. [AC]

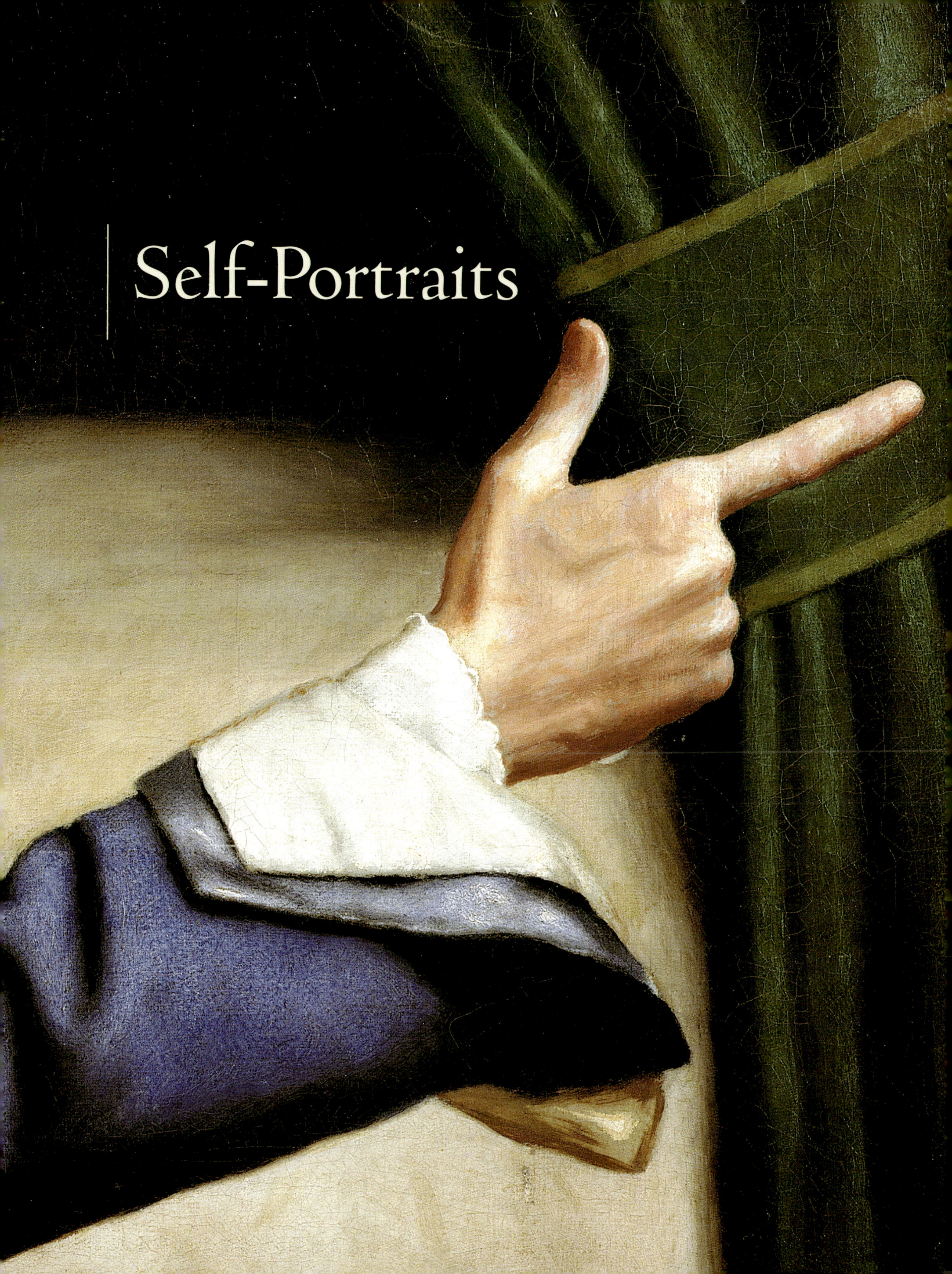
Self-Portraits

Claire Stoullig

Few things are more fascinating than painters who limn their portrait on canvas or paper at the risk of producing an image as likable as devastating. The self-portrait is all about likeness and is the only pictorial genre to have a clearly defined "practical" purpose. Primarily a portrait, it becomes the expression of a subject, of a person's unique subjectivity.

We know of some twenty self-portraits by Liotard, seven of which are in the Musées of Geneva. But Liotard was certainly not the only artist of his day to be obsessed with himself. To look no further than the most famous pastelists of the eighteenth century, his contemporary and rival, Maurice Quentin de La Tour, and indeed Chardin, the great painter of still lifes, both explored the genre. What were they aiming at? In this genre, painters try to settle the totality of the painting all at once, dealing simultaneously with the questions of form and ground, the mental and the physical. But this eagerly sought global vision is rarely attained, since a painter's portrait of himself is only a fragment (of himself).

Fascinating for whoever looks at it, the self-portrait offers only the illusion of a direct encounter, of marked spontaneity, and greater intimacy. The beholder has no choice but to accept the painter's will to represent himself in the best possible light, or in the most "authentic" one, and to be seen "as he is." But how free the painter also is to deceive, to say more! More than just skin, it is a whole being that is unveiled for the other's gaze: the self-portrait can be seen as a double portrait. In any case, if the term self-portrait is in itself perfectly explicit, its meaning is open to a great variety of interpretations. Is this simply the most faithful representation that the artist can offer of his physical character, or of his moral one, or of both? How tempting simply to give up before such an impossible task! Thus, in order to circumvent the issue of resemblance, some artists opt for a whole variety of visual solutions, fleshing out their portrait with props, attributes, postures, and situations that are to a large degree tricks of representation, and often blur the image we are supposed to be looking at.

We find no such props in Liotard. The artist never cheats and engages willingly with his task. Indeed, he left behind a great number of self-portraits. The museum itself, with the Public and University Geneva Library, has eight: four pastels, one oil, and three drawings. He approached the genre using every technique, and this tenacity is logical enough in the case of an artist who, throughout his life, sought to achieve truth, to show human beings as they were, without deceit or flattery, and who, like any other mortal, longed for images and reflections of himself.

Between the first self-portrait (1727) and the last (1782) lie more than fifty years, a period punctuated by many other portraits that bear witness to the painter's development and compensate for the absence of archives and historiographic documents.

Liotard started painting self-portraits quite early in his career. The earliest such work in the museum (inv. 1934–12) dates from 1737, ten years after the first known example from 1727, which was painted in oils when the artist was starting out in Paris. The 1737 work is in pastel, Liotard's favored medium, and was executed in Florence, before the artist set off on the Grand Tour. Very much in awe of Rembrandt, who was a major influence, he chose to show himself in three-quarter view, as he would in most of the portraits painted throughout his career. The young man is still eager to resemble the men of quality

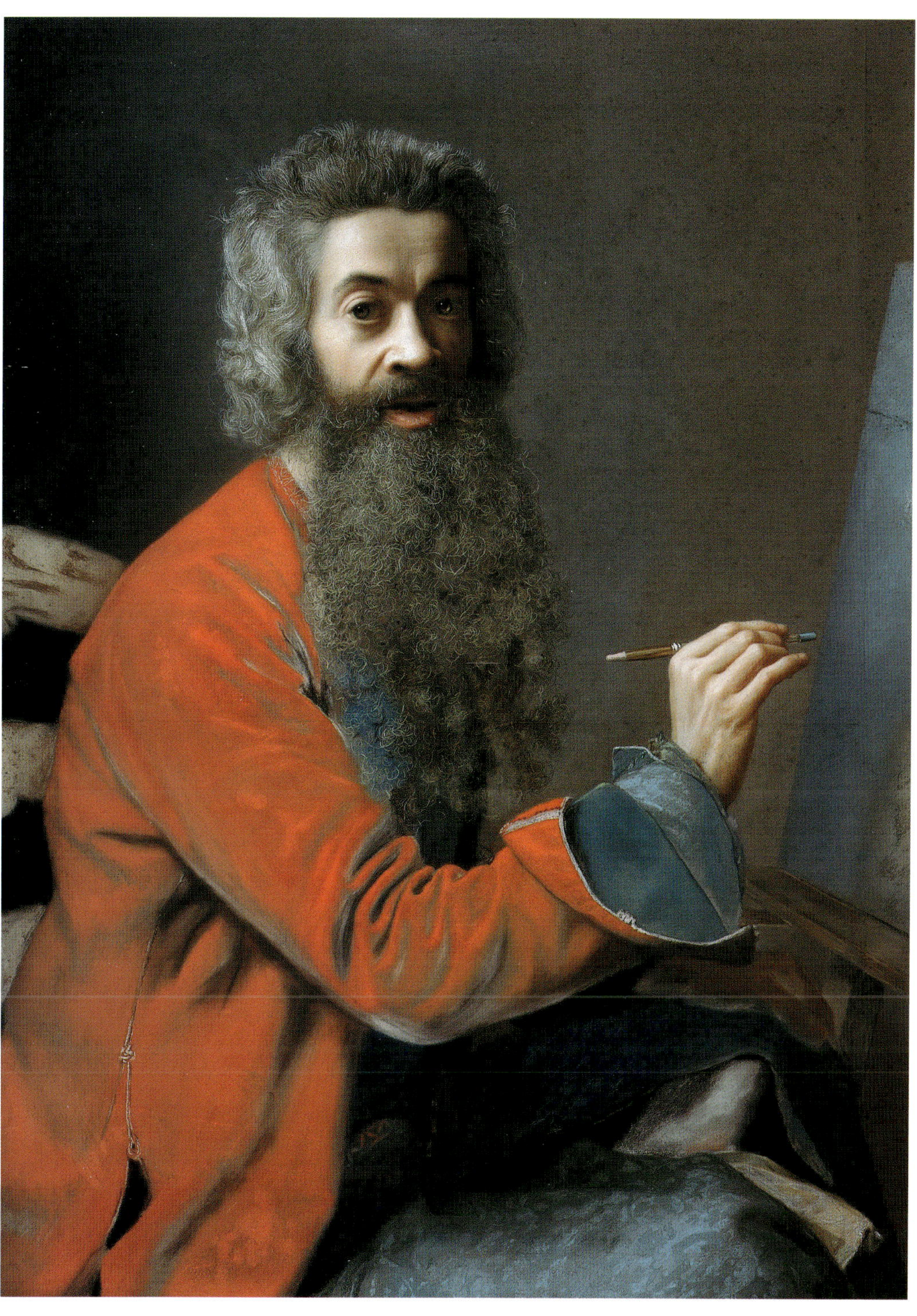

Self-Portrait, known as "Liotard with a Beard"

Circa 1749
Pastel on paper glued onto
canvas
97 x 71 cm
Bequest of the artist, 1789
Inv. 1843–5

Liotard bequeathed this self-portrait to the Geneva Library.
It was put on permanent loan at the museum in 1843 in
exchange for the *Self-Portrait, known as "in a Red Cap"*
(inv. 1827–20).

that he frequents, and so, in keeping with the fashion of the day, wears a wig and a formal outfit comprising a velvet coat, a jabot, and a cravat. This pastel follows the precepts regarding the distribution of light and dark laid down by the artist in his *Traité des principes et des règles de la peinture*. These relations of light and shade are a way of giving a physiognomy maximum character and relief, thus conveying the personality as effectively as possible. The artist must fix his image within fleeting time in order to gauge his inner state and so provide, at regular intervals, a genuine piece of self-analysis.

After his experience of the Grand Tour and the four years he spent in Constantinople, Liotard quickly abandoned this kind of "classical" portrait and sought to be identified as a "Turkish painter." Coming back from Asia Minor in 1743, in Vienna and then in Paris, he tried to make a name for himself in high society and court circles. He asserted his originality by presenting himself as a Turkish painter, dressed and groomed in the Middle Eastern way, that is to say, with a long beard. This was of course an effective way of not being ignored, indeed of getting noticed. His appearance met with mixed reactions, and some found it outrageous, but in adopting these peculiarities Liotard was certainly displaying an openness of mind and freedom of thought that were quite remarkable for a Genevan citizen with a Calvinist background. The *Self-Portrait, known as "Liotard with a Beard,"* from about 1749 (inv. 1843–5), presents a double identity. First, here is the painter, pastel in hand ready to be rubbed on the paper or parchment set on a stretcher (this element is visible only in this version), busy executing his portrait while looking at himself in the mirror—and, therefore, looking at us. Second, here he is posing in formal attire, in a superb red velvet caftan lined with blue silk, open to reveal a sumptuous material covering his thighs but leaving a glimpse of one leg. Looking more closely, we are intrigued to note that this fine piece of painting is also somewhat casual in its formal definition and that, surprisingly for a painter usually so meticulous in rendering what he sees, its morphology is rather approximate. This ceremonial costume was no doubt worn especially for the occasion and was the pretext for all kinds of liberties in terms of composition and color (the strong interplay between vermilion and blue) and in the pose of the painter, in mid-gesture, mouth open, as if taken by surprise and revealing something of the secret of his own painting, or as if pretending to be someone else. Here he affirms the full maturity of his art, which is also evident in the superb miniature from 1748 (inv. AD 8212), unfortunately stolen from the Musée de l'Horlogerie et de l'Émaillerie in 2002. In this highly precise self-portrait, he appears not as a painter, but wearing his Moldavian hat, thus indicating his readiness to embark on other adventures to other destinies.

This twofold question that intrigues the beholder is also manifest in the *Self-Portrait, known as "in a Red Cap,"* on permanent loan to the Geneva Library in exchange for the 1749 work, which was no doubt considered too large for its portrait gallery, and more representative of the genre. It is a strikingly bold work: the background, completely devoid of representation and unusually extensive in relation to the figure of the artist, dwarfs Liotard's face and seems to push the cap further down onto his head. It is as if Liotard would be literally crushed by the absent presence around him—knowledge, thought— were it not for the violent contrast of the red cap and blue clothing, which heightens the effect of the composition and reasserts the subject's dignity. That is the great feat here: to achieve extreme subtlety in a psychological portrait with the greatest economy of pictorial means.

From surprise we go straight to laughter in Liotard's self-portrait from 1770 (inv. 1893–9) in which, as intent as ever on the truth, he shows himself aged, wrinkled, and gap-toothed. This time, the hand is not holding the painter's tool but points outside the frame, past a curtain, as if to suggest his own exit from the stage of life. However, he is still laughing, stating his readiness to play a few more tricks, as in this painting itself, which seems to invite us to behold ourselves in a mirror hidden behind a curtain, as Liotard himself humbly does here.

The sheer quantity of Liotard's self-portraits shows how important this genre was to him as a way of bearing witness to his psychological development throughout his life. His chromatic approach is very deliberate, and he often limits his portrait to the primary colors blue and red, thus heightening the depth of the painting and bringing vibrancy to the almost monochrome shades of brown and gray in the background.

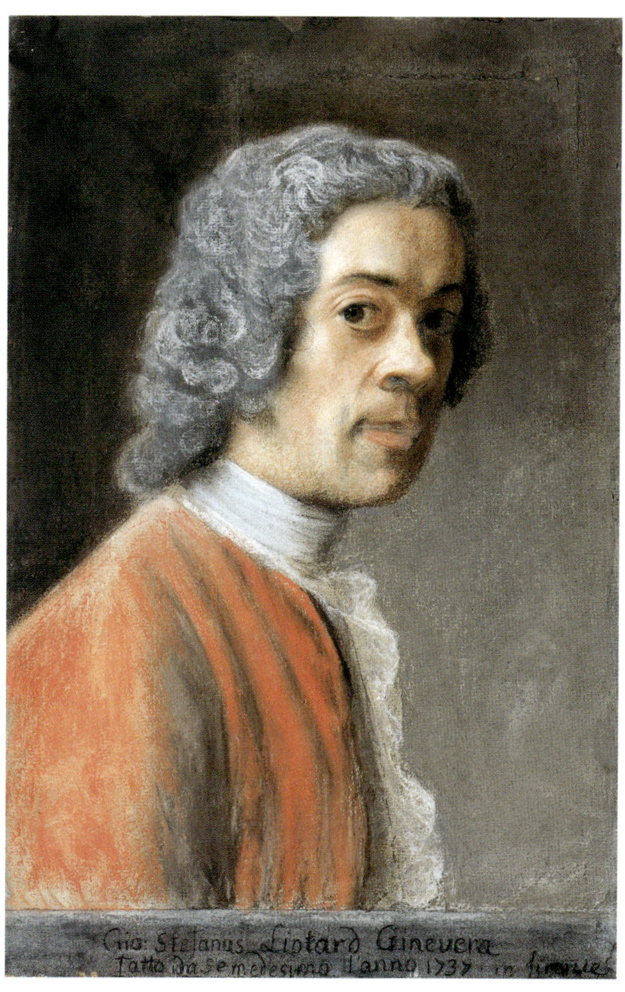

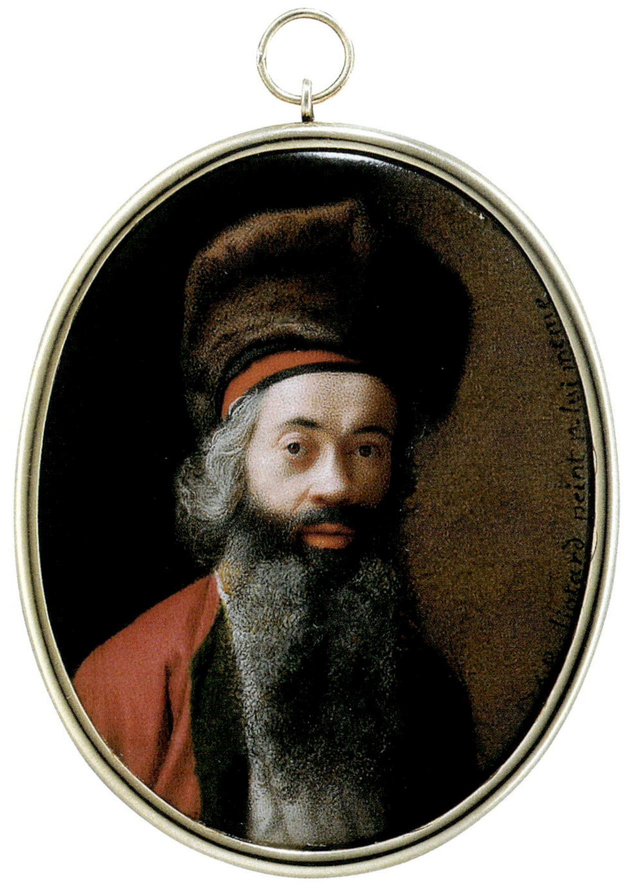

Self-Portrait

1737
Signed and dated
Pastel on paper glued
onto panel
38 x 24.7 cm
Purchase, 1934
Inv. 1934–12

After being held in several different private collections,
this pastel was acquired by Bernard Naef in 1934.

Self-Portrait, known as "with Beard and Moldavian Hat"

1748
Signed and dated
Painted enamel on copper
5.4 x 4.5 cm
Gift of Madame and Monsieur
Grégoire Salmanowitz, 1993
Inv. AD 8212

The famous English writer Horace Walpole (1717–97) was
a great admirer of Liotard's miniatures. He knew the painter
personally, and this enamel on a golden ground belonged to
the very fine collection that Walpole kept in his neo-Gothic
residence at Strawberry Hill, near Twickenham. The enamel
no doubt remained there during the first half of the
nineteenth century. In the description he wrote in 1784 of
his villa, with its furniture, paintings, and curiosities,
Walpole refers to this work as follows: "Liotard the painter,
in his Turkish dress, in enamel, by himself; given to
Mr. Walpole by his sister Lady Mary Churchill"
(Hans Boeckh, *Genava*, 1993, p. 153).
Work stolen from the Musée de l'Horlogerie et de
l'Émaillerie in 2002.

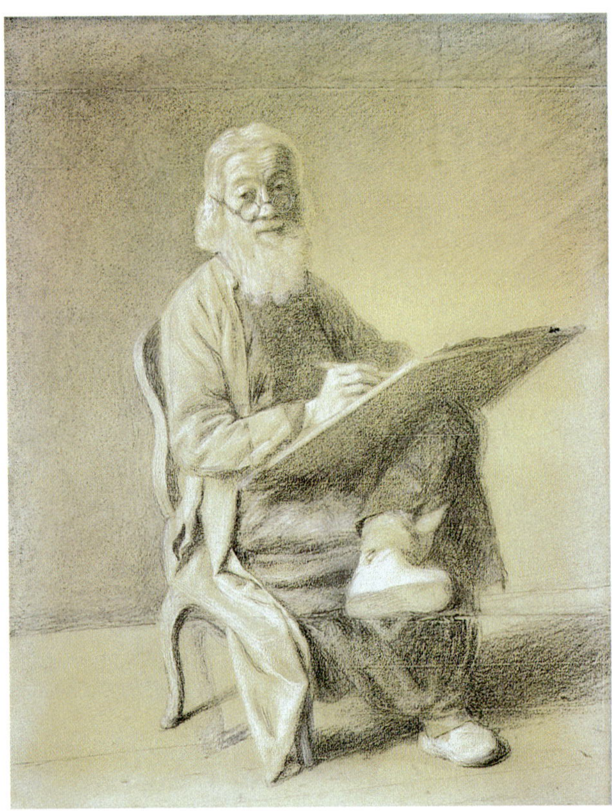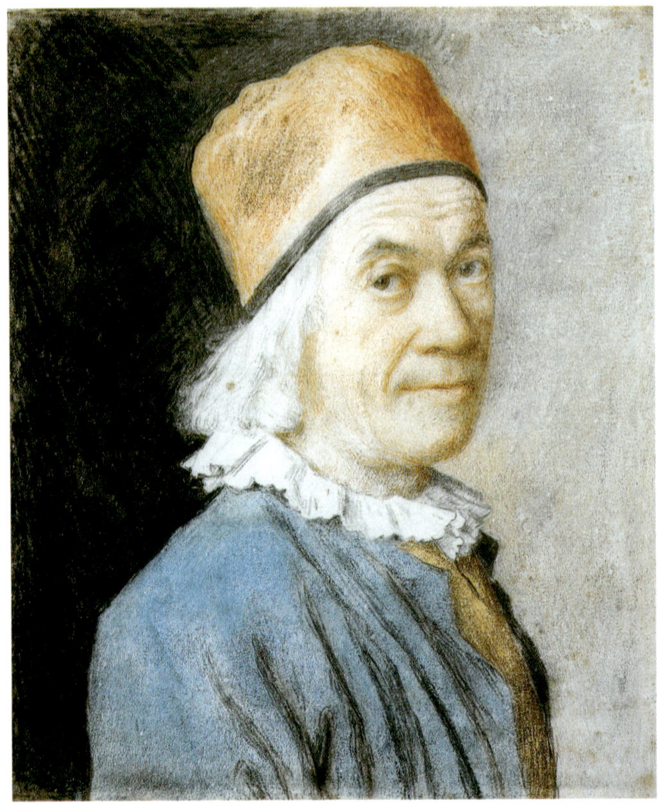

1782
Graphite pencil and black
chalk, stumping and
heightened with white chalk
on faded blue paper
54 x 43 cm
Donation, 1984
Inv. 1984–129

After having remained in the possession of the artist's
family in Amsterdam, this self-portrait was acquired by
Bernard Naef (Geneva).

1765–67
Black chalk, graphite pencil,
red chalk, and red and blue
pencil on vellum
12.1 x 10.2 cm
On permanent loan from the
Fondation Gottfried Keller,
1976
Inv. 1976–334

This work was kept by the artist in his personal collection.
It was inherited by his daughter Marie-Thérèse Liotard
(Geneva), then came into the possession of the Amsterdam
branch of the family before it was acquired by a private
collector in New York.

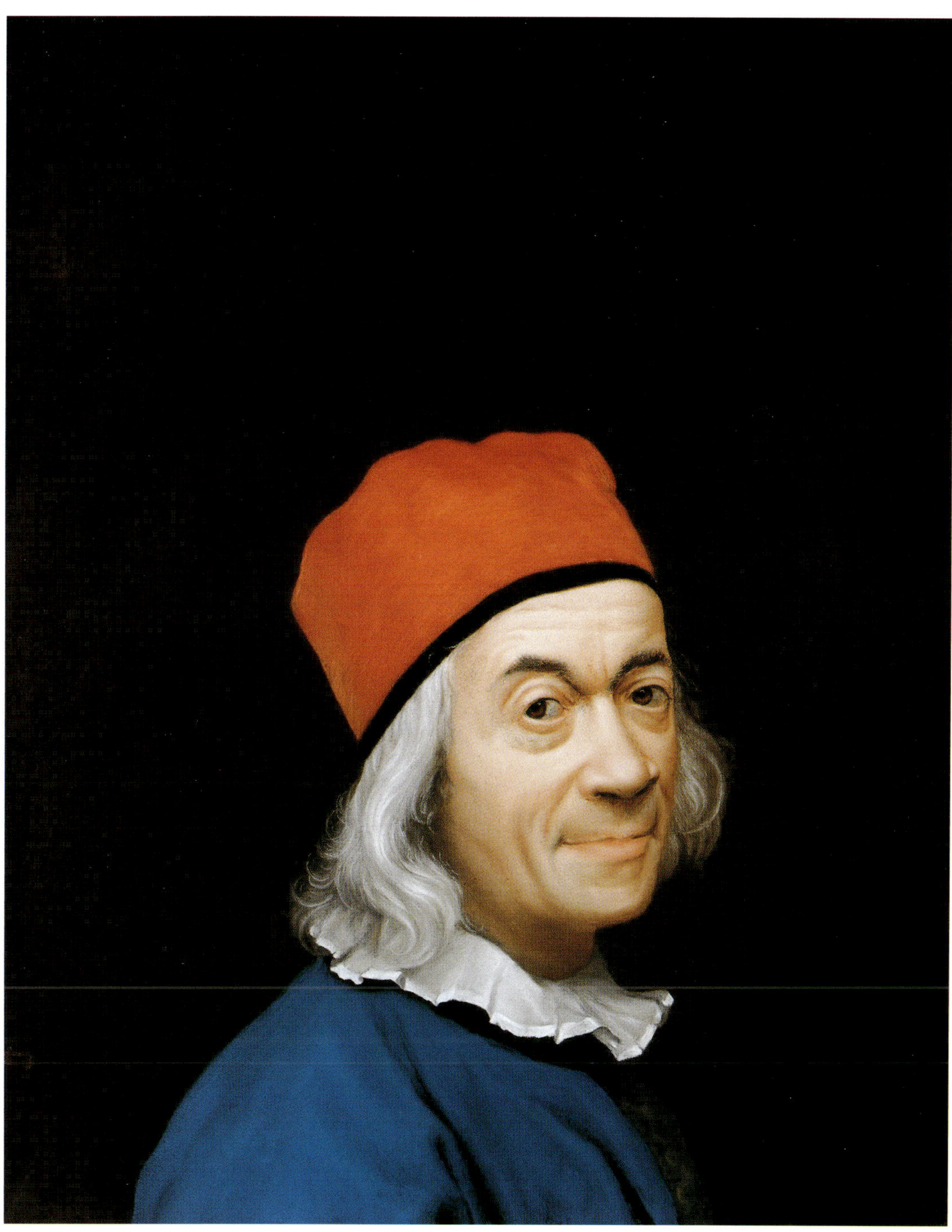

Self-Portrait, known as "in a Red Cap"

1767–68
Pastel on parchment glued
onto canvas
63 x 51 cm
Bequest of Madame
Louis Odier-Lecointe, 1827
Inv. 1827–20

This pastel was in the collection of Louis Odier-Lecointe and was then bequeathed by his wife in 1827 to the Musée Rath. It was put on permanent loan to the Geneva Library in 1843 in exchange for the *Self-Portrait, known as "Liotard with a Beard"* (inv. 1843–5), which had been bequeathed by the artist.

The different situations in which Liotard depicts himself, and the iconological character of his self-portraits clearly connect him with his French rival, Maurice Quentin de La Tour (1704–88), who also represented himself in seemingly unposed postures that challenge the usual spirit of the portrait genre. His *Self-Portrait in an Œil de Bœuf* (circa 1737, inv. 1917–27) aims to convey the model's psychology in addition to his physical likeness. Here too, a mischievous, playful expression and good-natured smile accompany a pointing hand, the index indicating another absent figure—the viewer, perhaps, or the artist's double. The modeling is supple and light, quite different from the almost photographic flatness of the Genevan painter. The soft, rich texture intensifies the impression of life that emanates from this portrait, while the hues and light application of the pastel heighten the intimacy of the moment.

Besides pastel, Liotard also made frequent use of black, red and white chalk in his self-portraits. The *Self-Portrait, known as "with a New Beard"* (1782, inv. 1984–129) is a rare full-length study. The figure of the artist does not occupy the entire sheet but instead seems lost in the page, hunched over itself, surrounded by lots of white. He is at work, wholly focused on his art and perfectly free, so much so that he has let his beard grow back in what may be a painful evocation of a bygone time remembered with longing.[1] Here he states his refusal of the spectacular, his determination to devote himself to his work and to create in the time he has left to live. In his *Self-Portrait, known as "with His Hand on His Chin"* (circa 1770, inv. 1925–5), he places himself firmly so as to fill the page, as if he wanted to expose himself to our gaze, and to move us by his state. The vision that he has here, and that he offers us, is full of compassion and pathos. Nearing his seventies, Liotard adopts the traditional Turkish gesture whereby, covering his throat with his hand, a man signifies his total submission to the woman he loves. These two drawings are very touching, for they give us perfectly authentic images of Liotard, an artist free in his mode of expression and in his life. In them he confirms his perfect understanding of his subject.

1. Anne de Herdt, *Dessins de Liotard*, ex. cat., Paris, Geneva, 1992.

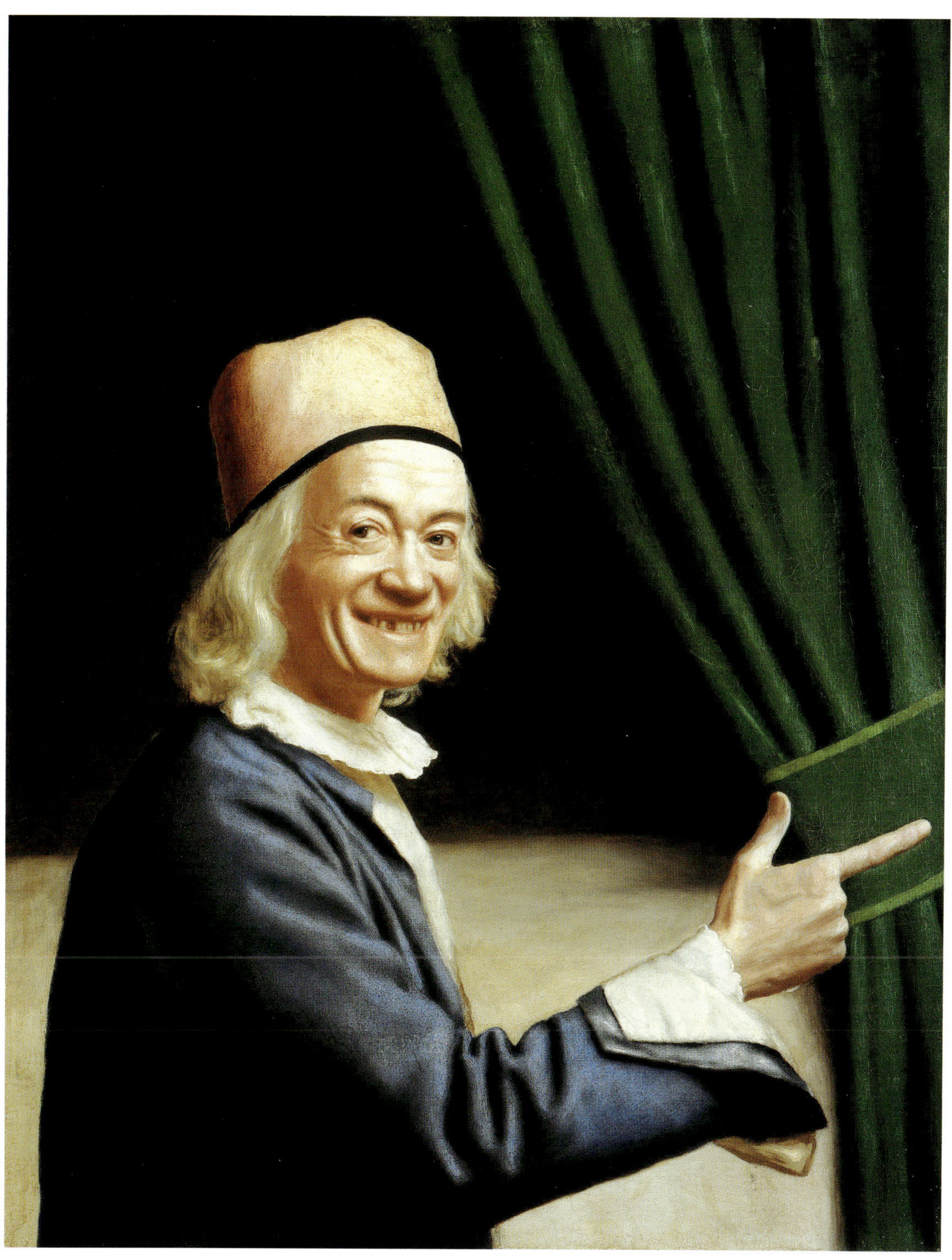

Liotard Laughing

Circa 1770
Oil on canvas
84 x 74 cm
Purchase, 1893
Inv. 1893–9

Kept in the artist's own collection, this self-portrait was
inherited by his daughter Marie-Jeanne de Bassompierre
(Geneva) in 1790; from her it passed to the Liotard family
in Amsterdam. In 1873 it entered a private collection in
Utrecht.

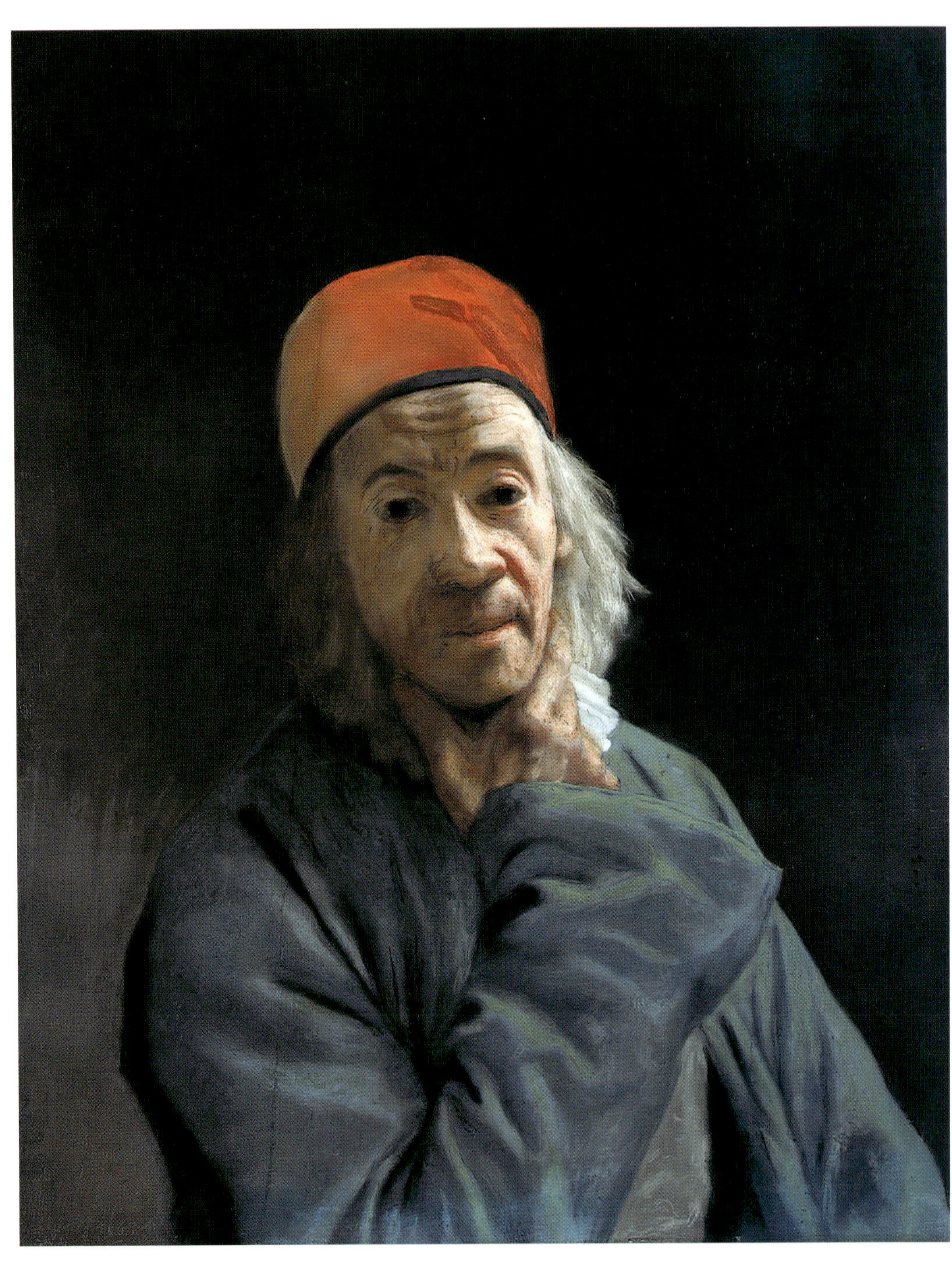

Self-Portrait, known as "with His Hand on His Chin"

Circa 1770
**Pastel on paper glued
onto canvas**
63.5 x 51 cm
**Purchase, 1925
Inv. 1925–5**

From the Earl of Bessborough's collection (London), this
pastel was inherited in about 1773 by relations in the
Ponsonby family (London).

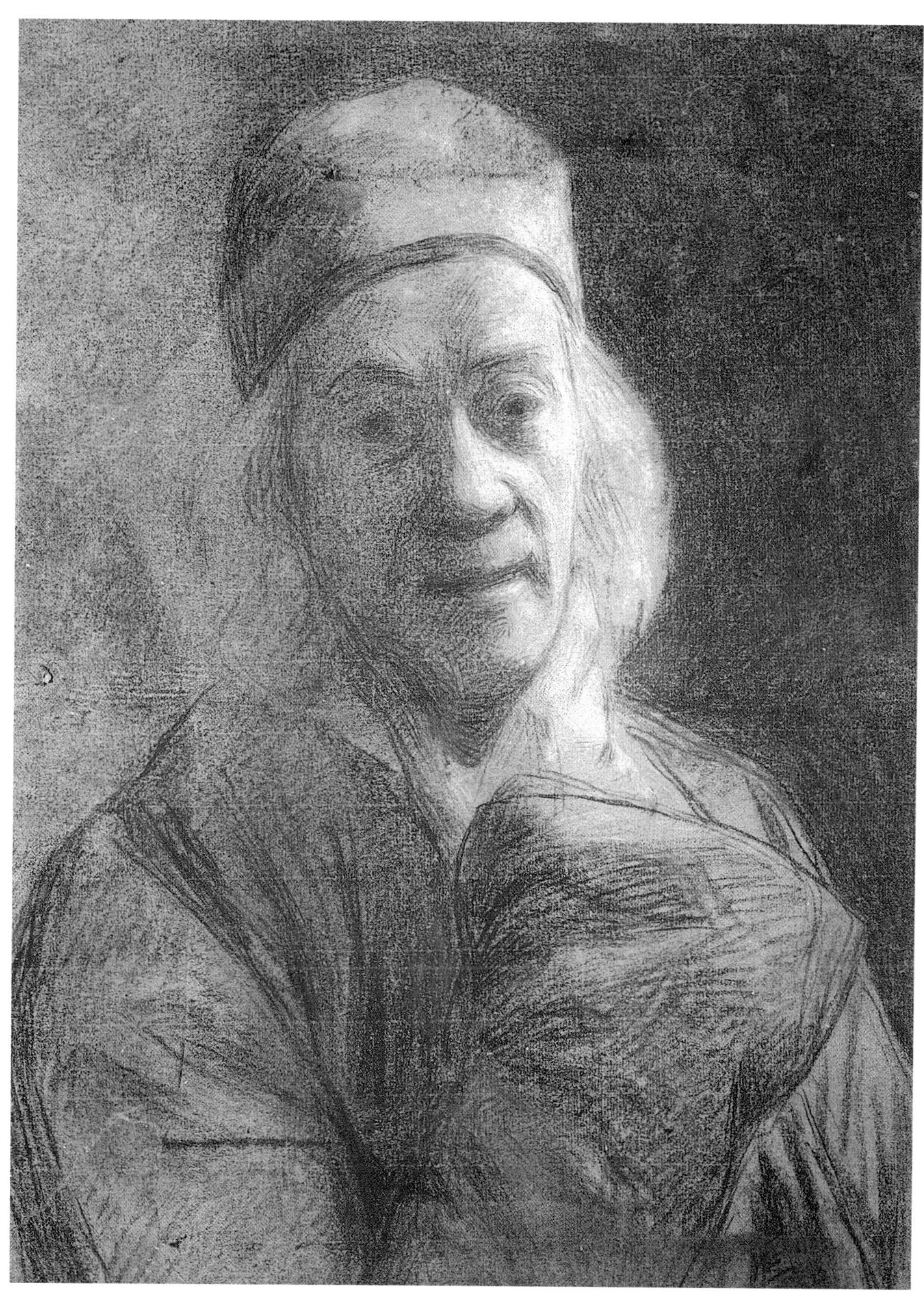

Self-Portrait

Circa 1770
Black and white chalk,
heightened with red chalk
on blue paper glued to
cardboard
48.8 x 35.9 cm
Purchase, 1960
Inv. 1960–32

This drawing was in the artist's personal collection
(Geneva). After that, its location was unknown until the
early twentieth century, when it reappeared in a private
collection.

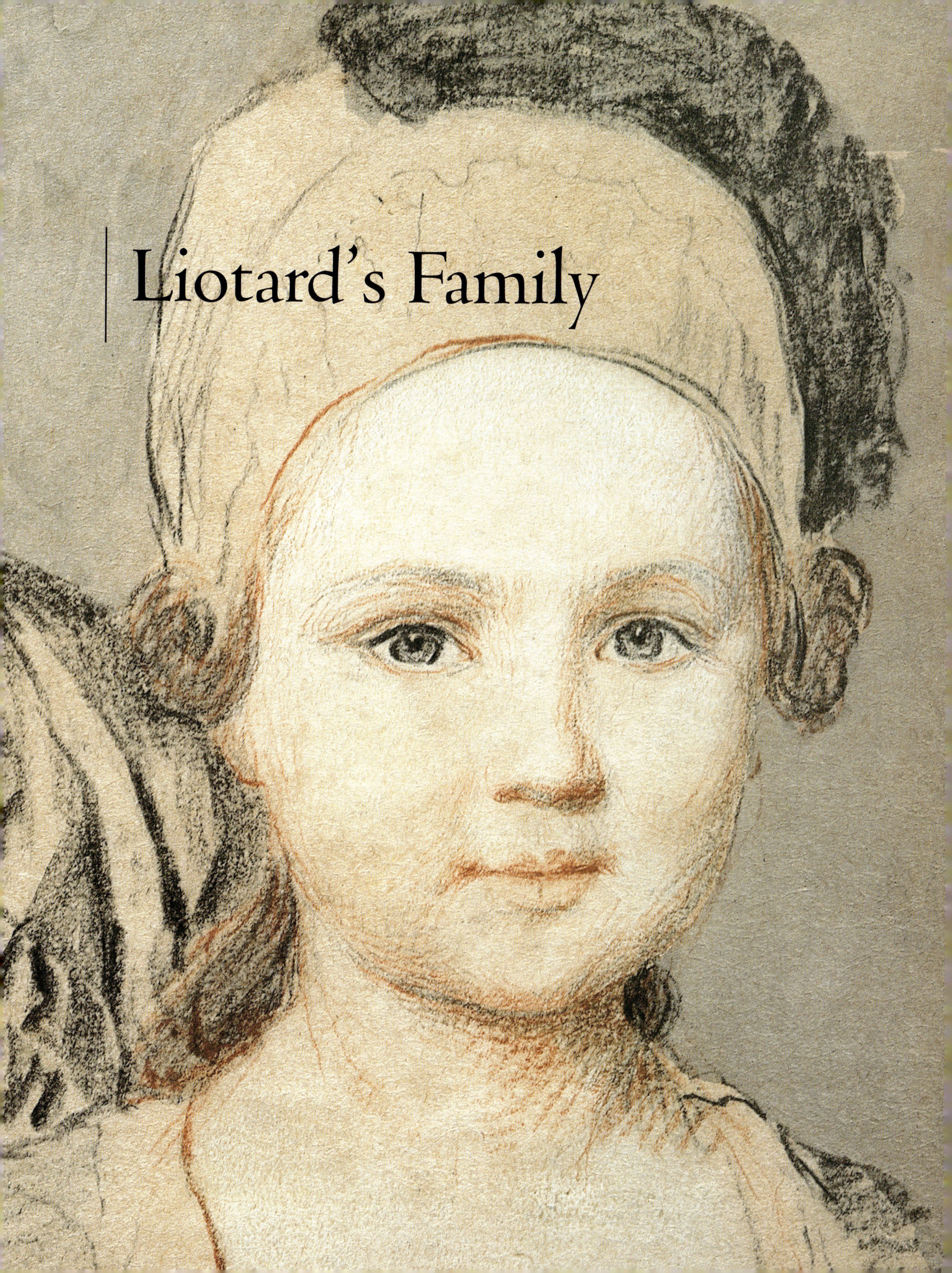

Liotard's Family

Isabelle Félicité Bleeker

Liotard undertook his first drawn portraits, depicting members of his family, back in the days of his apprenticeship as a miniaturist and enamelist. The watercolor portrait of his twin brother, Jean-Michel Liotard, made in about 1718–20, exemplifies these early works. This is the second known drawing by the artist. A few years later he produced a very different depiction of his brother in his *Presumed Portrait of Jean-Michel Liotard* (before 1738, inv. 1865–1). This was a bravura piece, remarkable for its freedom of execution and for the contrast between the vigor and stylistic diversity in the rendering of the jacket with the smooth, graphic quality of the face. Between 1723 and 1735, Liotard returned to Geneva from Paris and made a portrait of his father (*Antoine Liotard*, circa 1727–30, private collection).

In 1755 the painter traveled to Holland and stayed with his nephew, the pastor Jean-Louis Maisonnet, in Delft, and painted a magnificent portrait of him as well as one of his wife, both of which are in the museum (*Jean-Louis Maisonnet, a Pastor in Delft*, 1755, inv. 1969–9, and *Madame Jean-Louis Maisonnet, née Marie-Anne Marconnay*, 1755, inv. 1969–10). In these two pastels we may note the care taken over the details, the quality of the finish, and the unity and clarity that were characteristic of the realistic, bourgeois conception shared by Liotard and the Dutch portraitists. We should also remember that most of the paintings in the artist's personal collection were Dutch; he used these works as both examples and models.

After Delft, Liotard stayed in The Hague, where he was introduced into Dutch aristocratic circles. Finally, he ended his tour of the Netherlands in Amsterdam, where he met Marie Fargues, the daughter of an émigré French merchant, whom he married in 1756. The museum has a very fine drawing of her (circa 1762) with her eldest son, Jean-Étienne (1758–1822), sitting on her lap. Liotard produced numerous studies of his wife, children, and other members of his family. The first known portrait of one of his children was painted in 1760 and shows Jean-Étienne, at the age of twenty-two months.[1] The museum collection includes another depiction of him (inv. 1934–28) and a number of portraits of Liotard's daughters.

His eldest daughter, Marie-Jeanne or Mariette (1761–1813) married the printer François de Bassompierre in 1782, and Liotard went to live with them at Begnins in 1786. It was in the 1780s that he produced the mysterious and striking pastel of his daughter passing a dish of peaches. Donated to the museum by Baron Edmond de Rothschild in 1998, this composition combining the portrait and still-life genres in an interior setting is unusual in Liotard's work. This pastel is exceptional for the freshness and delicacy of the fruit, the mysterious expression of the face, and the bold composition, with the division of the background emphasizing the picture plane.

In about 1779, Liotard drew the profile of his second daughter, Marie-Thérèse, born in 1763 (*Marie-Thérèse Liotard*, inv. 1934–31) and, a few months later, a delicate preparatory drawing shows her looking at her own miniature portrait (*Marie-Thérèse Liotard, the Artist's Daughter, Looking at Her Portrait in Miniature*, 1779 or 1780, inv. 1935–7). The drawing is squared, in preparation for a mezzotint.

1. Anne de Herdt, *Dessins de Liotard*, ex. cat., Paris, Geneva, 1992, no. 110, p. 202.

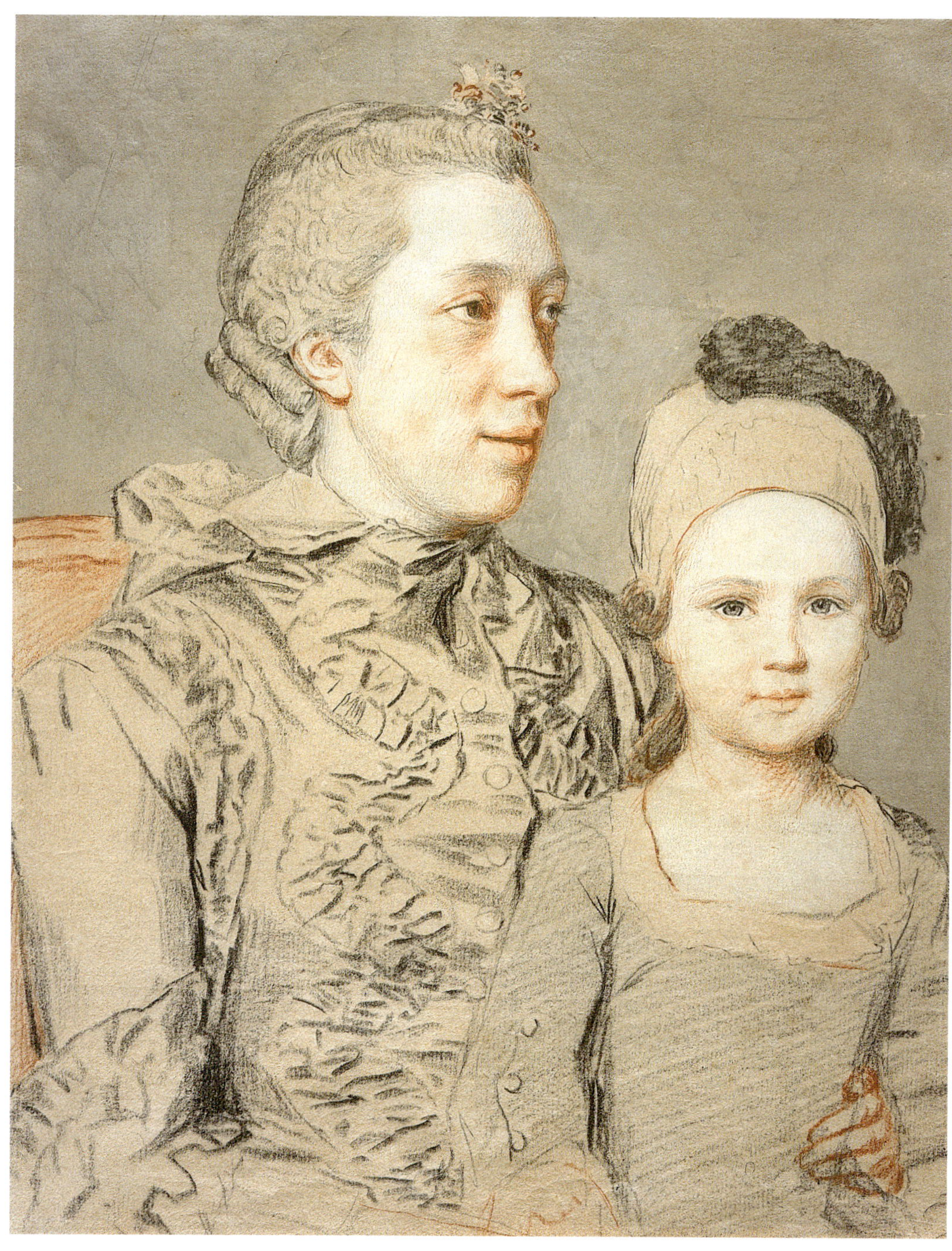

Circa 1762
Black and red chalk and
watercolor on paper,
heightened with color on the
verso
24.5 x 19.6 cm
Gift of the Société Auxiliaire
du Musée, 1934
Inv. 1934–32

This is an astonishing family portrait. As Anne de Herdt observes (1992, p. 238), the mother and her son here appear to be strangers. It is as if two independent portraits had been combined to form a single image, and this physical proximity was the sitters' only connection. Sitting on his mother's lap, wearing a charming bonnet, the young Jean-Étienne, the artist's eldest son, meets the gaze of the viewer, who is also the maker of the drawing: his father.

His elegantly dressed mother, meanwhile, gazes into the distance. The only connection between these two figures is the barely sketched motherly hand placed on the son's waist. Swiftly sketched in, the clothes take second place to the carefully drawn faces, which evince Liotard's characteristic concern for exactitude.

This drawing belonged to the Liotard family in Amsterdam.

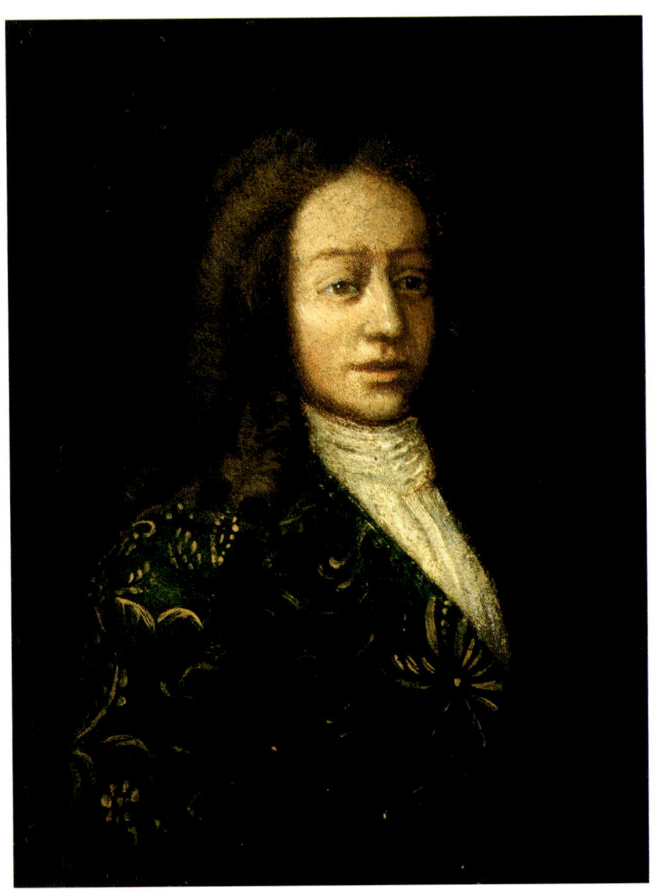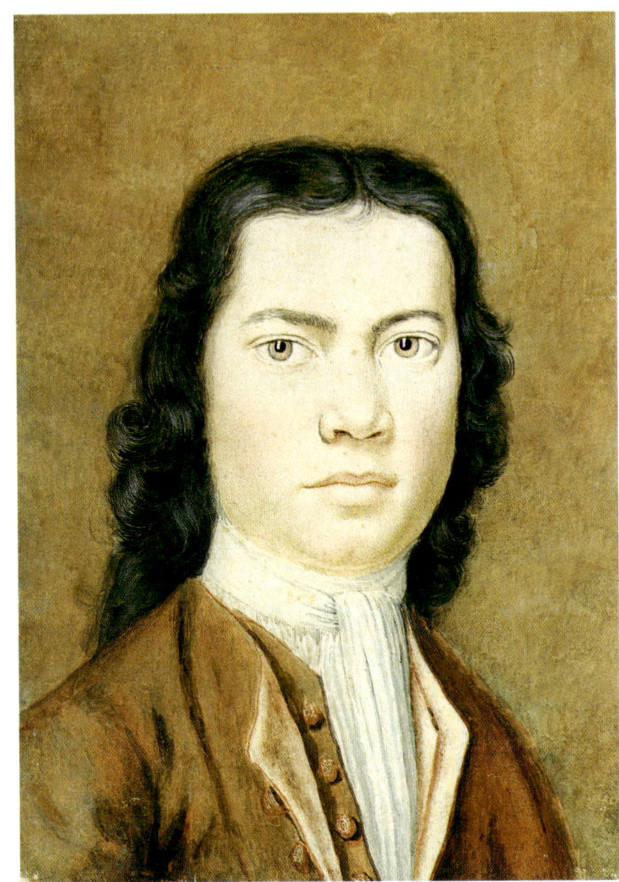

Antoine Liotard (1661–1740), the Artist's Father

Circa 1721
Oil on panel
15.8 x 12 cm
Purchase, 1987
Inv. 1987–1

The merchant Antoine Liotard came from Montélimar, in the province of Dauphiné, as did his wife, Anne Sauvage (1659–1731). He took refuge in Geneva after the revocation of the Edict of Nantes (1685) and was accepted as a bourgeois there in 1701. According to the son of Jean-Étienne Liotard, Antoine "was a man of wealth" but, ruined like many other Genevans by the financial debacle in Mississippi, was forced to sell his fine big house in the city. The artist represents his father in three-quarter profile, his gaze not meeting the viewer's. The sixty-year-old Antoine seems astonishingly young. He wears a wig and a green and gold damask coat.

Jean-Michel Liotard, the Painter's Twin Brother (1702–1796)

Circa 1718–20
Brush and watercolor, Chinese ink, and red chalk heightened with white gouache on paper glued to a board
23 x 16.5 cm
Gift of the Société Auxiliaire du Musée, 1934
Inv. 1934–30

A draftsman and engraver, Jean-Michel Liotard trained with Benoît II Audran in Paris. He also worked in Venice, where his brother visited him on his way back from Vienna in February 1745. In 1746, Jean-Michel married Marie, the daughter of the pastor Jean-Jacques Des Prez. Back in Paris, Jean-Michel made numerous engravings of works by other artists, notably Watteau and Eustache Le Sueur.
This early drawing is very different from Liotard's later pastel of his brother (p. 39). Although still somewhat stiff, it does reveal the artist's talent for detail, the sharpness of his vision, and the delicacy of his line. In the biography of his father, Jean-Étienne Liotard *fils* mentions a portrait of his uncle executed by Liotard when he was training with Daniel Gardelle (Louis Gielly, *Genava*, 1933, p. 192): "Liotard started painting portraits from life, of his family or of other persons prepared to take part, and when they paid him a *mirliton*, a Louis d'or, he was very pleased. [...] Several of these portraits still exist and one can admire their most exquisite naturalness, among them the portrait of his twin brother, who was then very young and still looks like him." This portrait was kept in the artist's own collection and remained with his family in Amsterdam until 1934.

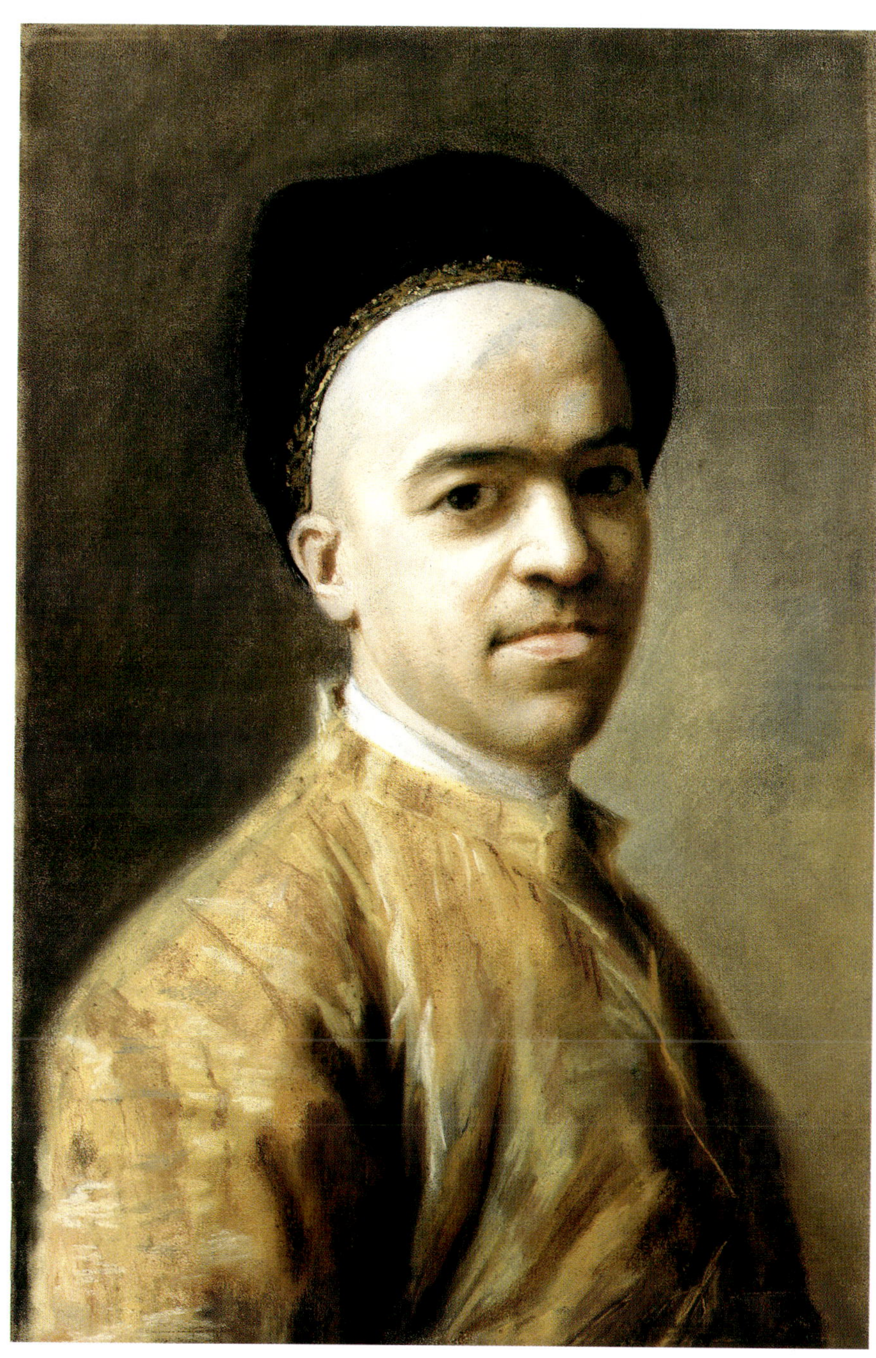

Presumed Portrait of Jean-Michel Liotard (1702–1796)

Before 1738
Pastel on parchment
55 x 38.5 cm
Bequest of David Claparède,
1865
Inv. 1865–1

Originally considered a self-portrait, this pastel was first identified as a portrait of the artist's twin brother, Jean-Michel, by Numa S. Trivas (1936). This is one of the works inherited through kinship by Théodore Claparède and bequeathed by David Claparède to the Musées d'Art et d'Histoire in 1865.

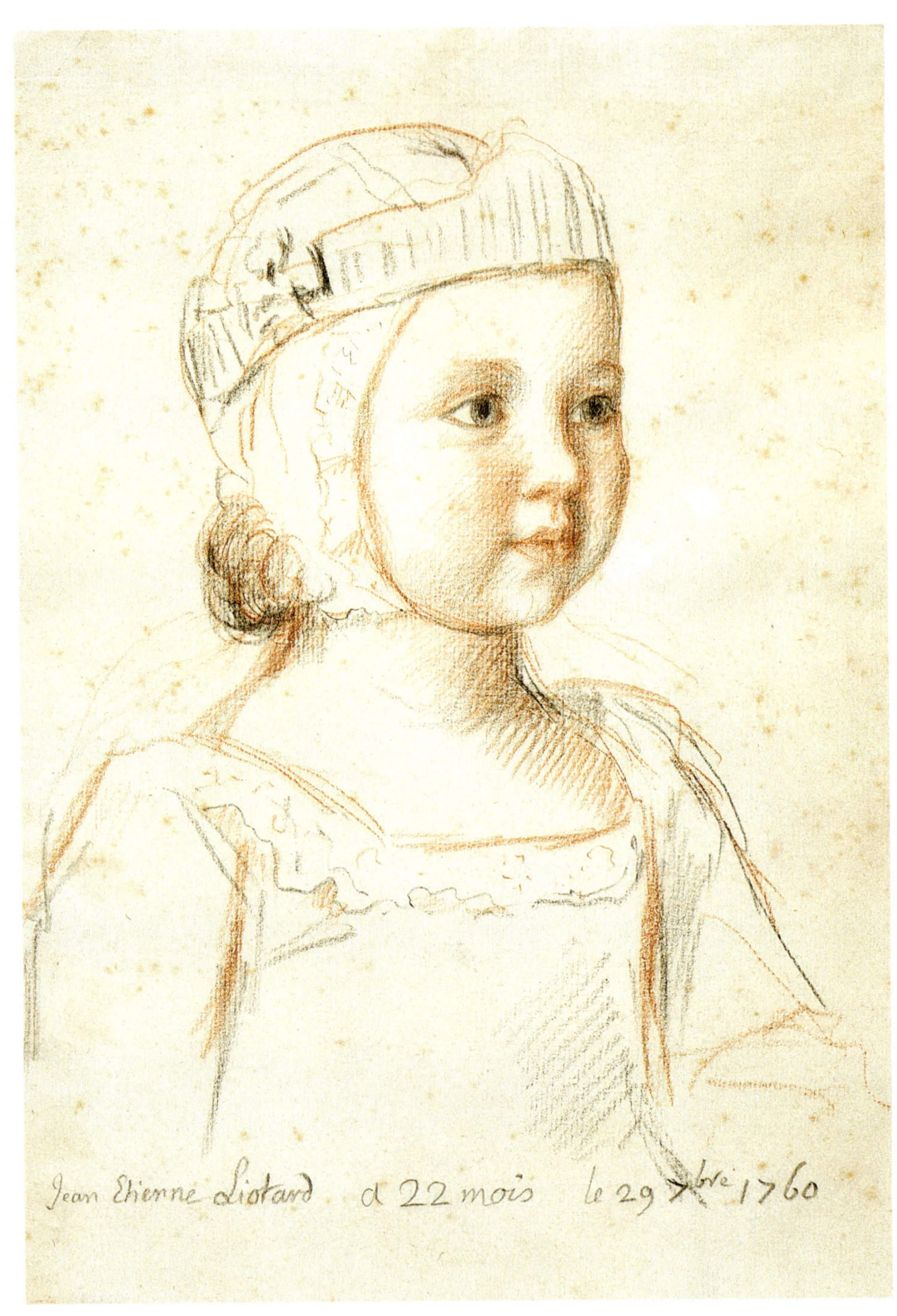

Jean-Étienne Liotard (1758–1822), the Artist's Eldest Son, at Twenty-Two Months

1760
Red and black chalk, and
graphite pencil on paper
23.5 x 17.1 cm
Gift of the Société Auxiliaire
du Musée, 1934
Inv. 1934–36

As Anne de Herdt has suggested (1992, p. 202), this very
plain and truthful work brings to mind the master
draftsmen of the sixteenth century, such as the Clouets and
Holbeins. The pared, precise expression of Liotard's work
has much in common with theirs.
This work passed from the artist's own collection to his
family in Amsterdam.

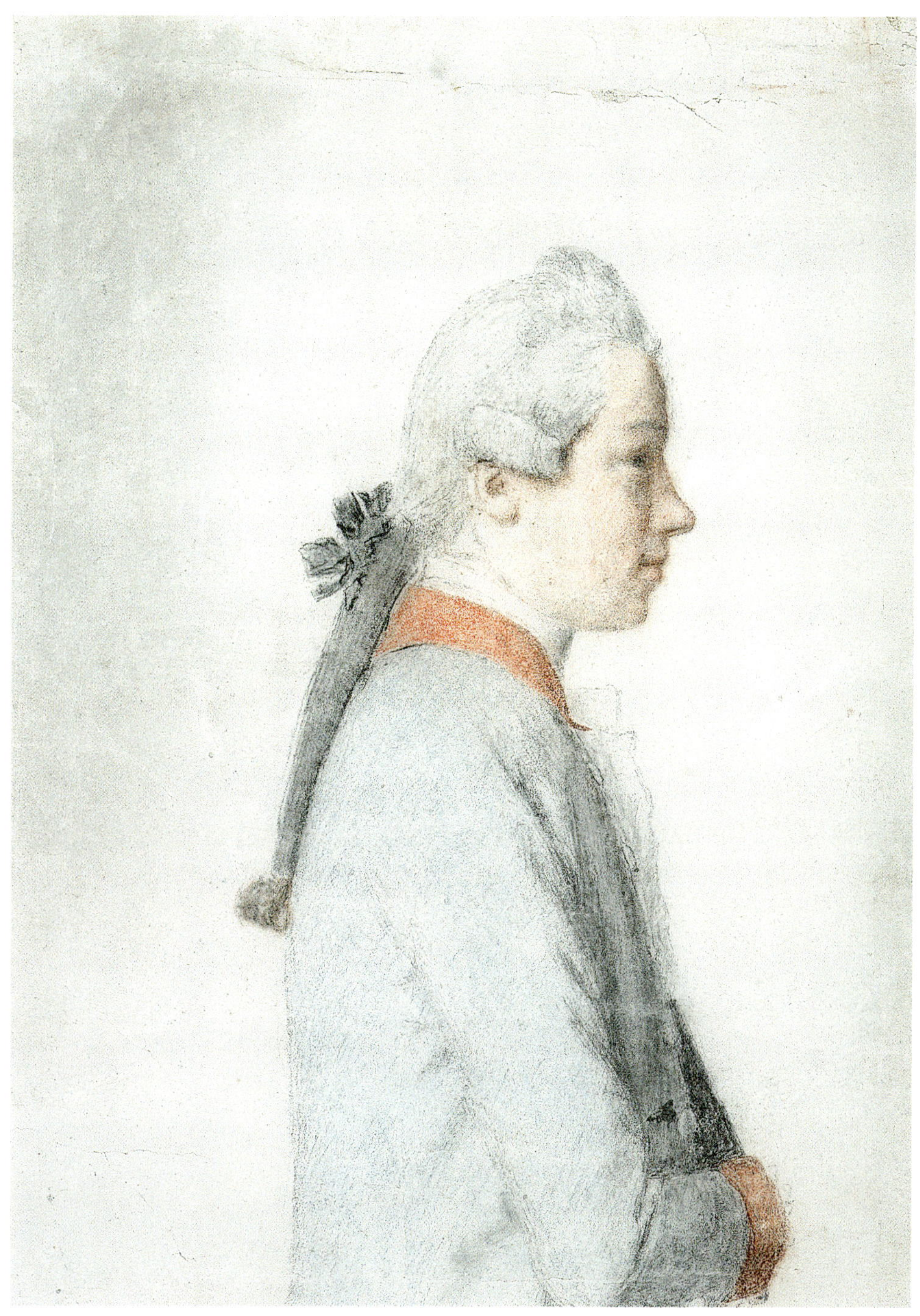

1777
**Red and black chalk
heightened with pastel on
canvas prepared with a white
ground**
28.1 x 21.4 cm
**Gift of the Société Auxiliaire
du Musée, 1934**
Inv. 1934–28

In October 1777 Liotard set off for Vienna in the hope of finding a good position there for his son, then aged nineteen. They arrived in the Austrian capital on November 5. Although received by the most influential figures there, and welcomed with great kindness by the empress, who offered them accommodation in her palace, the two travelers failed to achieve the success they hoped for. Although Liotard did execute drawings and paintings, they were mainly for the imperial family. He also produced this portrait of his son in court clothing, tricorn hat in hand, which the sitter alluded to as follows in his journal entry for November 28, 1777: "My father experimented with painting my likeness on prepared canvases [*sic*] (November 27, 1777); [he] worked a lot on my head."
This drawing was one of the works that was kept in the artist's own collection and remained with his family in Amsterdam until 1934.

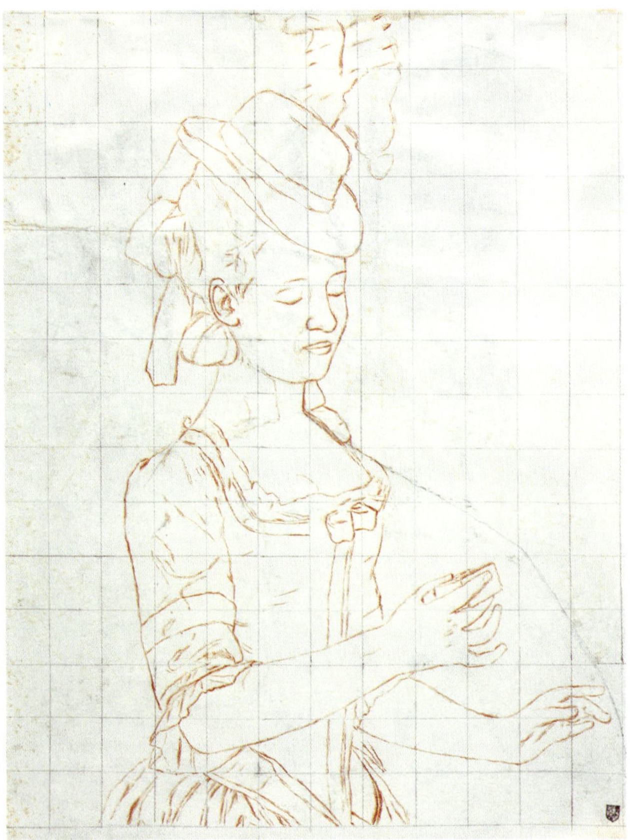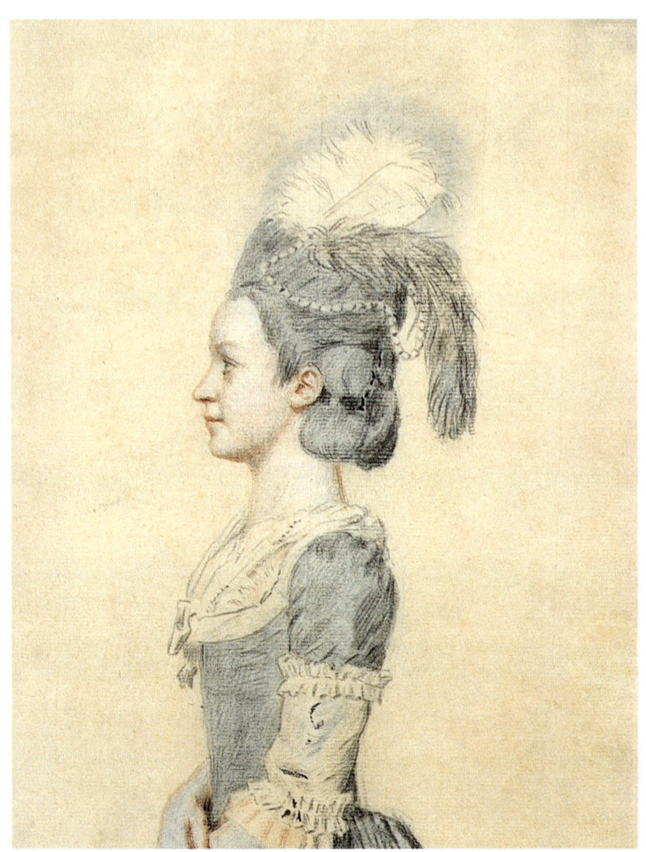

Marie-Thérèse Liotard (1763–1793), the Artist's Daughter, Looking at Her Portrait in Miniature

1779–80
Red chalk on paper squared
with graphite pencil
41.3 x 32.6 cm
Gift of the Société Auxiliaire
du Musée, 1934
Inv. 1935-7

Marie-Thérèse was Liotard's second daughter. Born in January 1763, shortly after her father's return from Vienna, she was the goddaughter of Maria Theresa of Austria. Despite this auspicious start, Marie-Thérèse was to have a very sad life. In 1784 her brother refused to allow her marriage to the Danish miniaturist Hans Henrik Ploetz, and she died in 1793, aged only thirty.

This preparatory drawing, squared by Liotard for a mezzotint engraving, shows her contemplating a miniature of herself, which she holds gracefully in her right hand. It was based on a drawing in mixed chalks (private collection) in which Liotard pursued his exploration of light effects. In the chapter on grace in his treatise, Liotard discussed the print as follows: "The foremost quality for a painter is to put grace in everything he does. […] In print IV of my daughter Marie-Thérèse, my intention was to depict a young woman in a simple, naïve and pleasant posture, smiling graciously and looking at what we take to be a portrait on a snuff box that she is holding."

This drawing belonged to the Liotard family in Amsterdam.

Marie-Thérèse Liotard (1763–1793), the Artist's Daughter, Seen in Left Profile

Circa 1779
Graphite pencil, and black and
red chalk heightened with
faint blue watercolor and
traces of white gouache on
yellowed white paper,
heightened with color on the
verso
24.2 x 18.9 cm
Gift of the Société Auxiliaire
du Musée, 1934
Inv. 1934-31

Marie-Thérèse was sixteen when her father drew this portrait. The freedom of touch and contrasts between the different pencils give this work a singularly fresh feel. This piece went from the artist's own collection to his family in Amsterdam.

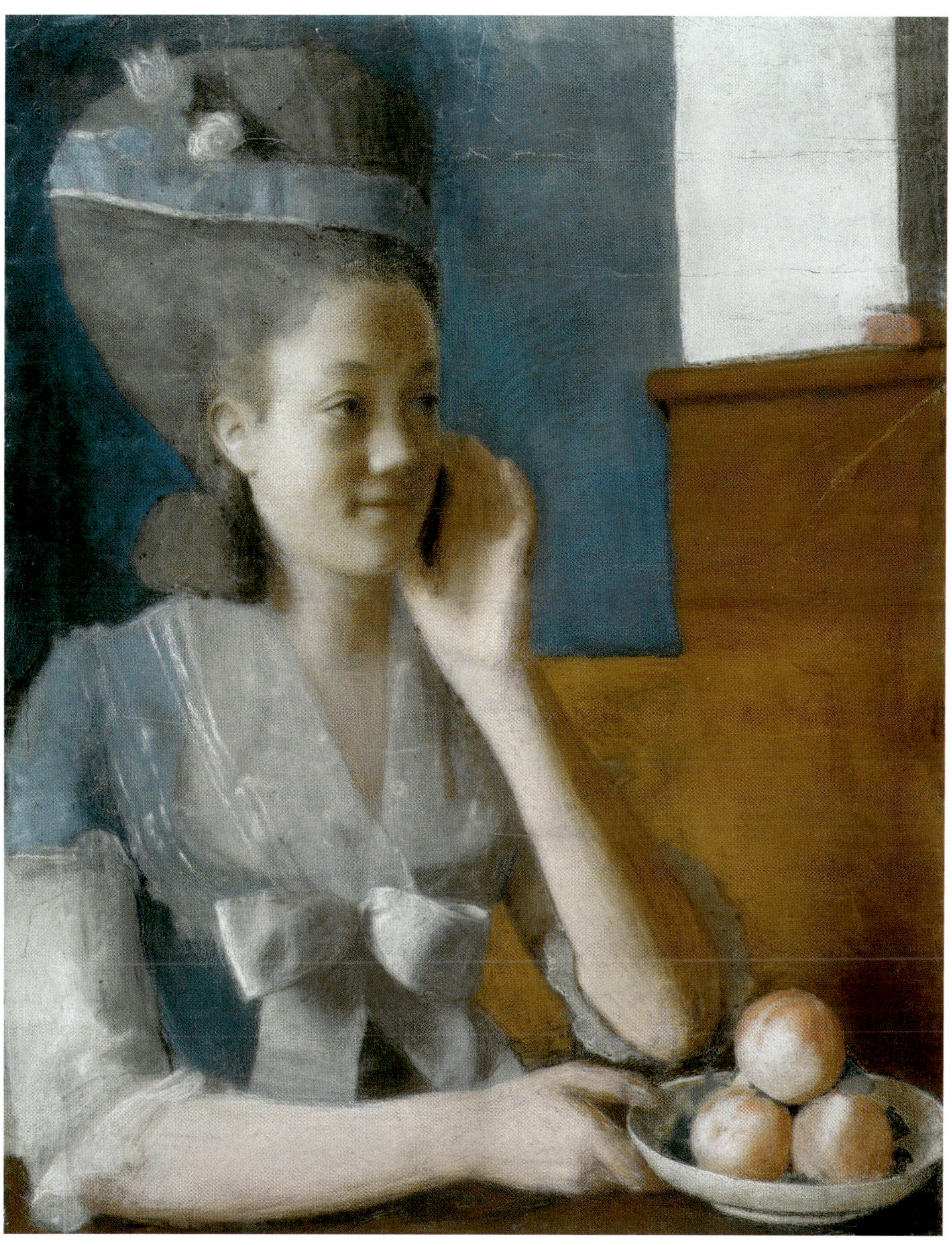

Marie-Jeanne, known as Mariette, de Bassompierre (1761–1813)

1779
Pastel on paper glued onto
canvas
69 x 55 cm
Bequest of Baron Edmond de
Rothschild, 1998
Inv. D 1998–501

Liotard's eldest daughter, Marie-Jeanne, married the Liège-based printer François de Bassompierre in 1782 but divorced him in 1799. She died in 1813.

This pastel went from the sitter's collection, by way of inheritance and kinship, to the Vignier family in Geneva and was later acquired by Baron Edmond de Rothschild in Geneva.

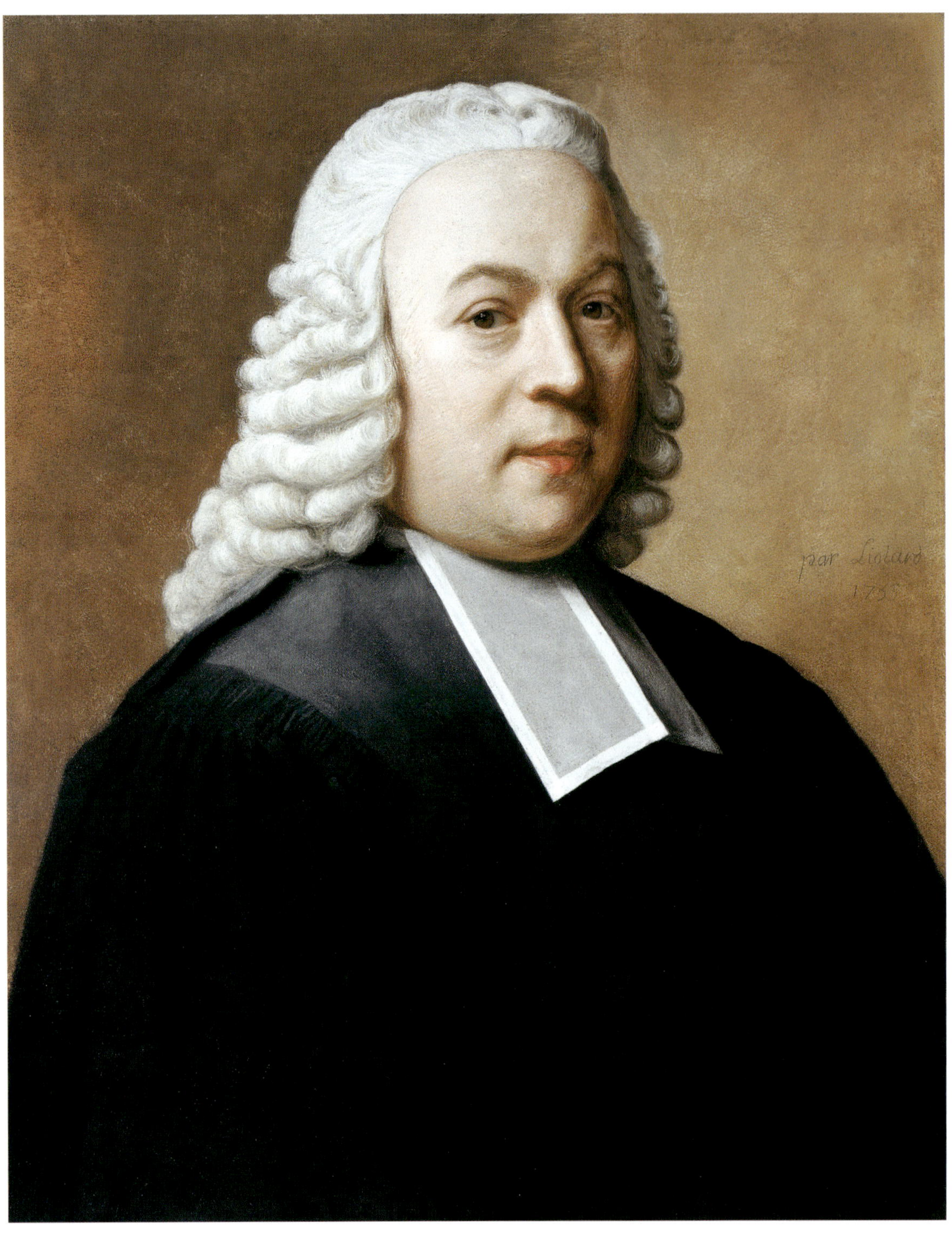

Jean-Louis Maisonnet, a Pastor in Delft (1713–1789)

1755
Signed and dated
Pastel on parchment
57 x 45.6 cm
Gift of Madame E. Dapples,
1969
Inv. 1969–9

The son of one of Liotard's sisters, his nephew Jean-Louis
Maisonnet was born in Geneva. He became a pastor in
Delft, and in 1744 he married Marie-Anne Marconnay, from
a family of French refugees. Liotard stayed with him during
his Dutch sojourn in 1755, and the pastor commissioned
him to do portraits of himself and his wife. He would later
act as witness at Liotard's marriage to Marie Fargues
(Amsterdam, August 1756). He is shown here in his black
pastor's clothing, bewigged, against a solid background.

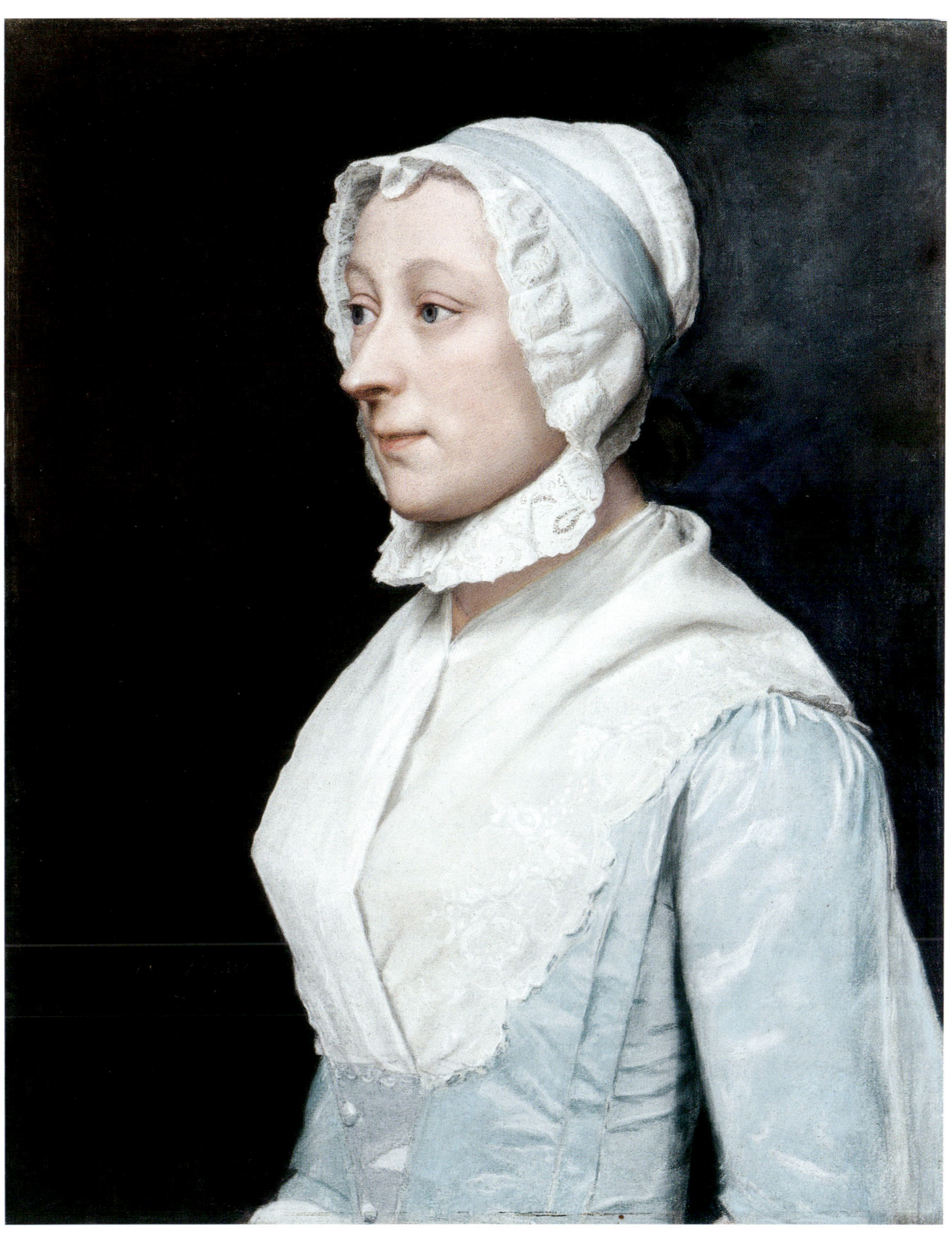

Madame Jean-Louis Maisonnet, née Marie-Anne Marconnay (1721–1812)

1755
Signed and dated
Pastel on parchment
56.5 x 46.5 cm
Gift of Madame E. Dapples,
1969
Inv. 1969–10

Marie-Anne Maisonnet faces her husband. A fine, still
figure, dressed in light colors, she is depicted in full light,
without compromise.
From the Maisonnet home in Delft, these works went to
private collectors in Leiden and Florence.

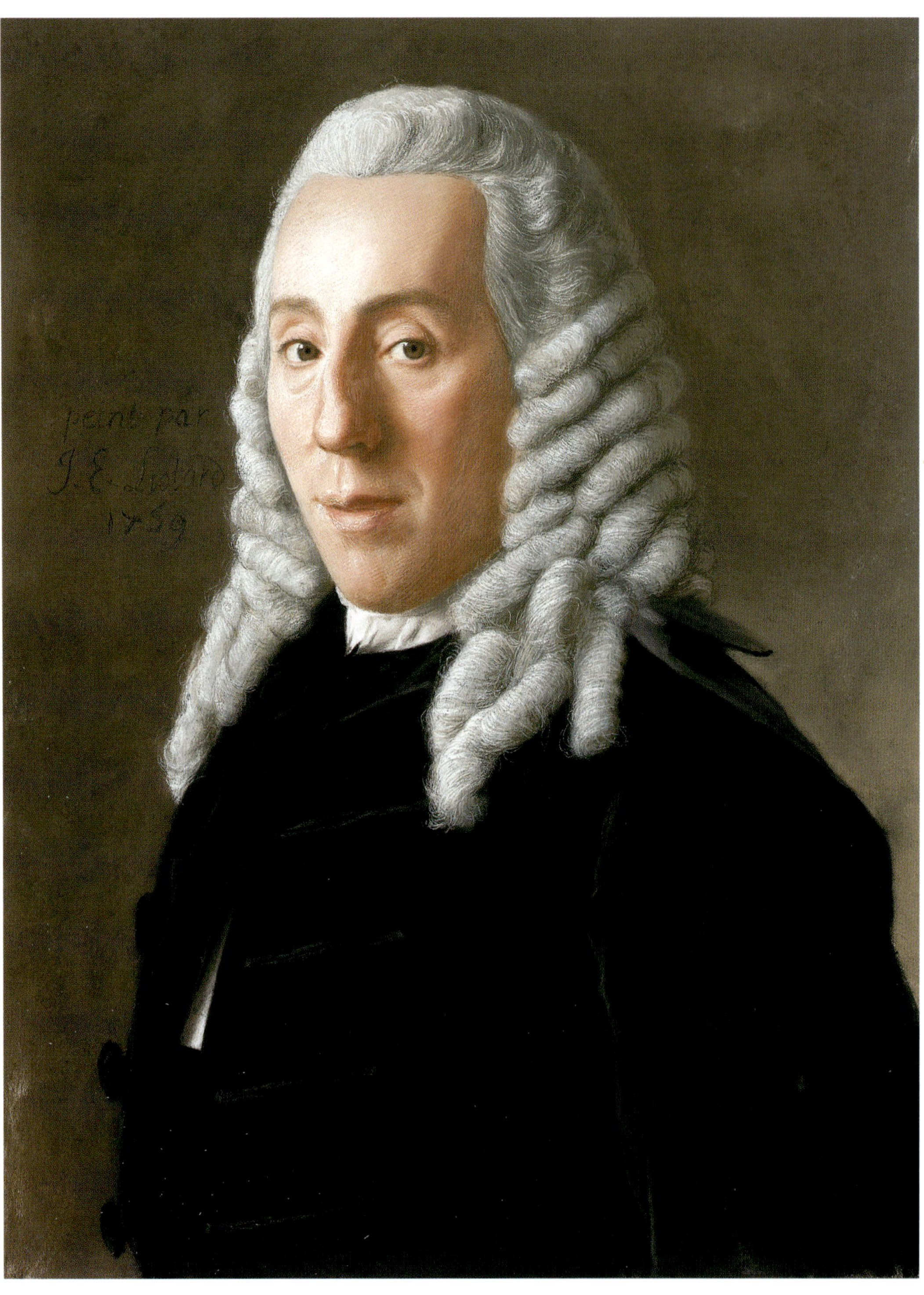

Jean Sarasin (1722–1798)

1759
Signed and dated
Pastel on parchment
60 x 46.5 cm
Bequest of David Claparède,
1865
Inv. 1865–5

The son of the pastor Jean Sarasin (1693–1760) and brother of Marianne Sarasin-Liotard (see p. 50), Jean Sarasin married Marie-Jeanne Liotard, the artist's niece, in 1752. Jean Sarasin became auditor of justice and a member of the Council of Two Hundred in 1758, and it is in the attributes of his office that this future owner of Peney Castle (1763), counselor (1767), and syndic (1773) chose to be represented.

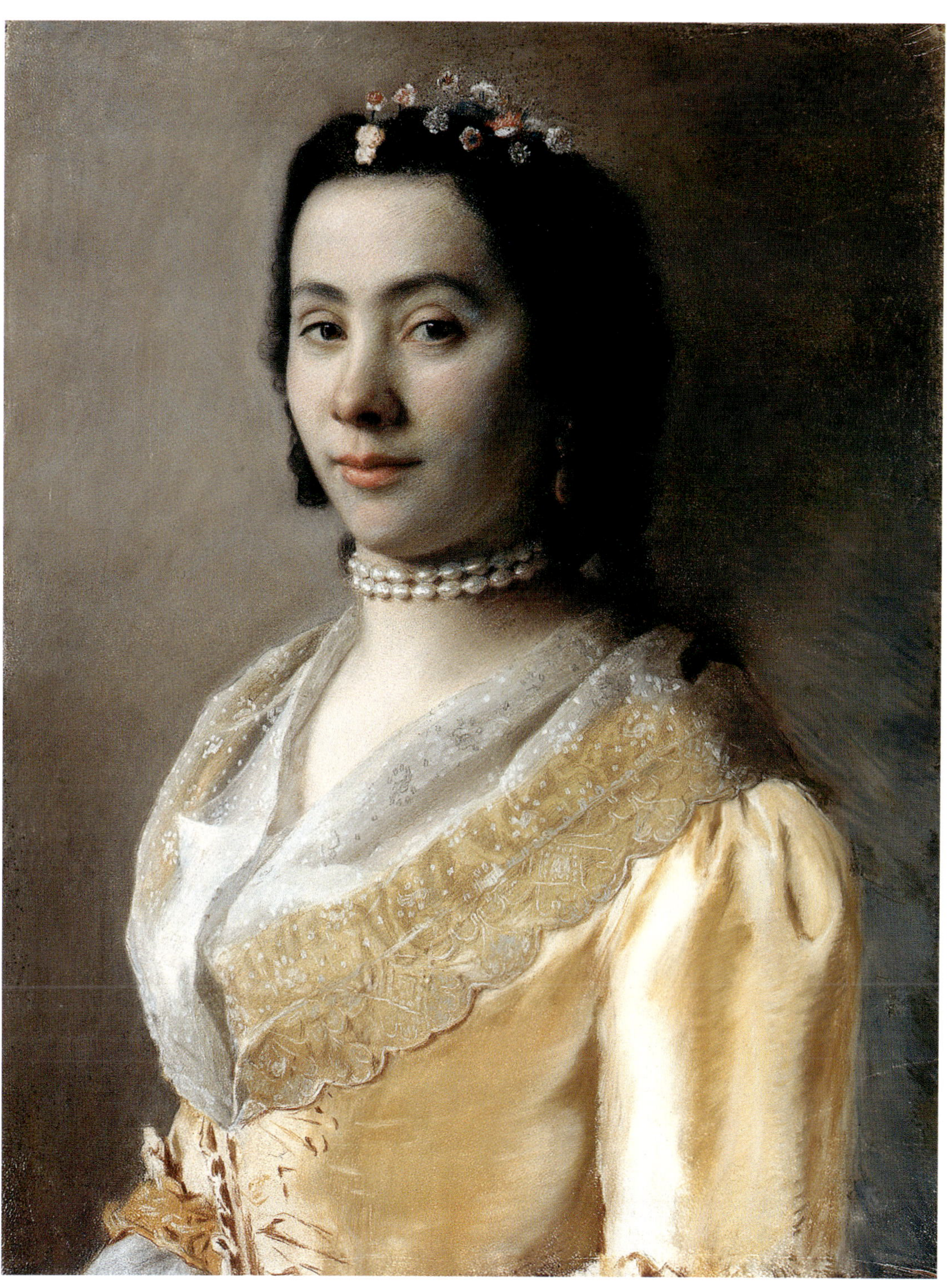

Circa 1752
Pastel on parchment
42 x 33 cm
On permanent loan from the
Fondation Gottfried Keller,
1940
Inv. 1940–20

This portrait of Liotard's niece is not a pendant to the larger one of her husband, the future syndic Jean Sarasin. The young woman, whom Liotard had already depicted in pencil, is rendered here in pastel on the occasion of her wedding in 1752. The palette is rich, the tones golden. Wearing a yellow dress with a kerchief, bedecked with a pearl necklace and with delicate flowers standing out in her dark hair, Marie-Jeanne is resplendent in this portrait, which is nevertheless uncompromising, both noble and intimate. Here, Liotard combines supple strokes of pastel with a great sense of detail. He is extremely subtle in his rendering of the transparency of Marie-Jeanne's complexion and of the texture of the fabrics. The pictorial qualities of this pastel make it one of the artist's outstanding works. It went by inheritance and kinship to the Claparède Collection and remained in that family until 1940.

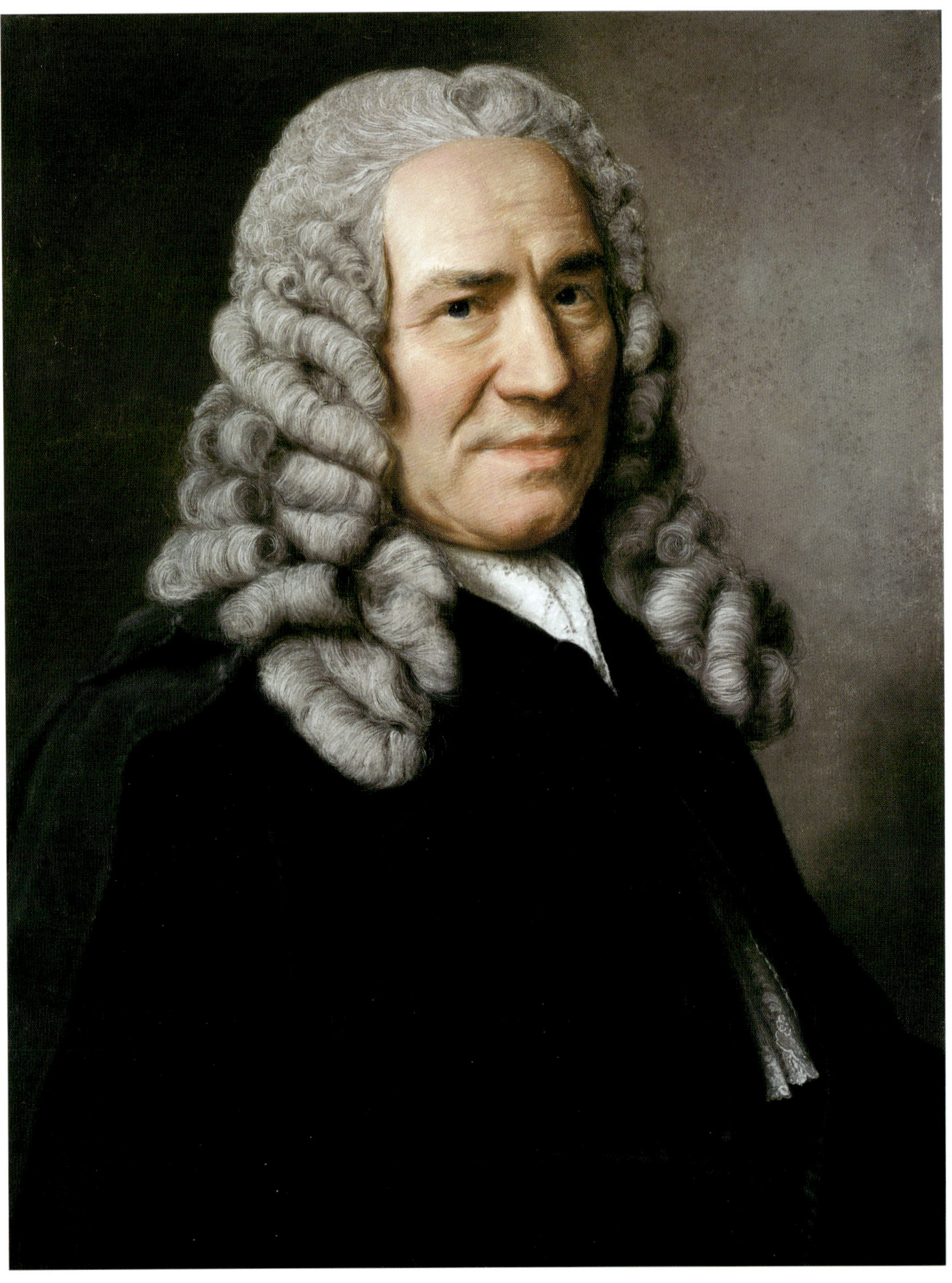

Pierre Mussard (1690–1767)

1763
Pastel on parchment
63.5 x 50.5 cm
Purchase, 1894
Inv. 1894–1

A famous magistrate and professor of law, Pierre Mussard became Liotard's relative when his sister Jeanne married the artist's older brother, Jean, in 1710. A member of the Council of Two Hundred since 1721, a counselor in 1735, secretary of state from 1738 to 1749, and syndic on several occasions (1750, 1754, 1758, and 1762), he was also a deputy for the Republic in Paris and Turin. Like Jean Sarasin (p. 46), he is depicted in a black robe, jabot, and wig. In February 1763, he presented the painter's daughter,

Marie-Thérèse, for baptism. She was named after Empress Maria Theresa, who had agreed to be her godmother. Since the august sovereign forgot to thank her representative at the ceremony, Liotard offered the syndic this portrait. It was to this member of one of the Republic's most powerful families that Montesquieu entrusted the manuscript of his *Spirit of the Laws* for publication.

From the sitter's collection, this pastel passed into a private collection in Geneva.

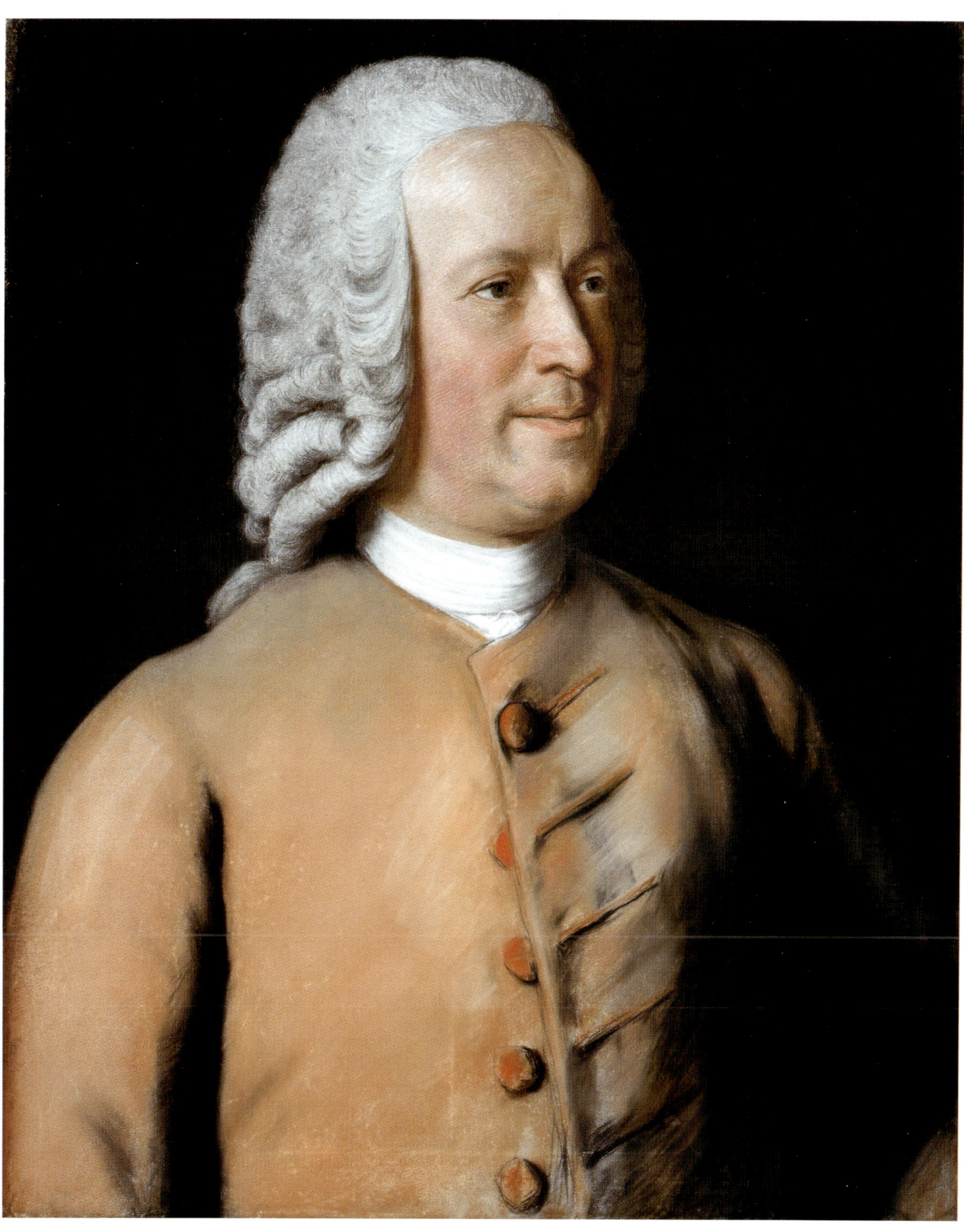

Monsieur Liotard de Plainpalais

Circa 1762 or 1775
Pastel on parchment
60 x 48 cm
Bequest of David Claparède,
1865
Inv. 1865–2

Liotard de Plainpalais was a cousin of the artist's. Like most
of Liotard's portraits of family members, this pastel evinces
great freedom of execution.

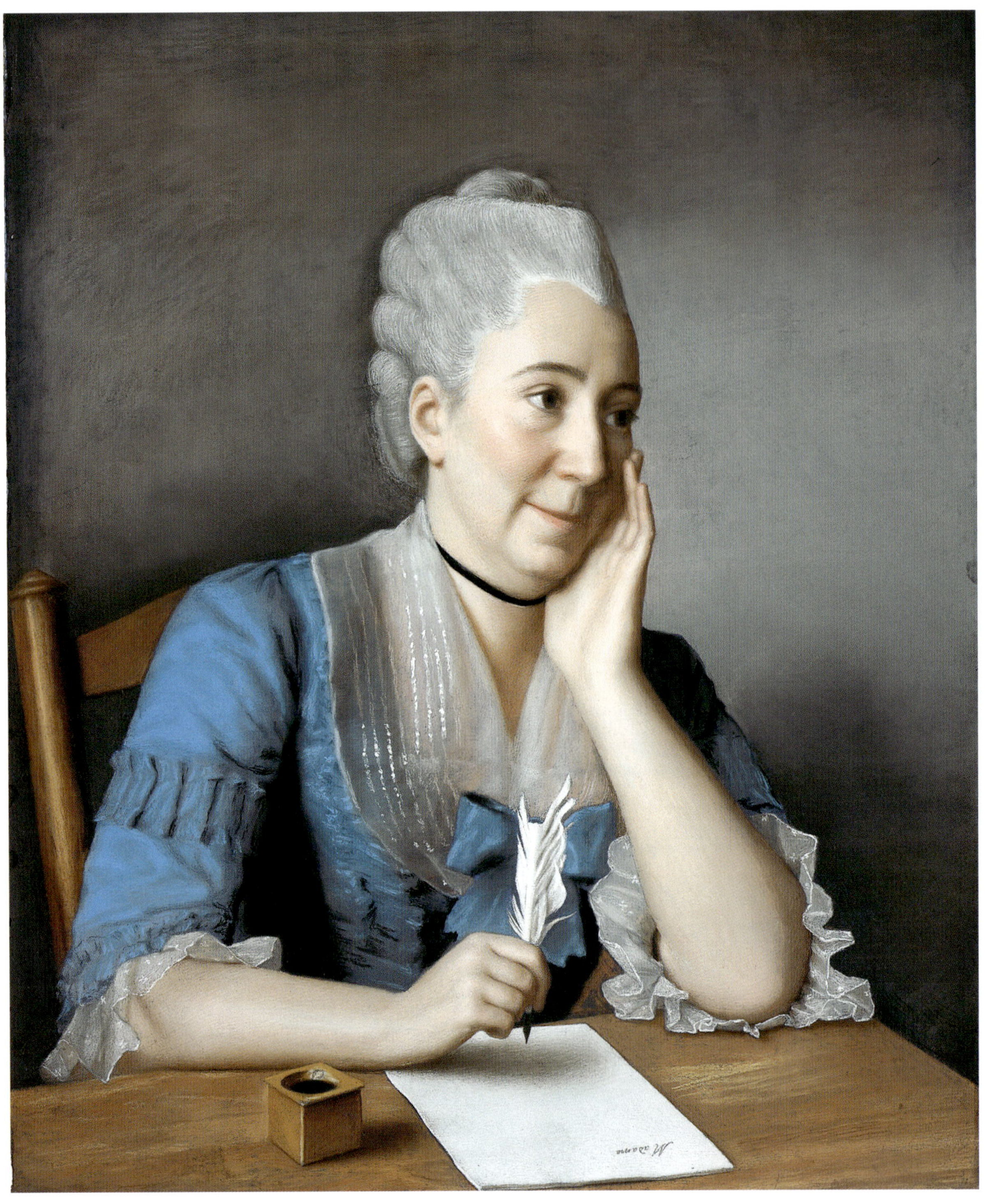

Madame Marc Liotard de la Servette, née Marianne Sarasin (1733–1827)

1775
**Pastel on paper glued onto
canvas**
66.2 x 55.2 cm
**Bequest of David Claparède,
1865**
Inv. 1865–3

Marianne Sarasin became a familiar figure in the Liotard
household after her brother Jean (p. 46) married Liotard's
niece, Marie-Jeanne, the subject of a delightful portrait by
the artist (p. 47), in 1752. In 1768, Marianne herself
married Marc Liotard de la Servette, the son of the painter's
older brother Jean.
Leaning on a table, quill pen in hand, she is pensive, ready to
write a letter, which she has begun with the word "Madame."

The theme of letter writing, which implies an elevated social
milieu, is picked up in the companion portrait of her
husband and helps confer a certain unity on the two works
in spite of the differences in composition and posture.
Whereas Marianne sits behind a table and is pensive, Marc
Liotard is in the foreground of the picture, looking out at
the viewer.

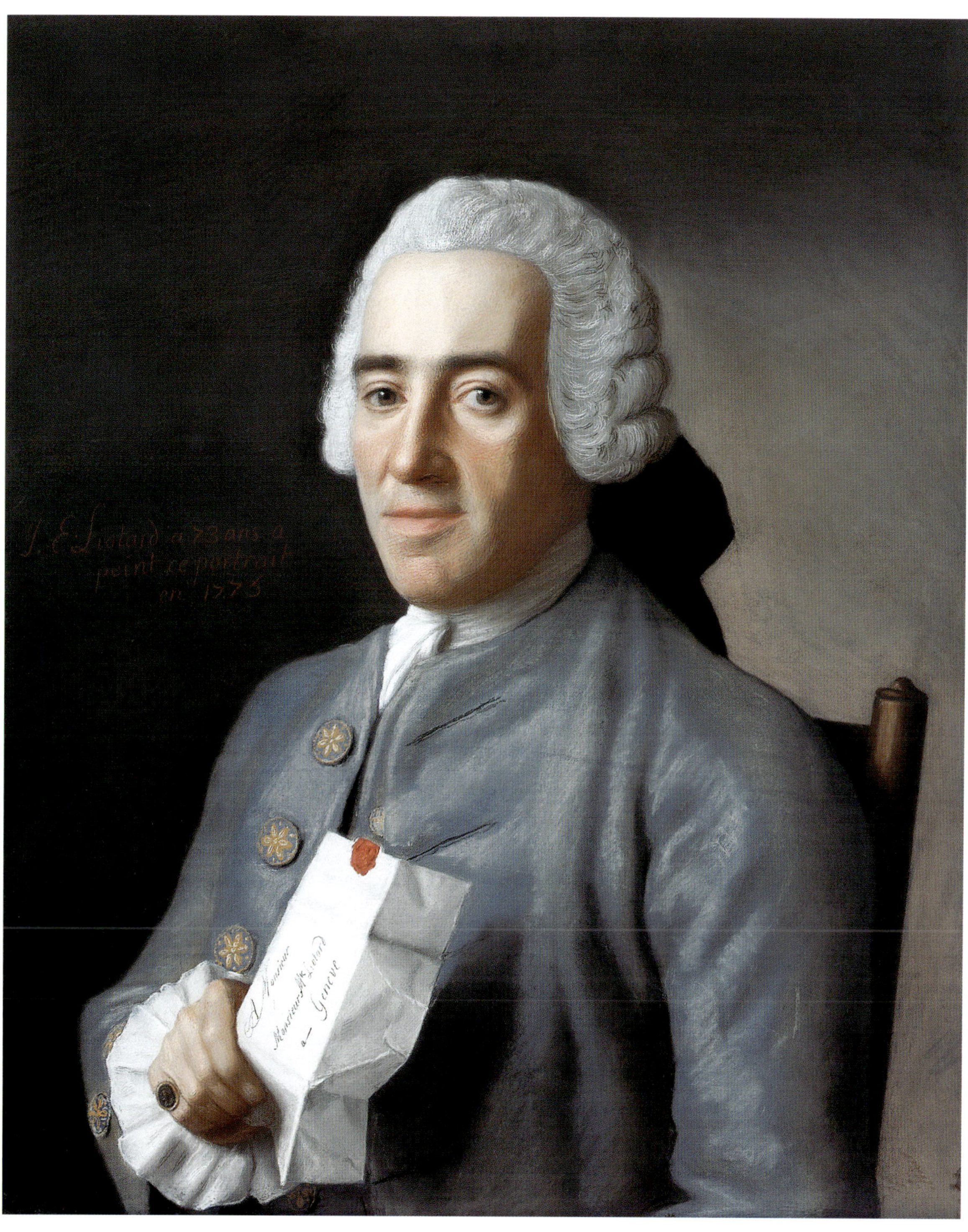

Marc Liotard de la Servette (1717–1792)

1775
Signed and dated
Pastel on paper glued
onto canvas
65 x 53 cm
Bequest of David Claparède,
1865
Inv. 1865-4

Marc Liotard, the painter's nephew, was a merchant and banker in London, where he founded the house of Liotard, Aubertin & Rivier. He made his fortune there and then returned to build a home at La Servette, in his native city. From that point on he became known as Liotard de la Servette.

In this portrait, the pendant to the picture of his wife, Marc Liotard is holding a letter addressed to him. It bears the inscription "to Monsieur / Monsieur Mrc [*sic*] Liotard / in Geneva." This pastel is handled in the same way as the one of his wife: shades of blue and parallel hatching emphasize the modeling of the face, which, like the wig, is carefully drawn. The rendering of the clothes is also meticulous.

As we have already seen in the case of the Maisonnets, Liotard also executed portraits of his nephews and nieces. Thus, Marie-Jeanne Sarasin inspired her uncle's remarkable 1752 portrait, which was acquired by the Fondation Gottfried Keller in 1940 and put on permanent loan at the museum (*Madame Jean Sarasin, née Marie-Jeanne Liotard*, 1752, inv. 1940–20). The daughter of Liotard's brother Jacques-Antoine, in 1752 she married Jean Sarasin, who was later to play an important political role in Geneva. Note this work's warm, subtle, and harmonious colors, its golden tone, and its supple, broad facture. The museum also holds Liotard's portrait of Jean Sarasin (*Jean Sarasin*, 1759, inv. 1865–5). The sitter is wearing his magistrate's clothes, with a heavy wig and black velvet coat. His imposing presence, dignity, and severity perfectly express his function, as well as his future political and social role. The same qualities are in evidence in the museum's portrait of another relation by marriage, the syndic Pierre Mussard (1763, inv. 1894–1). In 1710 Liotard's older brother, Jean, married Jeanne Mussard, the sister of this man who would become one of the Republic's most enlightened magistrates. Also noteworthy is the pastel of Marc Liotard, Jean's son, which he commissioned from his uncle in 1775 along with a portrait of his wife (*Marc Liotard de la Servette*, 1775, inv. 1865–4, and *Madame Marc Liotard de la Servette, née Marianne Sarasin*, 1775, inv. 1865–3). These two pendant pieces marvelously illustrate the artist's talent for more intimate, familiar depictions.[2]

2. Ibid., p. 230.

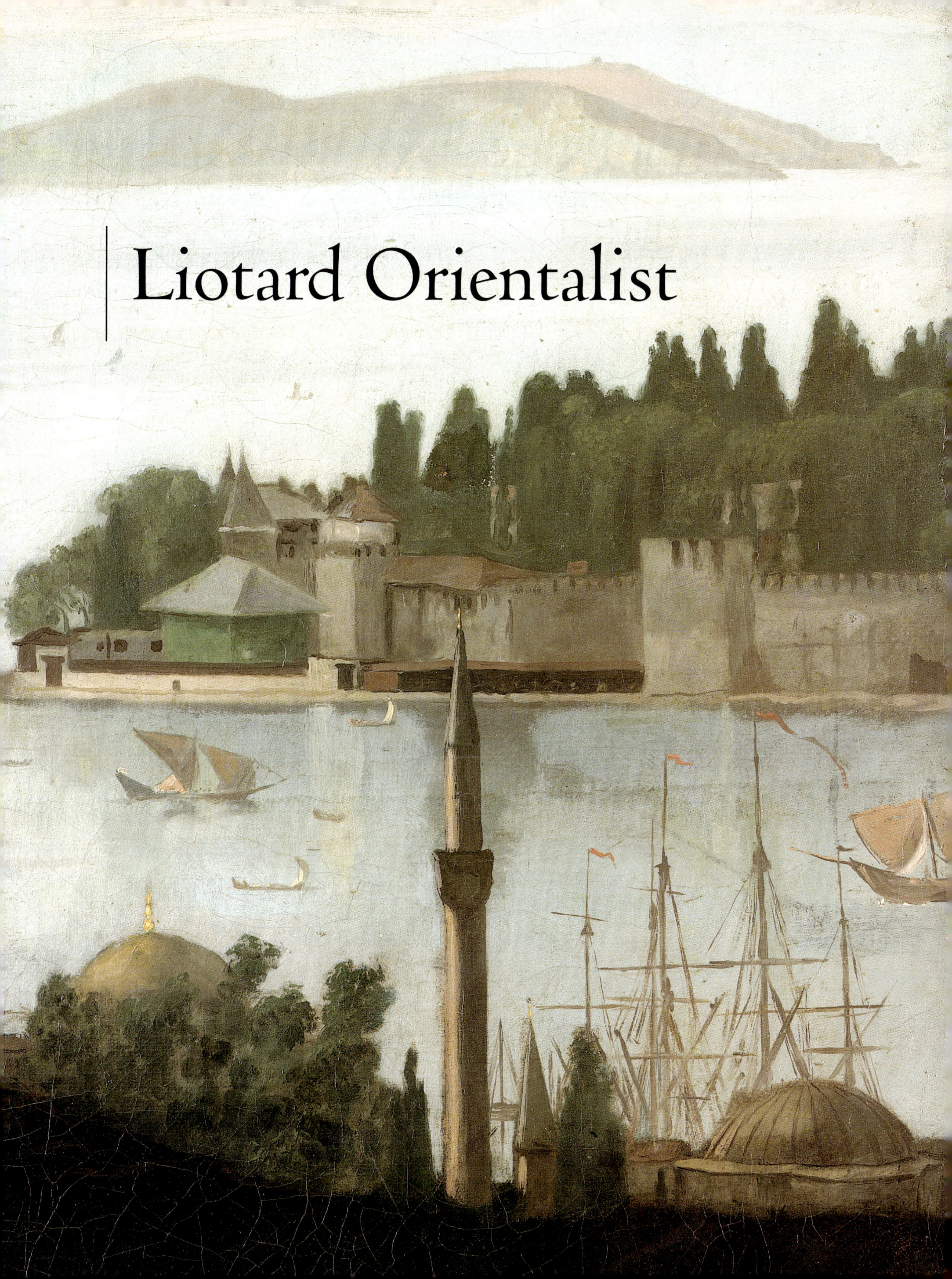
Liotard Orientalist

Claire Stoullig

Liotard spent many years in the Levant and was so fascinated by it that he adopted a number of Turkish customs. His numerous contacts with both Western diplomats and local figures were the source of many commissions. However, the museum itself has relatively few works from this Oriental period—in all, about ten, including four pastels, two oil paintings, and four drawings. This modest number reflects the difficulty of tracing works from this period of his career, many of which have been lost or forgotten.

In his *Frankish Woman and Her Servant* (1742–43, inv. 1936–17), Liotard achieves the quality of Persian miniatures with the freshness and variety of his colors, the precision of the details and the naturalness of the light. He also innovates with his subject, for he not only presents full-length portraits of two women but puts them in an interior, as in a genre painting. The Frankish woman is a stranger to this Islamic world and no doubt lives in the most Westernized quarter of Constantinople, Galata. She is accompanied by her young slave, and both are preparing for a bath. The beige-pink background unifies the scene, giving every element equal weight, be it the faces of the two figures and their attributes or their accessories and clothes. The meticulous, accurate observation gives this drawing a documentary quality, especially in the depiction of the *salvar* (baggy pants), *cepken* (jacket), *yemeni* (scarf), and *takunya* (wooden shoes) that constituted the traditional costume. The deep luminosity—diffuse and dense, not violent—of the pastel indicates the overhead light entering the room and the humid atmosphere of a Turkish bath. Liotard was trying to grasp and penetrate a civilization that he found fascinating, but, faithful to his principles of truthfulness, never idealized or let himself be seduced by the exoticism of the Near East. This attitude is also evident in the women's very reserved gestures and expressions.

The *Frankish Woman from Pera, Constantinople* (1738–43, inv. 1931–5), referred to by J. W. R. Tilanus as the "grande dame de Smyrne," does indeed make for an imposing presence, what with her posture and her rich clothes. But her presence is nothing beside that of *Richard Pococke (1704–1765)* in the full-length portrait painted, atypically for Liotard, in oils and, unusual in his corpus, life size (inv. 1948–22). The British archaeologist and theologian was above all an illustrious traveler who went on the Grand Tour and wrote about it in a book covering economics as well as archaeology and history. Here, Liotard draws on his skills as both a great painter and a miniaturist. He represents Pococke in an Ottoman costume, standing out against a cloudy sky and leaning on an ancient altar, looking over to the city of Constantinople from the hill at Pera. The view of the Bosphorus, the Tophane Mosque, and the city walls, as well as the bandstand, are a distillation of that magical city. The paint, with its very discreet strokes (as advocated by Liotard in his treatise on painting) and the blended colors, herald the Neoclassical style that will succeed the Rococo art then very much in fashion in France.

The second of the four oil paintings held by the museum also belongs to this ensemble: *Woman with a Tambourine Dressed in Turkish Costume* (1738–43, inv. 1939–8) shows a young woman engaged in an amusing activity. As if to add to the scene's musical timbre, Liotard plays on the brightness of the colors and the oppositions between complementary tones (the red of the divan and the green of the gold-embroidered caftan). However, the young woman's reserved expression and lofty bearing suggest that she is posing more than actually playing. In fact, Liotard is more concerned with catching the golden

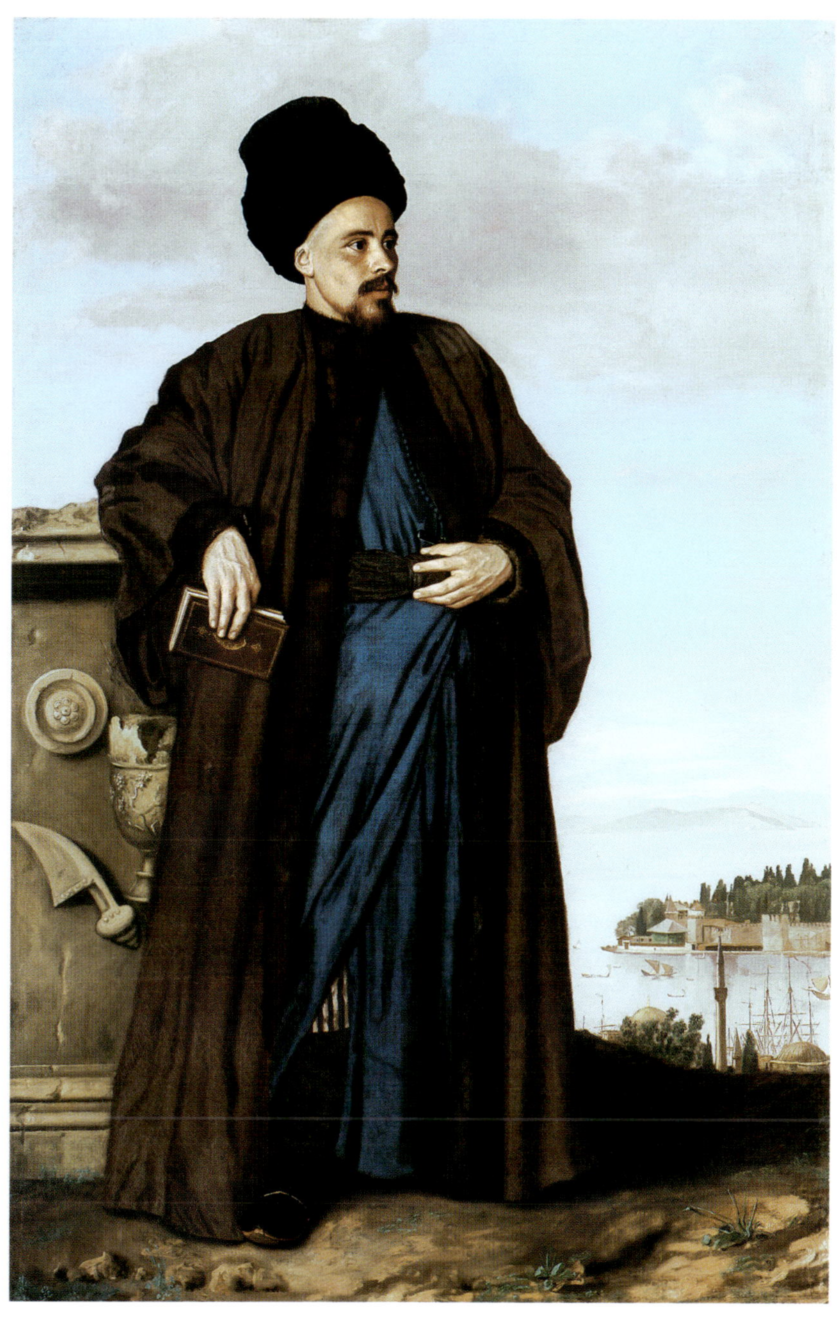

Richard Pococke (1704–1765)

1740
Oil on canvas
202.5 x 134 cm
On permanent loan from the
Fondation Gottfried Keller,
1948
Inv. 1948–22

The Englishman Richard Pococke was a pioneer of Egyptian and Middle Eastern archaeology. This attraction to the East was something of a family tradition: his grandfather taught him Hebrew and classical literature, and his great uncle Edward Pococke was an eminent professor of Arabic at Oxford University.

After studying theology, Richard Pococke set out on a Grand Tour with his cousin, Jeremiah Milles, the future president of the Society of Antiquaries in London, to whom he bequeathed this portrait. They spent four years traveling through Europe, especially in Italy and France. In 1737, Pococke set out for the Middle East, a journey that he recounted in the two volumes of his *Description of the East and Some Other Countries* (1743–45). He first made the

acquaintance of Liotard in Constantinople in June 1740. The artist's first portrait of him was a drawing in pencil and red chalk (Musée du Louvre, Paris) that is described as follows in the catalogue of Liotard's collection of pictures published in Paris in 1771: "The Englishman Bishop Pococ [*sic*], with the Armenian habit [it is in fact a Turkish one] that he wore when traveling in the Levant." This was the basis for the oil painting here. After a short stay in Geneva, Richard Pococke set out to see the glaciers at Chamonix in June 1741. He was one of the first foreigners to climb up to the Sea of Ice. After returning to England in 1742, he became bishop of Ossory and then of Meath. He died in 1765.

This painting passed from the sitter's collection to that of his family in Alston.

light that reveals the richness of the setting than with rendering the atmosphere of a musical moment or the soft, sensuous feeling procured by such pleasures. To accentuate the atmospheric would be to risk the picturesque and obviously contradict the painter's way of looking at Asia Minor.

Contrary to the previous painting, the pastel entitled *Portrait of a Young Woman in Turkish Dress Sitting on a Divan*, executed in about 1750 (inv. 1930–2), goes beyond the meticulous depiction of a setting and offers an intimate everyday scene, with a young woman lost in thought, indifferent to everything around her. The interior is Turkish, with a low divan, a Persian carpet with Usak motifs, and luxurious fabrics and clothing in harmony with the blues and reds of the composition. But the figure is clearly a European victim of—amorous?—disappointment after having read the letter that lies, torn into pieces, on the carpet. This scene echoes a classic theme in Western painting.

Frankish Woman from Pera Followed by a Little Girl (1738–42, inv. 1931–6) was executed during Liotard's Turkish sojourn using the traditional technique of red and black chalk to reinforce the relief and accentuate the pastel tones.

After four years in Constantinople, Liotard was invited by Prince Constantine of Moldavia to the court at Jassy. Arriving in 1742, he executed portraits of the prince's family and its close circle, and also depicted the literary characters who frequented the court (the prince was an enlightened figure, and his library was the envy of all Europe). The clothes indicate that the *Gentleman in a Fur-lined Robe at the Court of Jassy* (1742–43, inv. 1934–35) is a man of rank: ermine was worn by men in the legal profession or doctors, while the typically German beret had been very popular with learned men in eastern Europe since the sixteenth century. The elegance and distinction of this figure, his bearing, and the way he holds his head and meets our gaze are underlined by the scale of the drawing, which is excessive in relation to the format of the paper. The gentleman is rendered with Liotard's characteristic precision and sense of detail. More specifically, the fine dots of red chalk accentuate the drawing and enhance the light effects obtained by the play of the black and white of the graphite pencil and black chalk.

Because of its important trading activities in the Levant, the Netherlands had a consul in Smyrna. There Liotard was introduced into the Dutch colony and commissioned to depict the wife of a rich merchant. The painter considered this daughter of an English consul a true "Smyrnian" (as the caption to the drawing indicates), and indeed she had spent most of her life in Turkey. *Madame James Fremeaux, née Margaret Cooke*, (circa 1738, inv. D 1997–14) is the bust-length portrait of a European woman in Near Eastern costume, attesting to the mid-eighteenth-century fashion for Orientalism. The painter chose to highlight the richness of her clothing as a frame for the face, whose luminosity is masterfully brought out by the shades of pastel. Liotard has endowed her with an expression of melancholy fragility.

Liotard's Asia Minor series ends with *The Divan. Liotard's Bedroom in Constantinople* (about 1742, inv. 1934–33). This personal reference (the room was surely not without significance for him) and the absence of any human figure speak eloquently of the painter's mixed feelings. The red chalk combined with graphite adds intensity to the scene and suggests, as ever with great restraint, a few special moments, perhaps spent in pleasant company. But this empty room, while possibly not beloved, was the everyday setting of a life that was both exciting and painful. In Liotard's vision of Asia Minor, we find none of the fantasy, the "tourist" highlights and imaginary exoticism that inspired those who painted "Turqueries" from a distance. His paintings seek above all to convey a deeper intimacy, a more subtle charm that is closer to reality. And this is no doubt because the painter lived in Turkey for a long time and loved its mores and way of life— even thinking of making it his permanent home.

The seduction of the Near East was crystallized in the eighteenth century by the work of this Enlightenment painter who discarded ethnocentrism and had no use for folklore or the picturesque. Liotard conveyed his perception of this part of the world through an enduring and genuine emotion. He belongs in a long line of artists, inaugurated by Gentili Bellini, the first painter to travel from Venice to portray the sultan, and extended in the century after his own by Delacroix, Chassériau, and Decamps, and in modern times by Klee, Marquet, and Matisse.

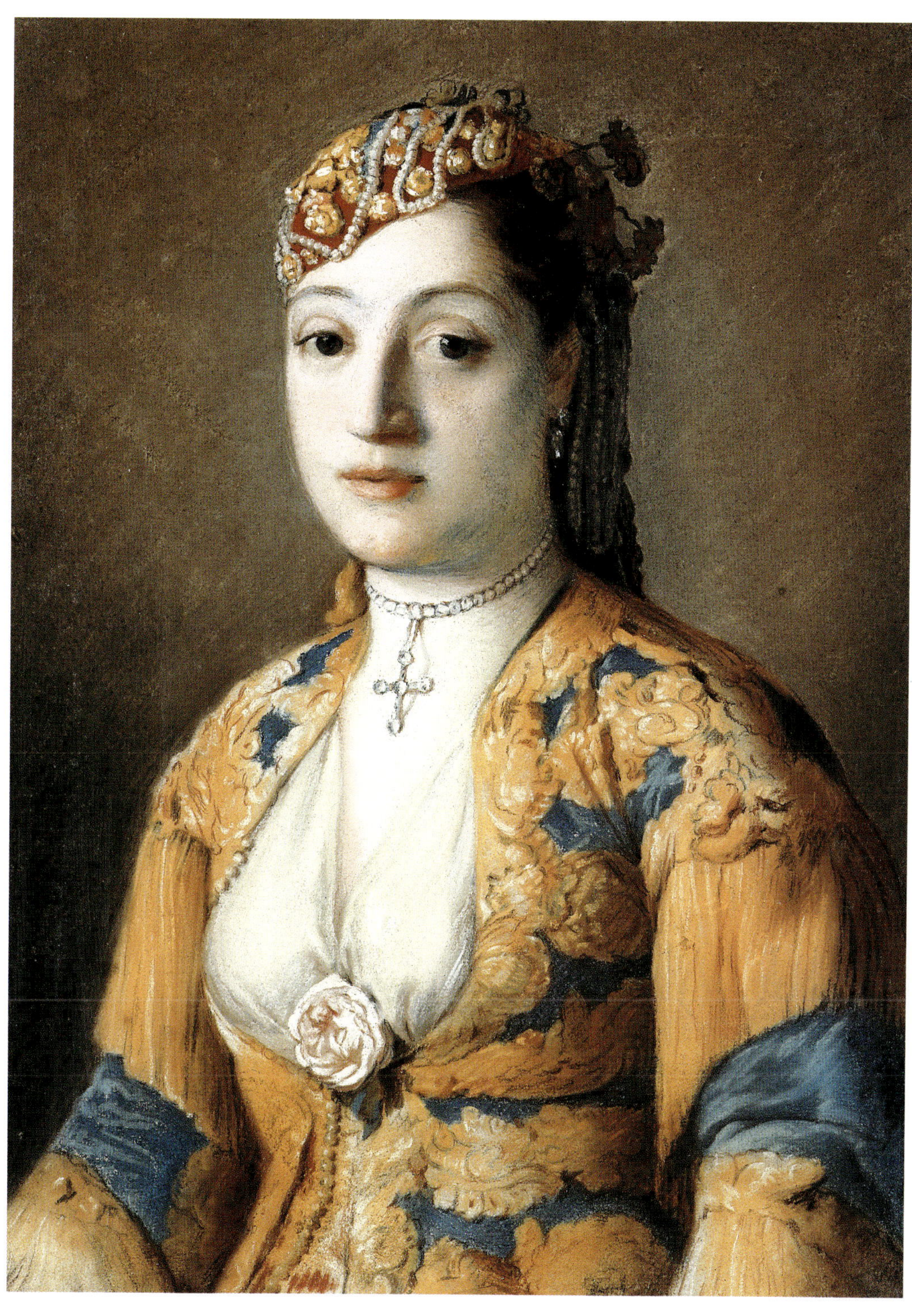

Madame James Fremeaux, née Margaret Cooke

Circa 1738
Pastel on paper glued
onto canvas
50.6 x 38.2 cm
Purchase, 1997
Inv. D 1997–14

In 1720 Margaret Cooke, granddaughter of the Dutch consul in Smyrna and daughter of the English consul in the same port, married James Fremeaux, a wealthy Dutch merchant who represented the cloth, silk, and cotton manufacturers of Leiden and Haarlem in the Levant. He commissioned a portrait of his wife in 1738, and Liotard made both this pastel and a drawing in black and red chalk (Musée du Louvre, Paris). In 1749 Margaret Cooke returned to England to live with her family at their property in Kingsthorpe.

This pastel remained in the sitter's family until 1997.

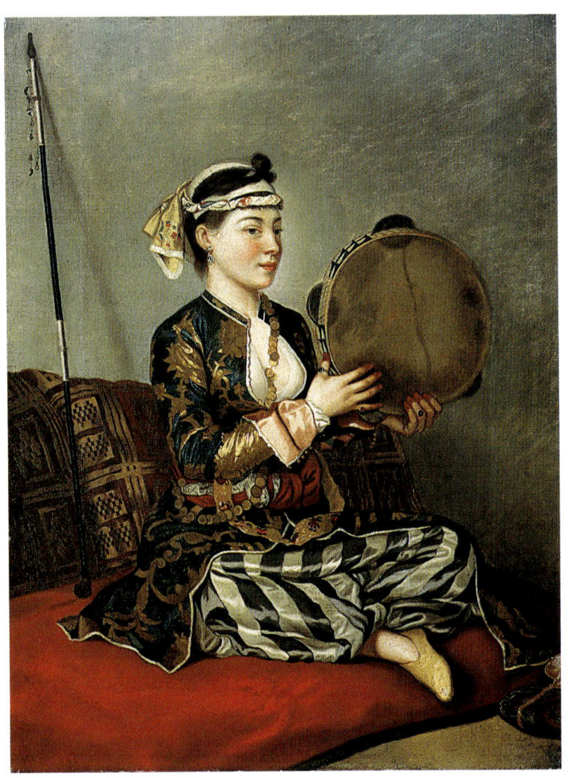

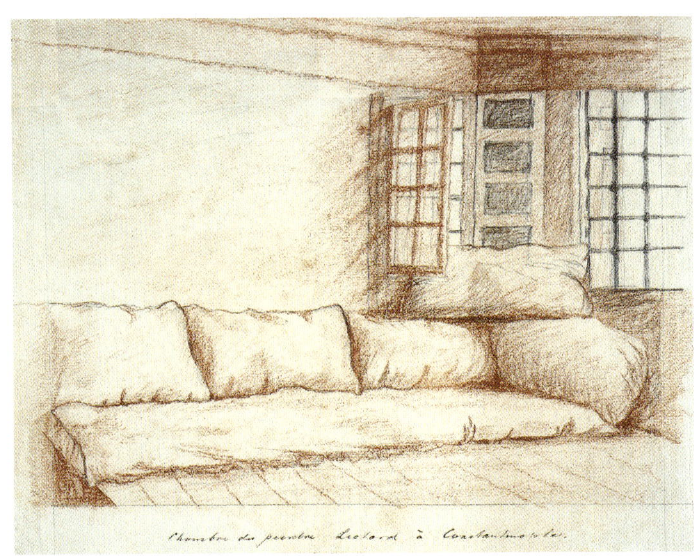

Woman with a Tambourine Dressed in Turkish Costume

1738–43
Oil on canvas
63.5 x 48.5 cm
Gift of the Société Auxiliaire
du Musée, 1939
Inv. 1939–8

This painting was in the collection of J. P. Heseltine
(London) and then in a private collection in Saint-Gall.

The Divan. Liotard's Bedroom in Constantinople

Circa 1742
Red chalk and graphite pencil
on paper
18.6 x 22.8 cm
Gift of the Société Auxiliaire
du Musée, 1934
Inv. 1934–33

This drawing was part of the artist's collection and remained
in his family in Amsterdam until 1934.

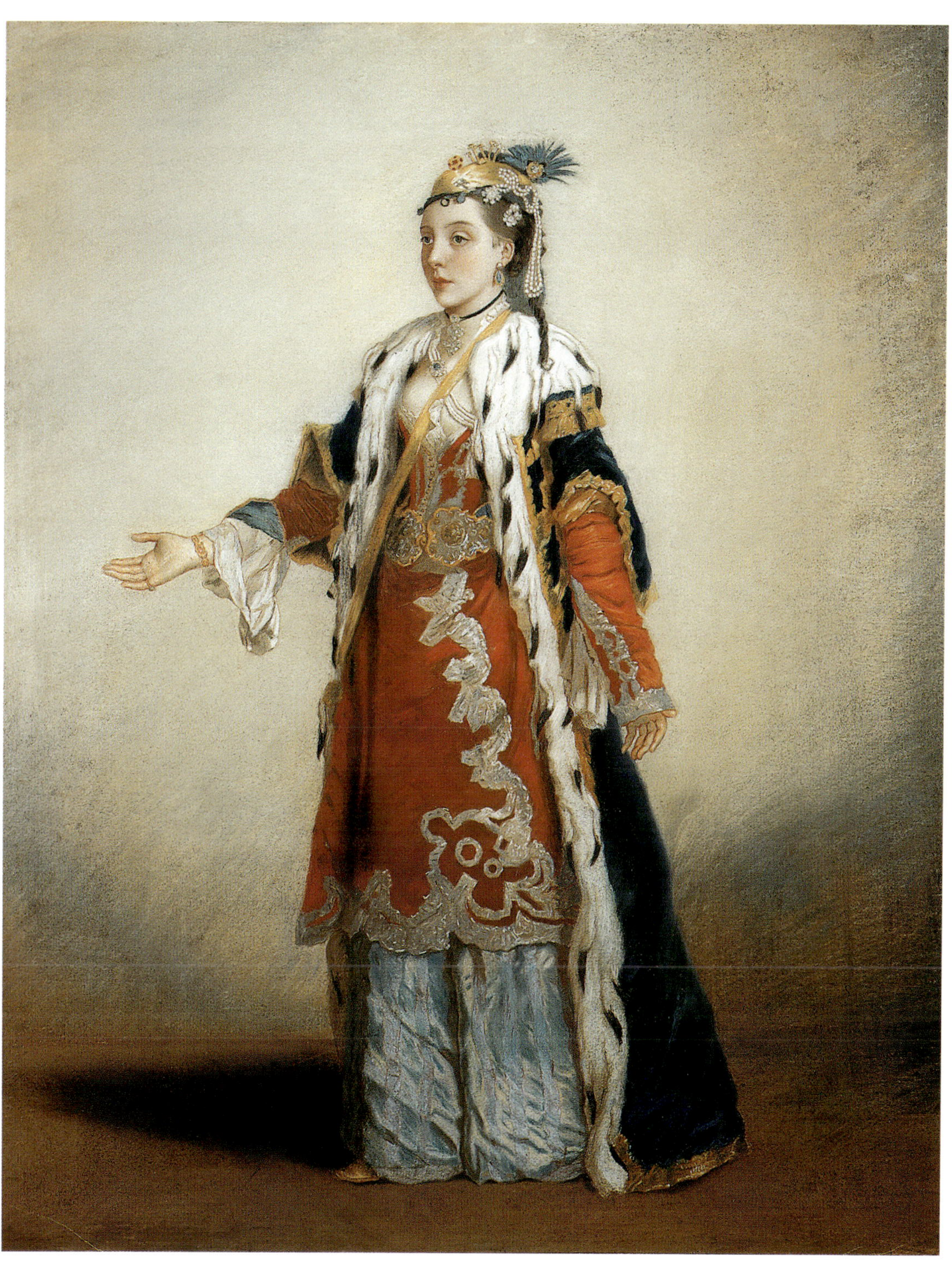

Frankish Woman from Pera, Constantinople

1738–43
Pastel on paper glued
onto canvas
63.5 x 48.5 cm
Purchase, 1930
Inv. 1931–5

This pastel was in the Beaumont Collection, Paris.

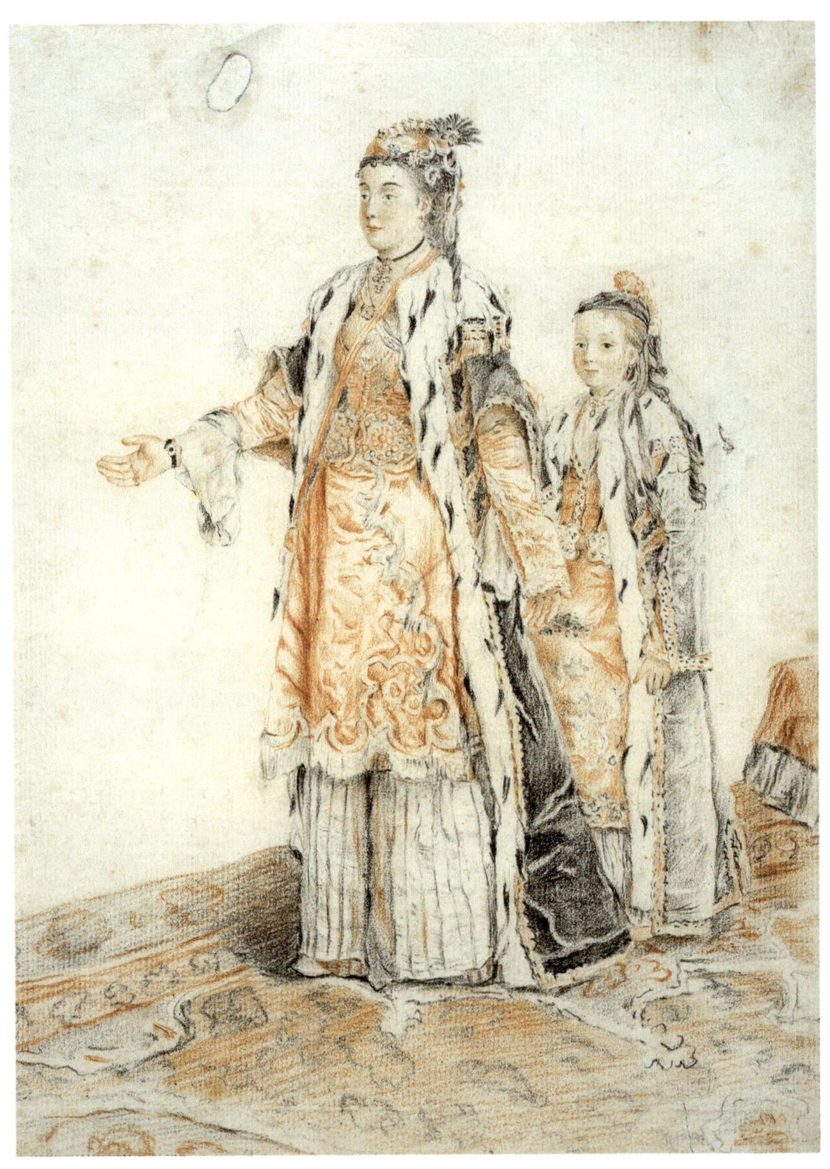

Frankish Woman from Pera Followed by a Little Girl

1738–42
Red and black chalk on paper
22.9 x 16.9 cm
Gift of the Société des Amis
des Musées d'Art et
d'Histoire, 1930
Inv. 1931–6

This drawing belonged, among others, to the Fargues and
Beaumont collections (Amsterdam and Paris, respectively).
It was acquired by the Société des Amis des Musées d'Art et
d'Histoire for the museum.

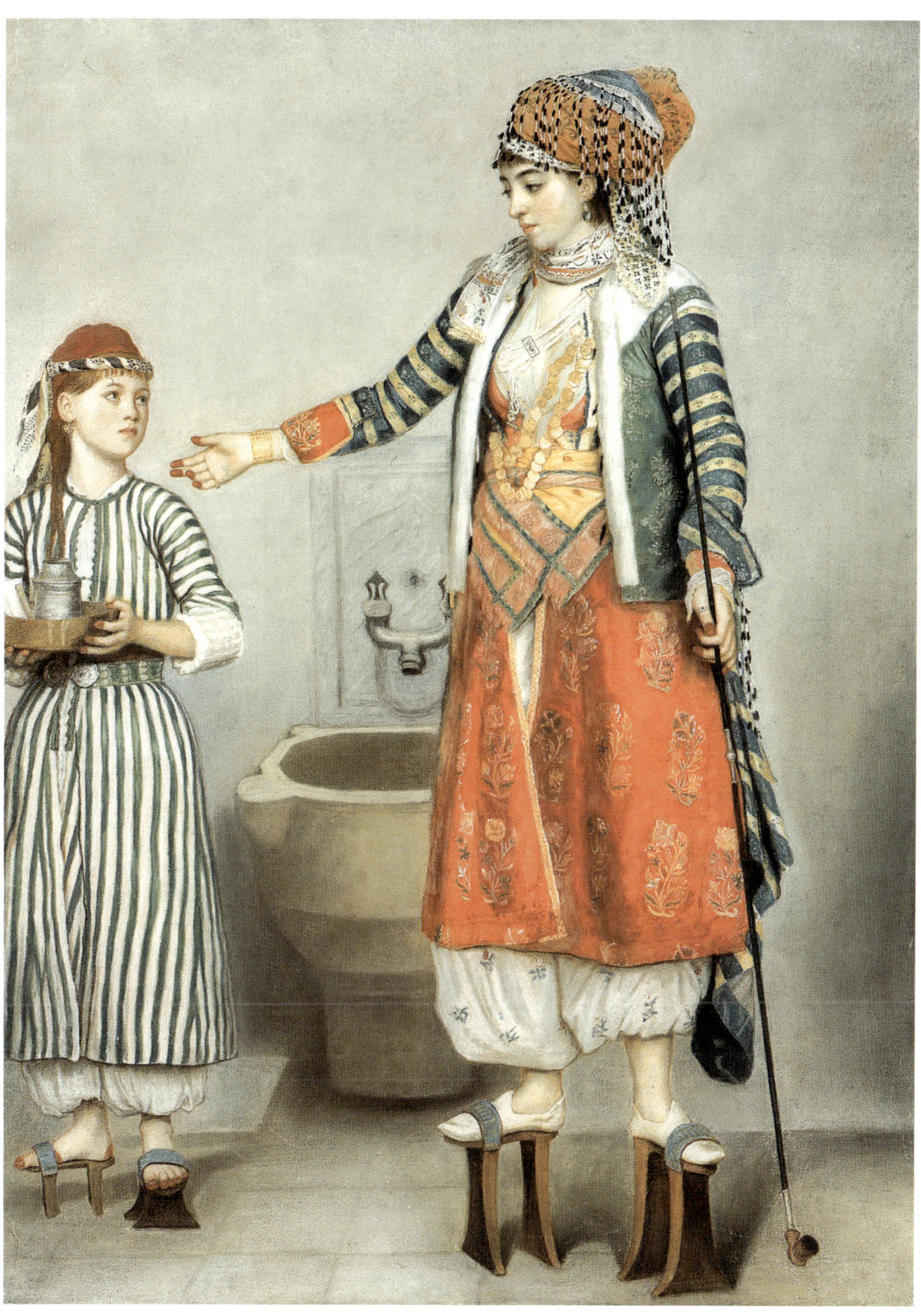

Frankish Woman and Her Servant

1742–43
Pastel on parchment
71 x 53 cm
Purchase, 1936
Inv. 1936–17

This pastel was in the collection of J. P. Heseltine in
London, then entered a private collection in Geneva. It was
acquired with the help of the Société Auxiliaire du Musée
and other generous donors.

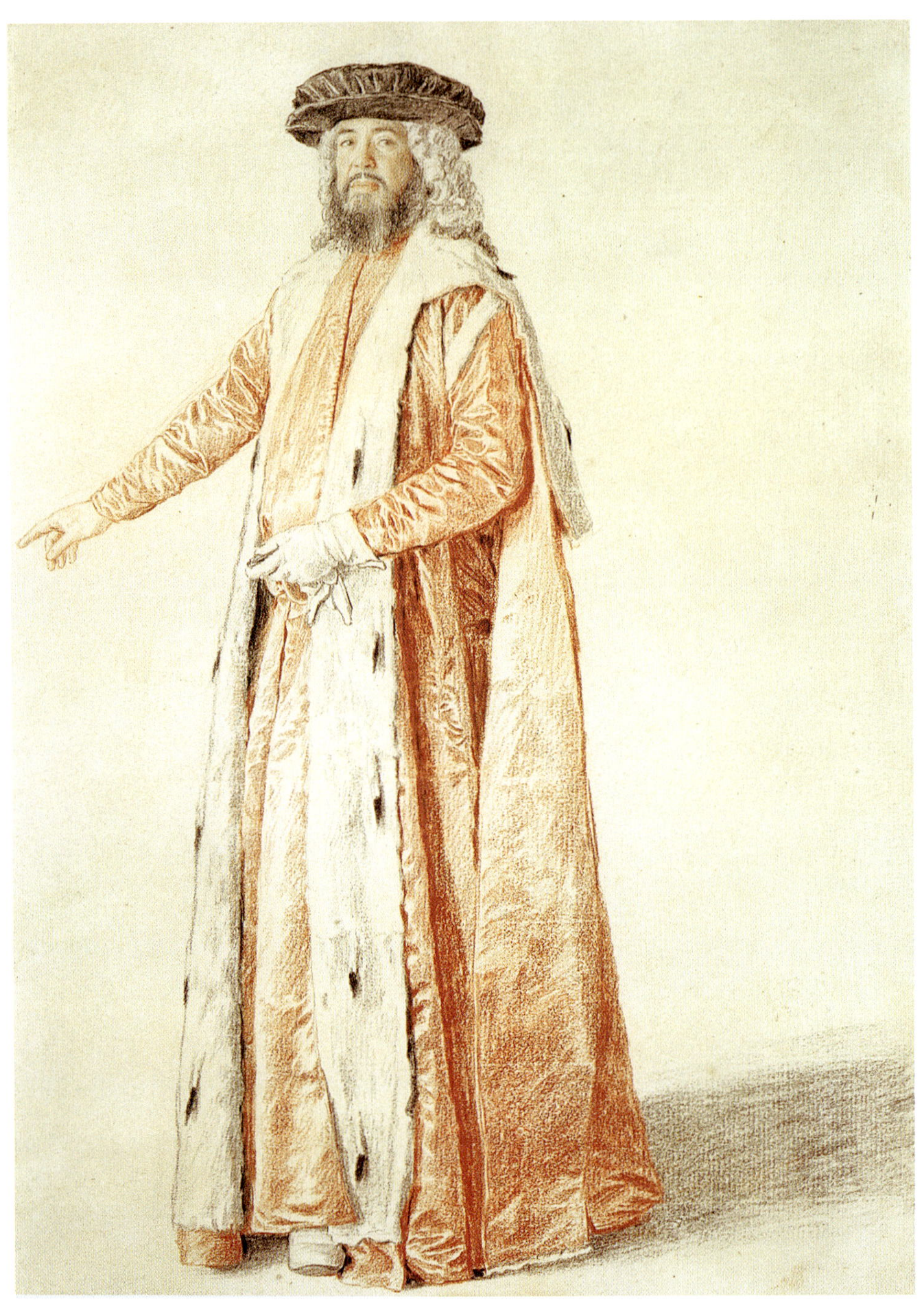

1742–43
Red chalk, graphite pencil,
and black chalk on paper
22.9 x 17.8 cm
Gift of the Société Auxiliaire
du Musée, 1934
Inv. 1934–35

This work passed from the artist's collection to that of his
family in Amsterdam, where it remained until 1934.

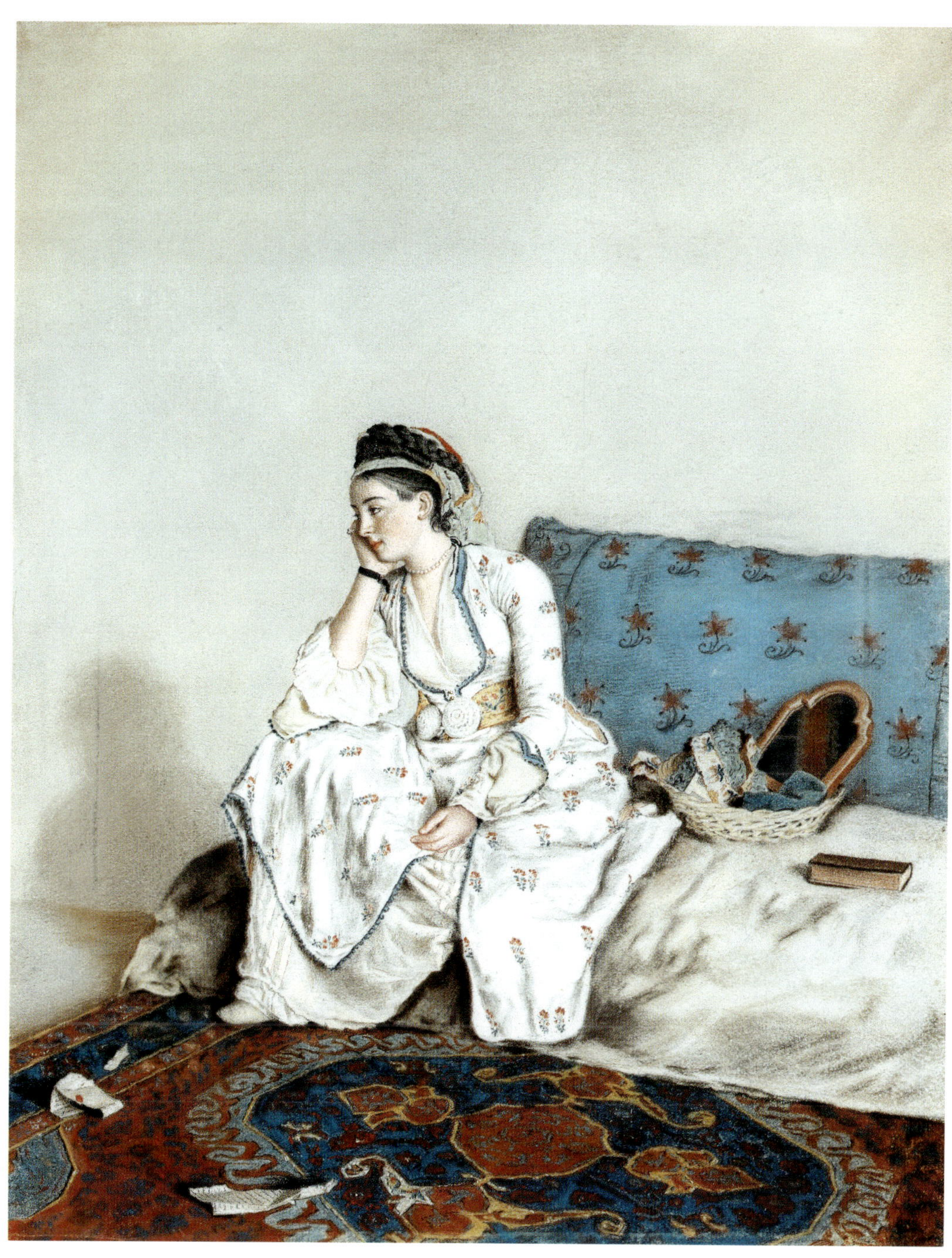

Portrait of a Young Woman in Turkish Dress Sitting on a Divan

Circa 1750
Pastel on parchment
23.5 x 19 cm
On permanent loan from the
Fondation Gottfried Keller,
1930
Inv. 1930–2

There has been a great deal of debate about the date of this work and the identity of the model. Liotard reproduced the image of this young woman in Turkish dress sitting pensively on a divan a number of times over the years, changing the face on each occasion. It was long thought that this pastel represented Maria Gunning (1732–60), who later married the Earl of Coventry. Today, however, it is generally agreed that, of all the variants on this image, the only one that depicts that famous Irish beauty is the one at the Rijksmuseum in Amsterdam. Indeed, the engravings made by Richard Houston after this work explicitly mention her name. This, one of the most famous pastels in the collection, was made after a drawing (location unknown) of which the Louvre holds a counterproof. A number of elements in the image, such as the mirror, the comb, the embroidery, and the torn letter have prompted Yvonne Boerlin to read it as a representation of Melancholy surrounded by attributes symbolizing transience (Anne de Herdt, 1992, p. 136).

This pastel was in the collection of François Turrettini (Geneva), and remained in his family until 1930.

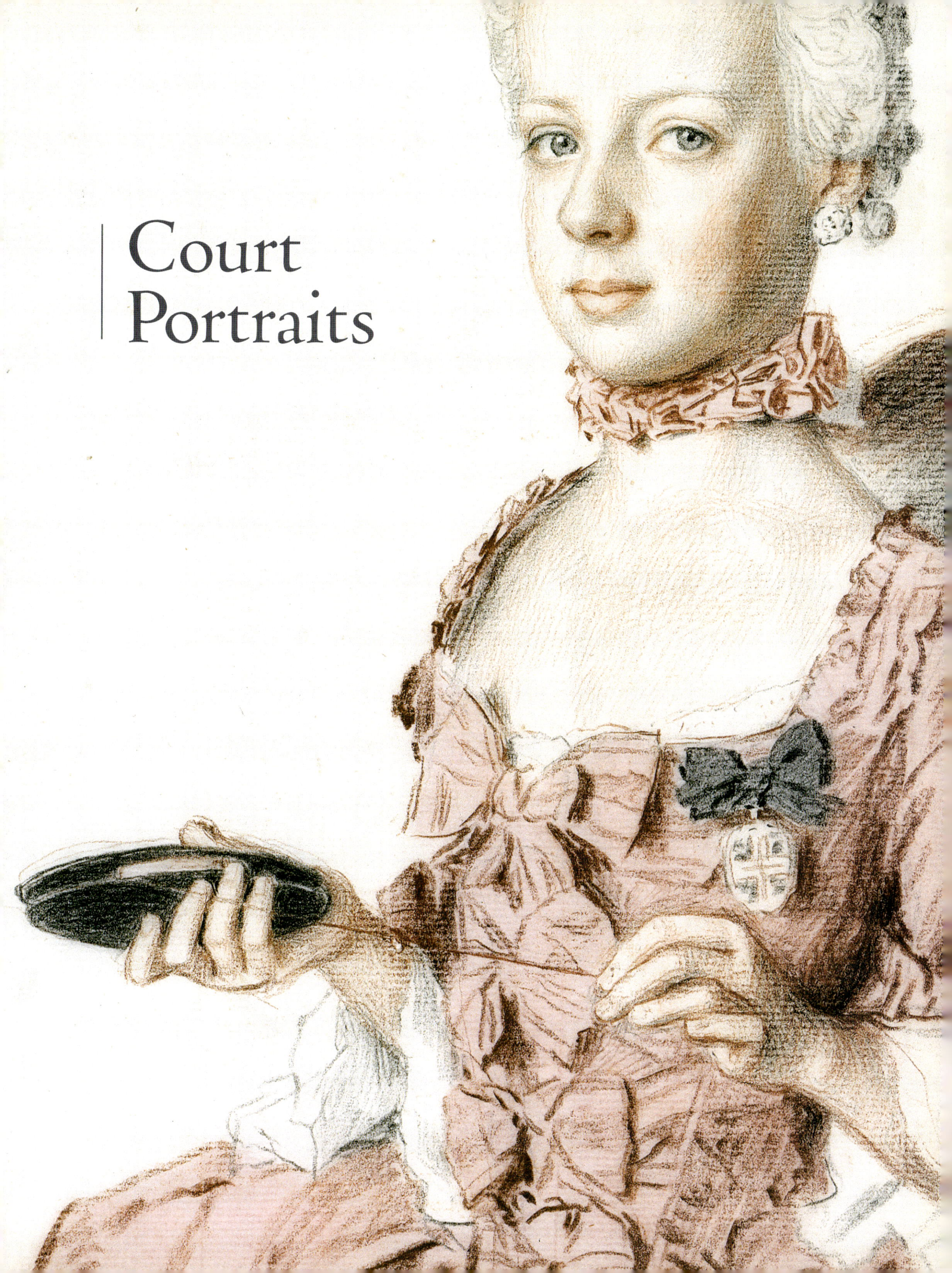

Court Portraits

Isabelle Félicité Bleeker

Almost everywhere in seventeenth- and eighteenth-century Europe, court art was solemn and majestic. Liotard worked in a world where the idea of the portrait was changing. In the Age of the Enlightenment, the theatrical conception of the model began to lose its dominance. Instead, the subject's psychology and identity became the central concerns. Artists now set out to convey a particular idea of their subjects, of their function and social status. Anxious to please their patrons, painters flattered their models. Representations of kings, princes, and princesses were all based on the prototype of the official commission that emerged at the turn of the seventeenth century, with sitters striking haughty poses, their finery mirrored in the pomp of their surroundings. The academic tradition called for idealization in portraiture. Liotard, who had a horror of virtuosity and never sought to display his own, went against these conventions. He represented princes and bourgeois as they were and resisted the obligation to flatter the holders of power. He gave the painted image another function and the painter a different place in society.

Liotard continued his artistic training in Paris from 1723 to 1735 and returned for another five years in 1748. In those days Hyacinthe Rigaud and Nicolas de Largillière were the masters of the official portrait, while Jean-Marc Nattier reigned supreme in the genre of the mythological portrait. Liotard met with a very positive response in Paris. He worked a great deal for the foreign community, especially the English, but also for the royal family and French high society. He was presented at the court in Versailles by the marshal of Saxony, who earlier had sat for his portrait by Liotard. Louis XV commissioned him to paint himself and the members of his family. Most of these portraits of the princesses of France are today kept at the Stupinigi palace, near Turin. They are completely different from Nattier's portraits, which depict the young women as goddesses.

The portrait of Madame Sophie de France, the sixth daughter of Louis XV, then aged sixteen, dates from this Parisian period. Liotard captures the princess's features with considerable realism, vigorously conveying the young woman's willful expression while giving his talent free rein in the rendering of her clothes, notably the lace of her dress and the velvet coat edged with ermine.

On his way back from the Levant in September 1743, Liotard stopped in Vienna. There, the art-loving Francis, Duke of Lorraine, recommended him to his wife, Empress Maria Theresa. Thus began a friendship that would endure for the rest of the sovereign's life and play an important role in Liotard's life and the development of his European career. Becoming a court painter in Vienna, he executed portraits of the imperial family and of many Austrian aristocrats. It was during his second Viennese sojourn, in 1762, that Liotard executed the famous portrait of the empress that she gave to the Genevan banker and jeweler Étienne Salles, and that his descendant Mademoiselle Salles-Pallard donated to the museum in 1839. Maria Theresa of Austria is represented as a monument, as both the mother of sixteen children and the respected head of state who governed the Hapsburg empire for nearly fifty years.[1] At the same time, she is portrayed very simply, without any of the attributes of her rank. Here we can see the originality and independence of the artist, who had no time for academic conventions and insisted instead on the claims of nature and truth.[2] Rather than treat this representation as a royal portrait, he approached it in light of his own friendship and intimacy with Maria Theresa.

1. Anne de Herdt, *Dessins de Liotard*, ex. cat., Paris, Geneva, 1992, no. 111, p. 204.
2. Renée Loche, "Jean-Étienne Liotard dans les collections genevoises," *Le Livre du Richemond IV*, 1990, p. 16.

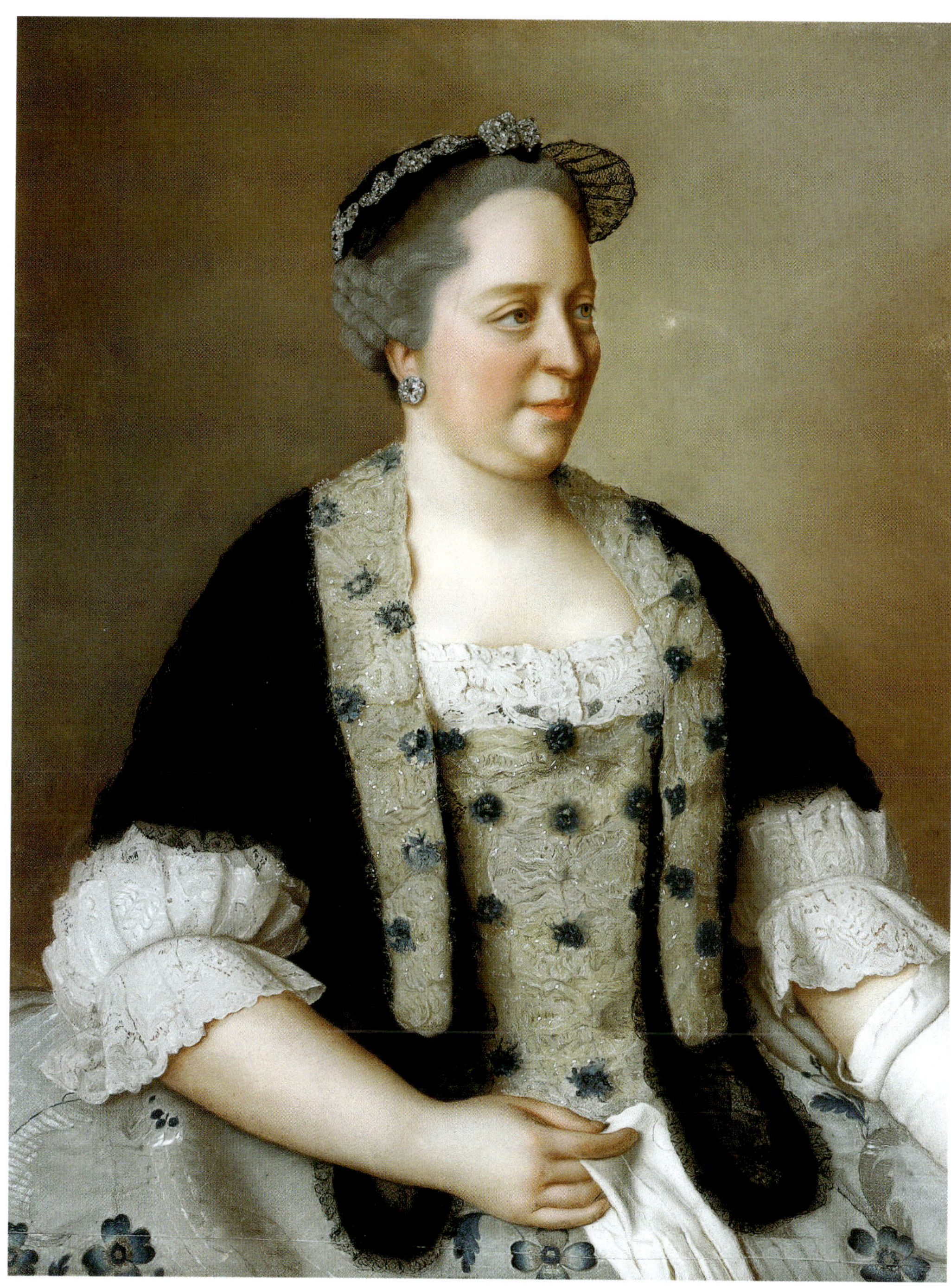

Maria Theresa of Austria (1717–1780)

1762
Pastel on parchment
89 x 72.5 cm
Gift of Mademoiselle Salles-
Pallard, 1839
Inv. 1839–10

More bourgeois than royal (the empress wears neither royal attributes nor elaborate jewelry, and is shown against a neutral background), this surprising portrait was commissioned in 1762 by Maria Theresa, who gave it to the Genevan jeweler Étienne Salles (1739–65). Flaubert saw this pastel on show at the Musée Rath when passing through Geneva in 1845, and wrote: "Museum. Maria Theresa (pastel), woman of around 45 to 48, fresh, flesh somewhat flabby, still pink, sagging eyes, moist and good; expression too complex to describe; admirable intensity." (*Notes de voyage*, I, Paris, 1910.)

This portrait went from the jeweler's collection to that of Mademoiselle Salles-Pallard.

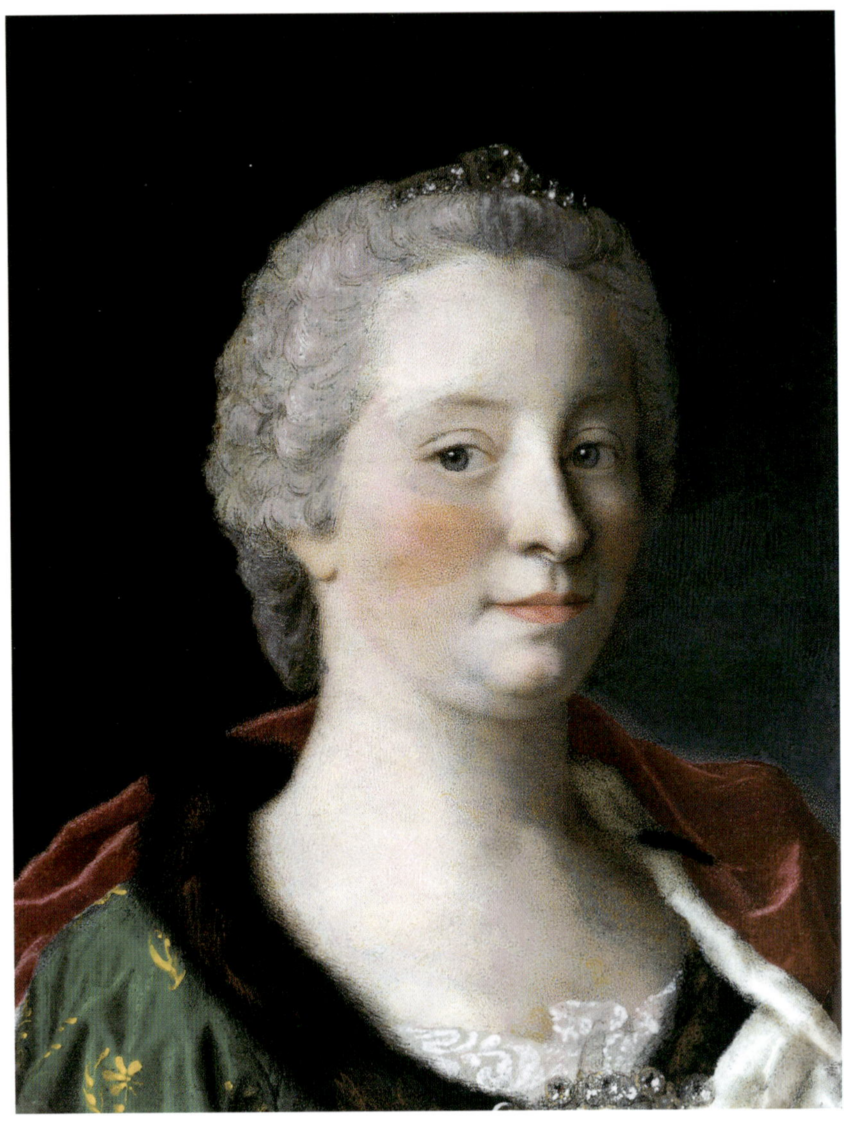

Maria Theresa of Austria (1717–1780)

Circa 1747
Enamel on iron
16.7 x 12.7 cm
Gift of Dr. Étienne Julliard,
1885
Inv. 1885–1

Maria Theresa of Austria, Queen of Bohemia and Hungary, succeeded her father, Charles VI, in 1740. Endowed with great political acumen, energetic and clever, she governed the country firmly while introducing a series of reforms that took it from an absolute to a parliamentary monarchy. In 1736, she married Francis of Lorraine, by whom she had sixteen children. A very popular ruler, she died in 1780. Among Liotard's many portraits of the empress, executed in a variety of techniques, the one in pastel kept at the Herzog Anton Ulrich-Museum in Brunswick seems to have been particularly important to the artist, who re-created it as a gouache (Bayerisches Nationalmuseum, Munich) and an enameled plaque (Rijksmuseum, Amsterdam). The enamel here is a preparatory version of the latter. Liotard started adapting his own works to different techniques during his first sojourn in Vienna. According to Hans Boeckh (*Genava*, 1989, p. 123), he continued these experiments through to 1747, the likely date of this enamel made in Lyons.

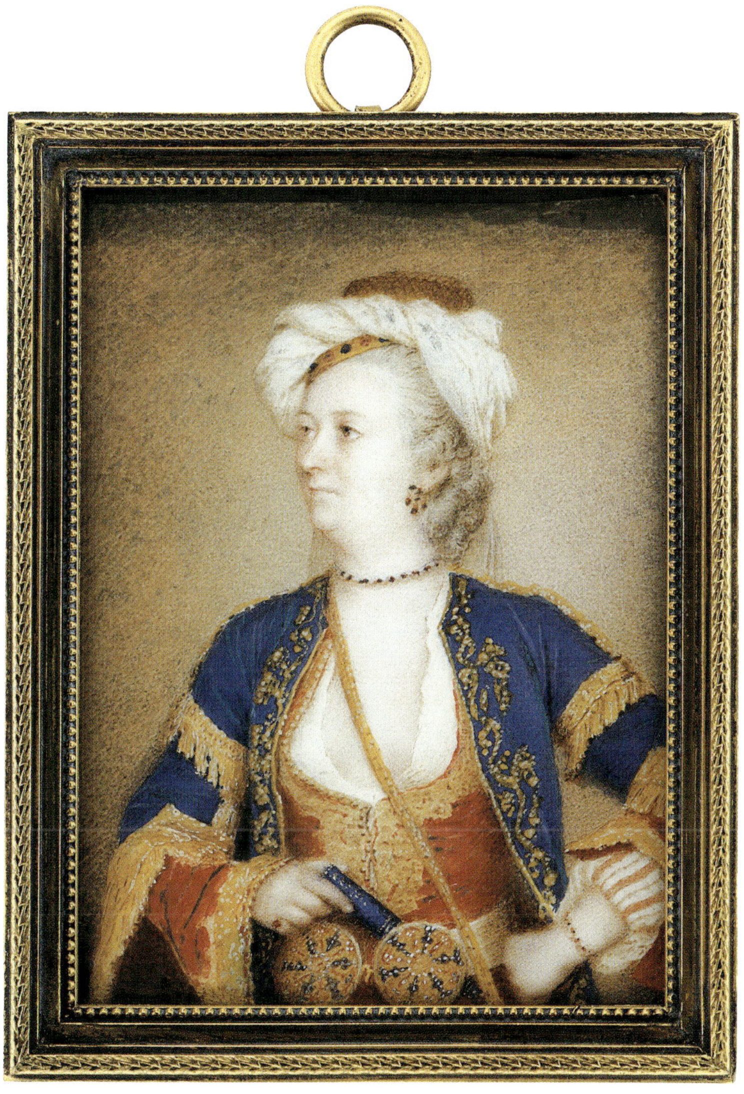

Presumed Portrait of Maria Theresa of Austria in Turkish Costume (1717–1780)

1743–45 (?)
**Watercolor and gouache
on vellum**
7.3 x 5.4 cm
Purchase, 1937
Inv. AD 40

Historically, this work has always been thought of as a portrait of Maria Theresa of Austria, but this identification is currently being challenged by historians and experts. Wearing a white turban, a blue caftan with gold trimmings, and a deep red dress, the model adopts a noble posture, with one hand on her dagger, the other on her hip. This surprising, glittering portrait reflects the European fascination with Oriental customs and costumes at the time. In Vienna in September 1743, Liotard, returning from Constantinople continues himself to wear Turkish dress.

[HM-EF]

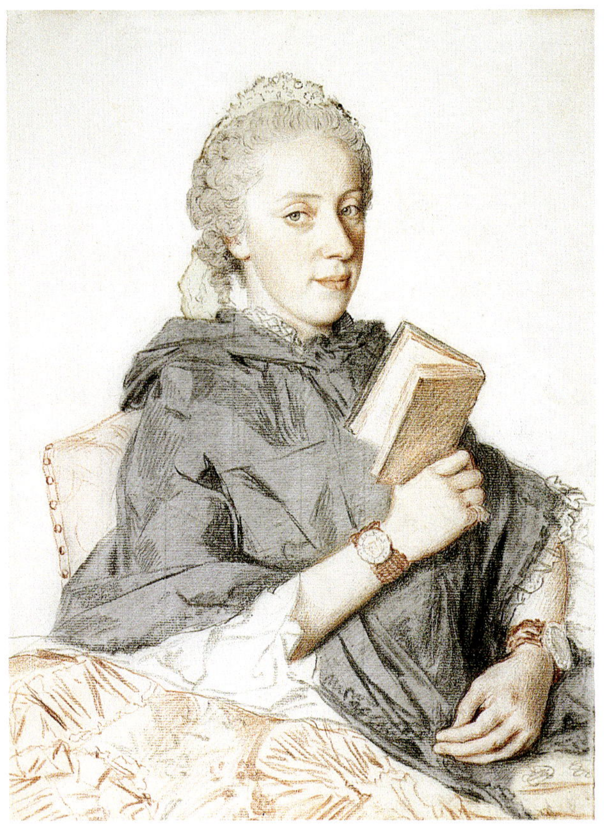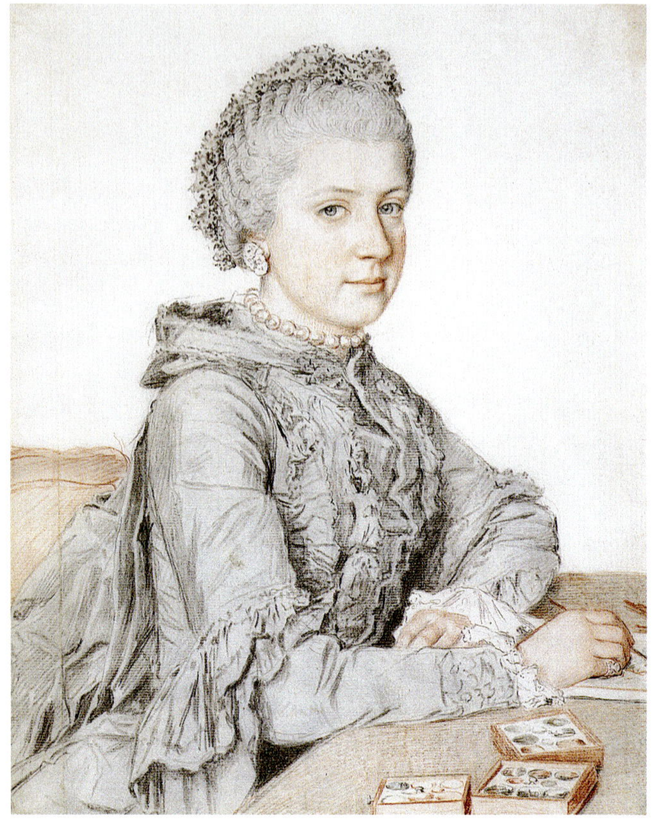

The Archduchess Maria Anna of Austria (1738–1789)

1762
Black and red chalk, graphite
pencil, watercolor, white
gouache glaze, and red chalk
wash on thin paper, heightened
with color on the verso
32 x 24 cm
On permanent loan from the
Fondation Gottfried Keller,
1947
Inv. 1947–36

Archduchess Maria Anna, the eldest of Maria Theresa of
Austria and Francis of Lorraine's sixteen children, was born
with a slight congenital deformation that gave her a stiff
arm. She also suffered from fragile health. Like her father,
and no doubt as consolation for the rejection she suffered at
court, she became fascinated by chemistry and physics and
amassed interesting collections of coins and minerals. She
also had a gift for the arts and drew and engraved on copper.
Four years after having her portrait done by Liotard, she

became abbess of the Convent for Noblewomen in Prague,
but her brother, concerned by her liberal positions and
influence in scientific and cultural circles, ensured that she
was kept away from court. She went to Klagenfurt and
became abbess of the convent, where she died in 1789.
Along with the other portraits of archduchesses and
archdukes of Austria commissioned by Maria Theresa in
1762, this drawing was sold by the imperial family in 1911.
It then entered a private collection in Vienna.

The Archduchess Maria Christina of Austria (1742–1798)

1762
Black and red chalk, graphite
pencil, and watercolor glaze on
thin paper, heightened with
color on the verso
32 x 26 cm
On permanent loan from the
Fondation Gottfried Keller,
1947
Inv. 1947–38

Her mother's favorite daughter, and like her in more ways
than one, Maria Christina had a real passion—and gift—for
drawing. She enjoyed making portraits of her brothers and
sisters and painted her family in gouache. In 1766 she
married Albert of Saxony, who was appointed governor of
Hungary on the same occasion. Her love of art made her a
valuable adviser when her husband created his very fine and
famous collection of drawings, which became the nucleus of

the Albertina Museum in Vienna. Liotard shows us the
archduchess at the age of twenty, brush in hand, looking up
from her art and apparently not distracted in the slightest.
Maria Christina died in 1798. Her splendid tomb, sculpted
after plans by Canova, at her husband's initiative, is still one
of the greatest treasures of the Imperial Crypt in Vienna
(the Herzgruft in the Augustinerkirche).

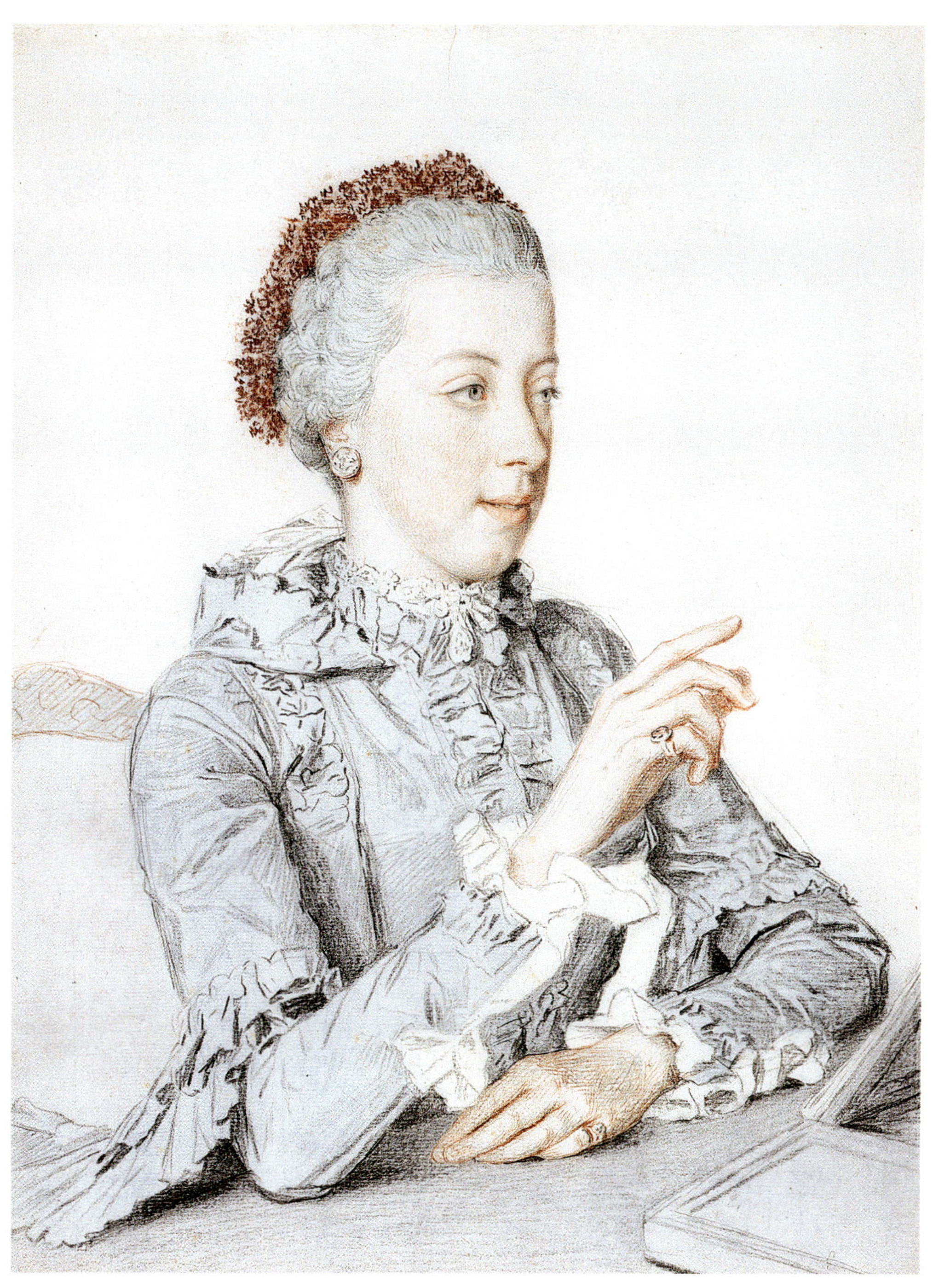

The Archduchess Maria Elisabeth of Austria (1743–1808)

1762
Black and red chalk, graphite
pencil, watercolor, and
watercolor glaze on thin paper,
heightened with color on the
verso
32.1 x 24.6 cm
On permanent loan from the
Fondation Gottfried Keller,
1947
Inv. 1947–35

The imperial couple's sixth child, the gracious and brilliant
Archduchess Maria Elisabeth was an excellent musician.
Sadly, she caught smallpox in 1767, five years after sitting
for Liotard. She survived but was permanently disfigured.
Condemned to solitude, the embittered Maria Elisabeth
lived with her mother until her brother's coronation in
1765. He sent her into exile in Innsbruck, where she became
the abbess of a convent founded by Maria Theresa.

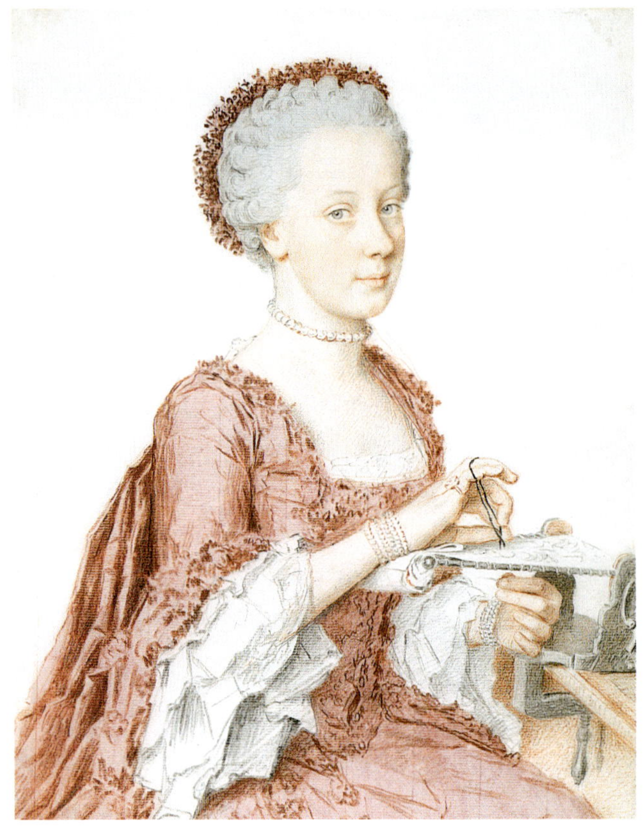 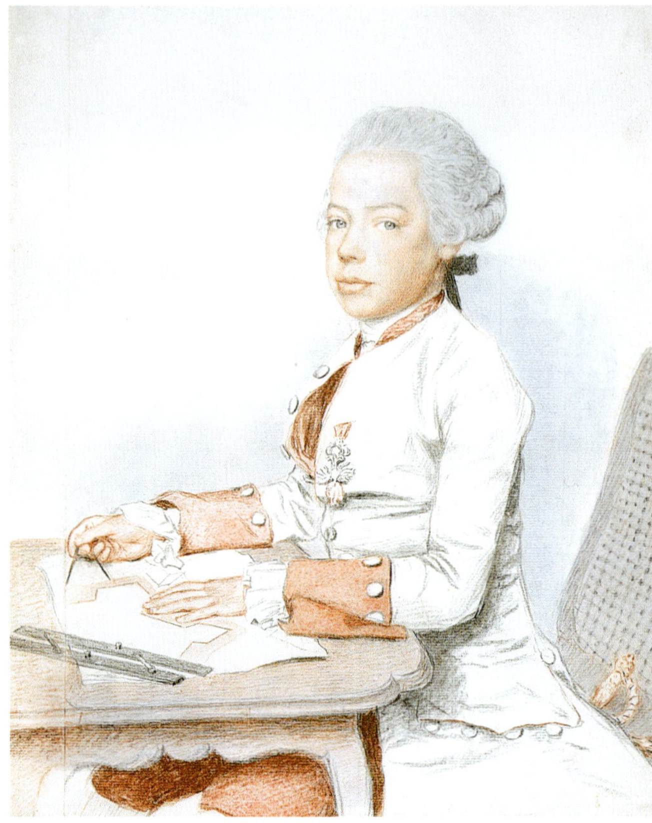

The Archduchess Maria Amalia of Austria (1746–1804)

1762
Red and black chalk, graphite pencil, and watercolor on thin paper, heightened with color on the verso
31.8 x 25.7 cm
On permanent loan from the Fondation Gottfried Keller, 1947
Inv. 1947–37

Sitting and working at her embroidery, the sixteen-year-old Archduchess Maria Amalia surprises the viewer with the intensity of her gaze, marked by skepticism but also conveying great inner strength. Indeed, that determination would be manifest a few years later when, pressured by her mother to make a political marriage, she put up a strong

fight—albeit a vain one. The empress chose as her husband the Infant of Spain, Ferdinand of Bourbon-Parma. Once in Parma, the young woman, who dominated her husband, soon took the reins of power. When Bonaparte's armies invaded, she fled to Prague, where she died without issue in 1804.

The Archduke Peter Leopold of Austria, Future Emperor Leopold II (1747–1792)

1762
Red and black chalk, graphite pencil, and watercolor on thin paper, heightened with color on the verso
32 x 26.5 cm
On permanent loan from the Fondation Gottfried Keller, 1947
Inv. 1947–44

Peter Leopold, the second of the imperial couple's sons, is depicted by Liotard in ceremonial apparel, sword at his side, busy drawing a Vauban-style fortress. In 1765, he married Maria Luisa of Bourbon, the daughter of Charles III of Spain, and became Grand Duke of Tuscany under the name Leopold I (1765–90). He governed the Duchy as a liberal,

enlightened despot. Called back to Vienna in 1790 to succeed his brother Joseph II at the head of the Holy Roman Empire, during his brief reign (1790–92) he managed to win back the Netherlands and then Liège and end the war against the Turks.

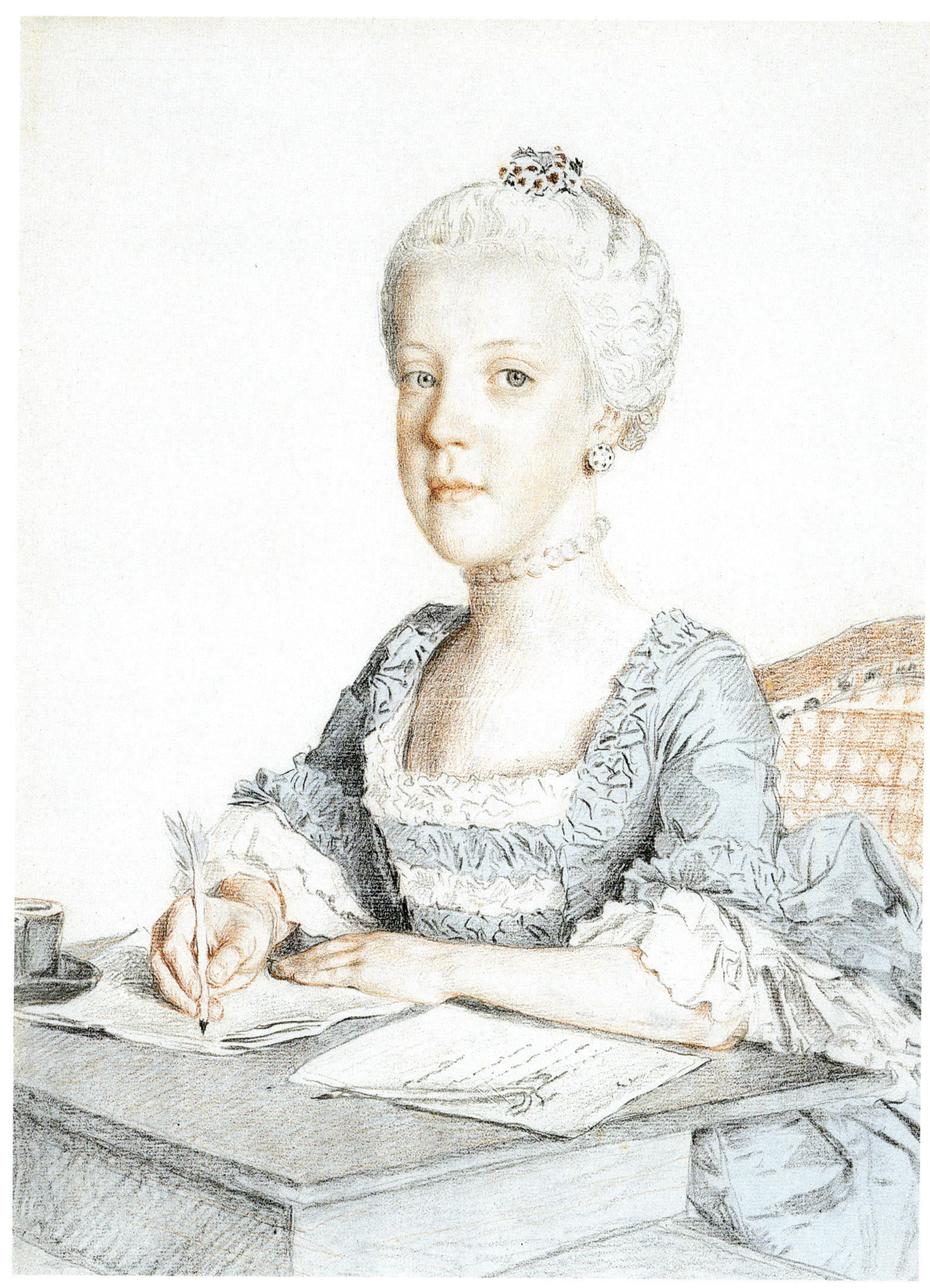

The Archduchess Johanna Gabriele of Austria (1750–1762)

1762
Red and black chalk, graphite
pencil, and watercolor glaze on
thin paper, heightened with
color on the verso
32.3 x 24.8 cm
On permanent loan from the
Fondation Gottfried Keller,
1947
Inv. 1947–39

Liotard here offers us a moving portrait of the eighth
daughter of Maria Theresa and Francis I. The little
archduchess, captured in the middle of writing a letter,
was to have a tragic destiny: she died at the age of thirteen,
not long after Liotard made this drawing.

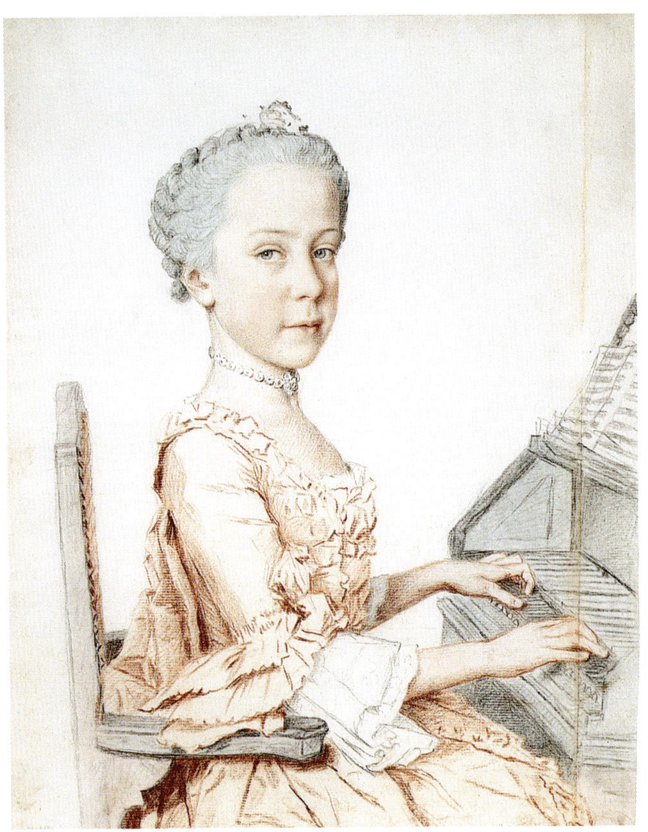 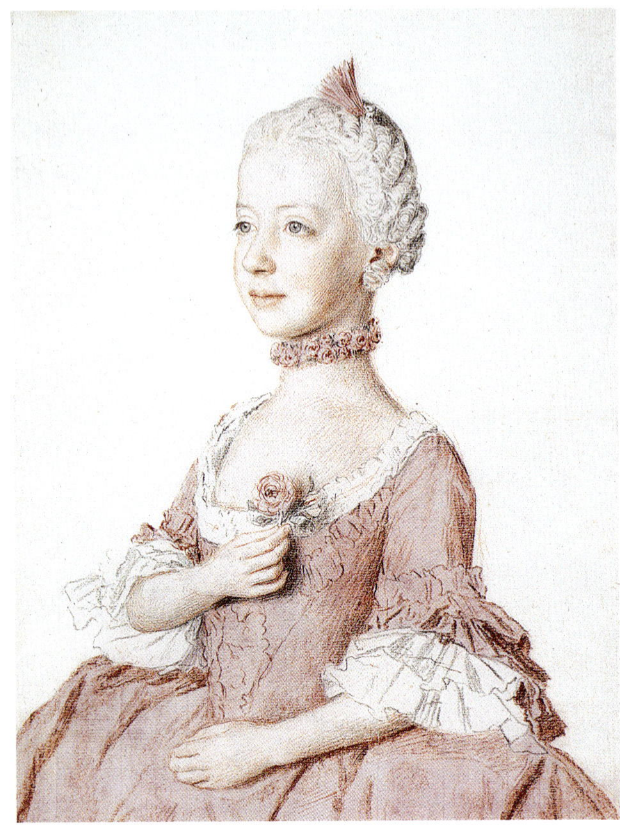

The Archduchess Maria Josepha of Austria (1751–1767)

1762
Red and black chalk, graphite
pencil, and watercolor glaze on
thin paper, heightened with
color on the verso
32.3 x 24.8 cm
On permanent loan from the
Fondation Gottfried Keller,
1947
Inv. 1947–40

Described by the empress herself as a "victim of politics,"
Maria Josepha was betrothed as a young girl to the son of
the Spanish king, Ferdinand IV, king of Naples and the Two
Sicilies. But then, on October 15, 1767, in the first flush of
youth, she died of smallpox. It was her sister Maria Karolina
who succeeded her on the throne of Naples and the Two
Sicilies, where she reigned for more than thirty years.

The Archduchess Maria Karolina of Austria (1752–1814)

1762
Red and black chalk, stumping,
watercolor, and pastel on thin
paper, heightened with color
on the verso
32 x 24.5 cm
On permanent loan from the
Fondation Gottfried Keller,
1947
Inv. 1947–41

Maria Karolina was the thirteenth daughter of Maria
Theresa and Francis I of Lorraine. Liotard skillfully conveys
the grace and dignity of this child, aged only ten, but
destined for great things. Her marriage to Ferdinand IV,
king of Naples and the Two Sicilies (previously betrothed to
her own sister Maria Josepha, who died young) made her
ruler of a state faced with both internal instability and
external threats. It was a role that she took on with great
courage, unlike her bumbling husband. She was twice forced
to leave Naples after victories by Napoleon's army, and she
remained the French emperor's most dogged enemy. She
died in 1814, shortly before the Congress of Vienna
restored her husband's kingdom to him. She witnessed the
deaths of thirteen of her seventeen children.

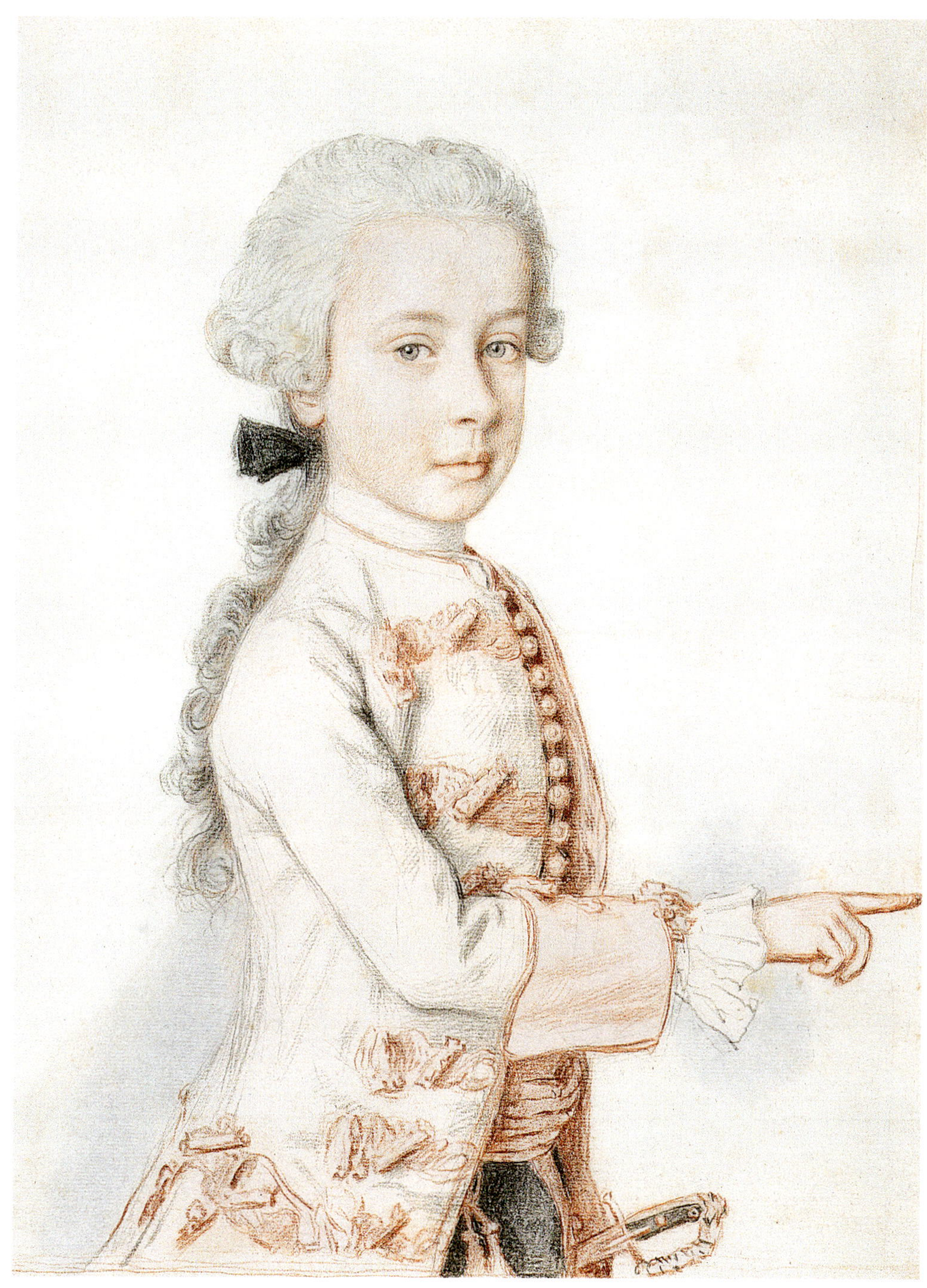

The Archduke Ferdinand Karl Anton of Austria (1754–1806)

1762
**Black and red chalk, graphite
pencil, and gray glaze on paper,
heightened with color on the
verso**
32.3 x 24.7 cm
**On permanent loan from the
Fondation Gottfried Keller,
1947**
Inv. 1947–45

Ferdinand is shown here at the age of eight and, his formal
clothes notwithstanding, in a much livelier, less official pose
than his brother Peter Leopold.

The imperial couple's penultimate child, the young archduke
was governor and captain general of Lombardy. Politically, he
was much less to the fore than his brothers and sisters until

his marriage in 1771 to Princess Maria Beatrice d'Este,
daughter of the Duke of Modena, whose dowry included the
rich Duchy of the House of Este. When the French army
occupied Lombardy, he took refuge in Vienna, where he died
in 1806.

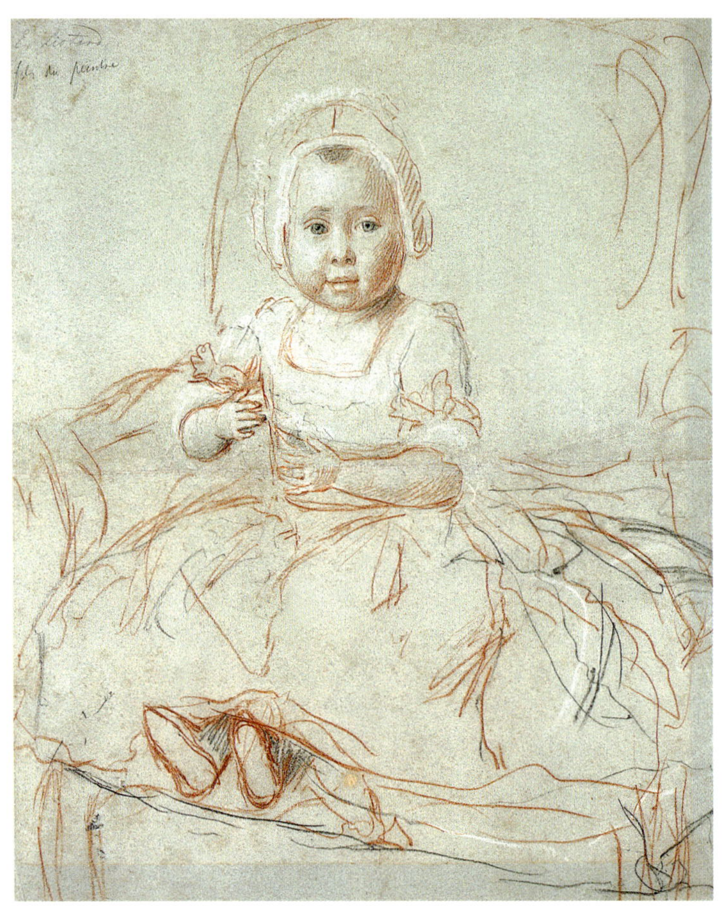 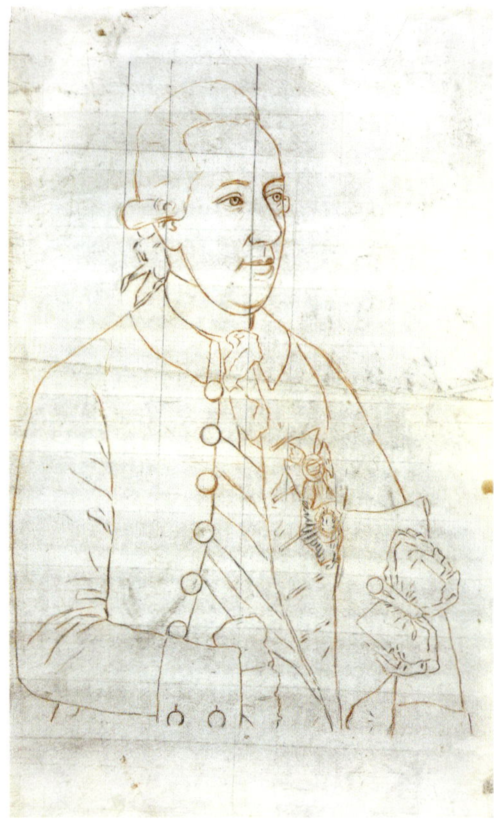

Portrait of Frederika Luise Wilhelmina of Orange-Nassau at the Age of Two (1770–1819)

1772
Black, red, and white chalk
with stumping on blue paper,
heightened with color on the
verso
62.5 x 51.7 cm
Gift of the Société Auxiliaire
du Musée, 1934
Inv. 1934–39

During his sojourns in the Netherlands, from 1755 to 1757 and from 1771 to 1773, Liotard acquired a sizable clientele, working, among others, for the Stadhouder, William V of Orange-Nassau, and his entourage in The Hague. In 1772, William commissioned a portrait of his infant daughter, Princess Frederika Luise Wilhelmina of Orange-Nassau. In this initial study for the pastel (previously kept at the Hohenzollern Museum, Berlin), Liotard depicts this lively, attentive child with just a few quick lines.

Until 1934, this drawing remained with the artist's descendants in Amsterdam.

The Emperor Joseph II of Austria (1741–1790)

1778
Graphite pencil and red chalk
on paper
40 x 25.5 cm
Gift of the Société Auxiliaire
du Musée, 1934
Inv. 1935–9

Between 1777 and 1778, Liotard executed several portraits of Joseph II of Austria, the eldest son of Empress Maria Theresa. Crowned in 1765 after the death of his father, Francis I of Lorraine, he had to share power in matters of foreign policy with his mother. A great admirer of Frederick II of Prussia, he was himself an enlightened despot. Under the name of Count Falkenstein, he visited Liotard in Geneva in 1777, after which the painter set off for Vienna with his eldest son. Among the portraits he made during this sojourn in the Austrian capital, several are drawings and some, yet to be located, are known only from Liotard and his son's letters to Marie Liotard-Fargues. Based on a pastel of the emperor (Rijksmuseum, Amsterdam), this drawing was squared so that Liotard himself could engrave it using a roulette ("Since he returned, your Papa has been engraving the emperor's portrait." Letter from Madame Liotard to her eldest son in Amsterdam, dated Geneva, December 2, 1778. Geneva Library, BPU, Ms. fr. 355, fol. 49–50). Apart from the choice of pencils, this work is very close to the artist's description of a portrait of the emperor done in 1777:
"I have finished the emperor in two sittings: very complete, very life like, drawn in black and white pencil. I wanted him to be in the pose of command and, while insisting that he would rather not, he made the gesture. He stayed standing for half an hour, his hand in his jacket, hat under his arm, lace and red collar with the ribbons of Maria Theresa and Saint Stephen. The empress would have preferred a more sunny air but he would have been angry if I had done so" (letter from Liotard to his wife, December 31, 1777).
Until 1934, this drawing was the property of the artist's descendants in Amsterdam.

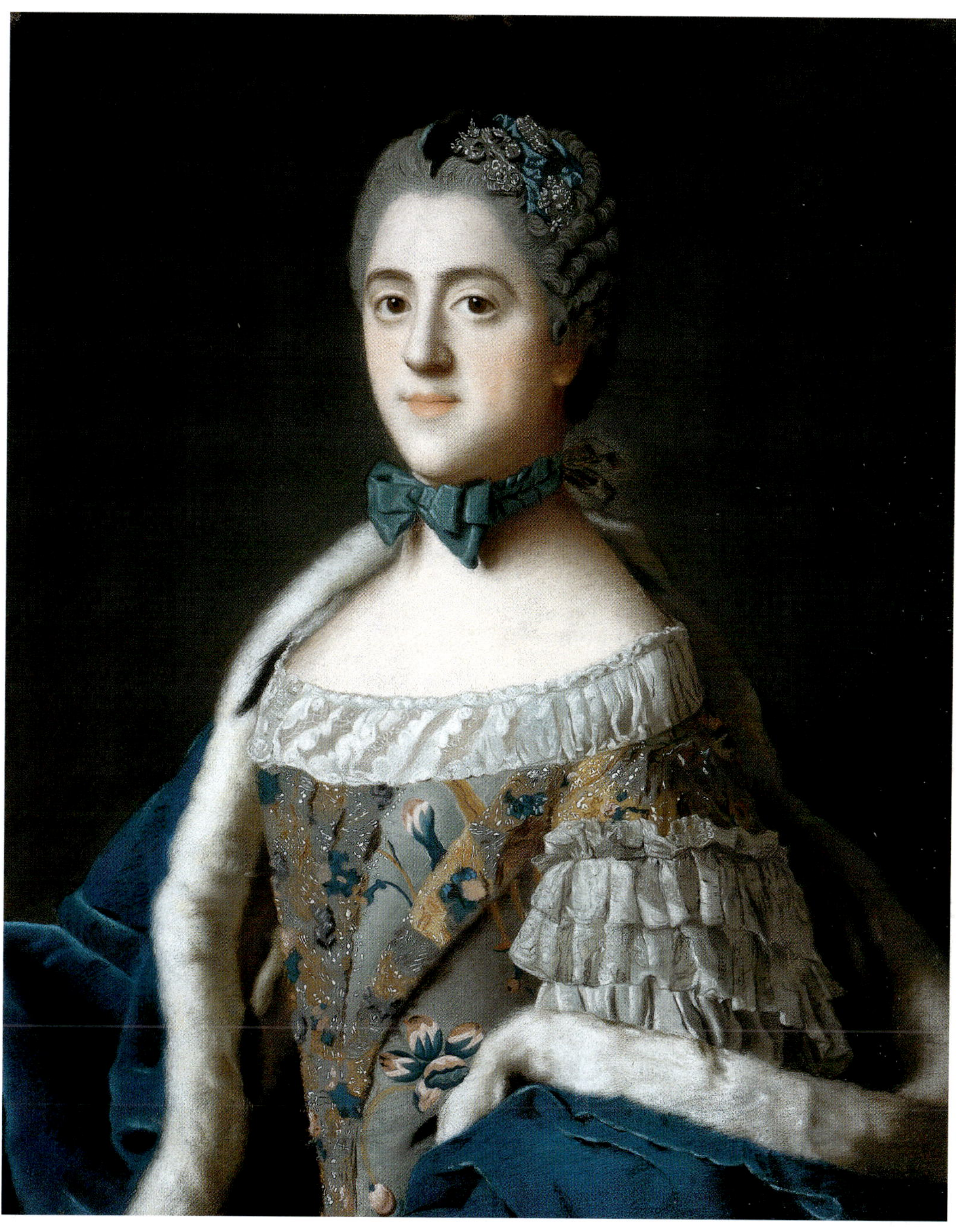

Madame Sophie de France (1734–1782)

1750–53
Pastel on parchment glued
onto canvas
60 x 50 cm
Purchase, 1963
Inv. 1963–58

Sophie-Philippe-Élisabeth-Justine, also known as "Madame Sophie" or "Madame Cinquième" (Madame the Fifth) after the death of her older sister, Madame Troisième (Madame the Third), was the sixth daughter of Louis XV and Marie Leczinska. With Victoire and her two younger sisters, she was raised at Fontevrault Abbey, which is where Jean-Marc Nattier painted their portraits in 1747. She returned to the court at Versailles in 1750. Condemned, like all but her oldest sister, Madame Infante, to celibacy, she lived at Versailles until the death of Louis XV. In 1775, with Mesdames Adélaïde and Victoire, she inherited the Bellevue castle, where the three sisters kept up the "old court." She died as she had lived, discreetly, amid public indifference. In this portrait, which no doubt shows her at the age of sixteen, the royal attributes are discreet but the ermine edging of her coat, the richness of her gown, and her lofty bearing all indicate that this is a royal princess. This pastel comes from a French private collection.

3. Anne de Herdt,
"Introduction à l'histoire du
dessin genevois de Liotard à
Hodler," *Genava*, XXIX, 1981,
p. 19.
4. Anne de Herdt, 1992,
op. cit.

During this same sojourn, the empress requested that Liotard draw portraits of her children.[3] These masterpieces were acquired by the Fondation Gottfried Keller in 1947 and put on permanent loan in the drawings collection of the Musées d'Art et d'Histoire. According to Anne de Herdt, this is one of the rare ensembles in the iconography of the Hapsburg-Lorraines to include nearly all the children of Maria Theresa and her husband, Francis I, all drawn at the same moment. These portraits were intended for the empress's personal collection. Their small format was designed to travel easily. They were considered to be "presentation drawings," that is to say, autonomous and definitive works. It is certainly clear that the high degree of finish and elaborate graphic rendering have nothing in common with preparatory sketches. Liotard played skillfully on the delicacy and transparency of his support. By heightening the paper with color on the back, and incising the contours of the faces, he achieved extraordinary effects of relief in his rendering of the models. These were Maria Theresa's favorite portraits, no doubt because in them she found her children's features captured with both humanity and authenticity.[4]

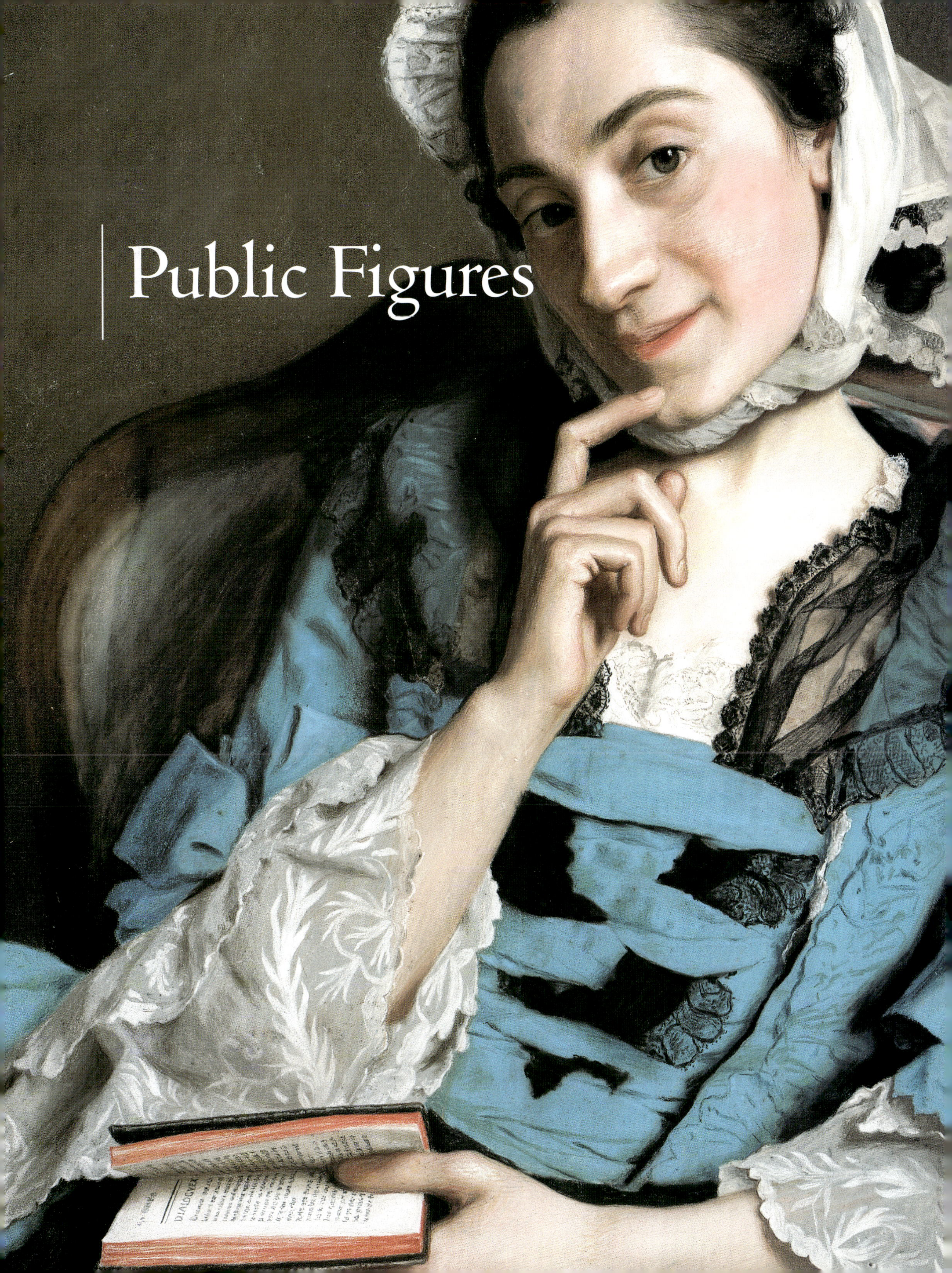

Public Figures

Isabelle Félicité Bleeker

This chapter examines Liotard's portraits of public figures resident in Geneva, and others he painted when they were in Geneva. Born into a French family that moved to Geneva after the revocation of the Edict of Nantes, Liotard was deeply marked by the Genevan character. Sharing a taste for moderation, reason, and truth with the scientists, writers, financiers, and magistrates in his social circle, he was particularly at ease when representing them, finding in them subjects especially suited to his art.[1] For all his frequent travels around Europe, Liotard remained deeply attached to his native city and settled there permanently in 1757. Rich and famous, he was welcomed by local notables who wished to have their portrait painted by the artist for whom so many crowned heads had posed.[2] In Geneva he produced his masterworks, providing at the same time a remarkably acute and vivid record of Genevan society in the mid-eighteenth century. The intellectual climate, we should recall, was intense. Madame d'Épinay, Baron Melchior Grimm, and many others came to the city for treatment by the famous Dr. Tronchin, whose cousin the counselor François Tronchin kept his remarkable collection of paintings available to other art lovers. Genevan scientists, with their insistence on the observation of facts as the sole means of discovering truth, had a profound impact on this society. Liotard's portraits of this wealthy and enlightened Protestant bourgeoisie, with whom he was in perfect harmony, are reflections of his own world.

Liotard worked in a world where the concept of portraiture was changing. The dramatic presentation of the model was beginning to lose its dominance, as the subject's psychology and social identity became central concerns for artists. The Genevan painter did not offer the ideal of grace and finesse strived for by most of the pastelists of the day. Flouting the conventions of the times, he refused to embellish his models or pose them in a flattering way. We see them as they are; nothing is hidden, no physical flaw omitted. By transcribing frankly and without compromise what he saw, he managed to convey something of the human soul.[3] Because he went against the ideas of his contemporaries, Liotard was something of an outsider. Driven by his concern for realism and his objective vision, expressed through his remarkable, consummate technique, he never produced a "desiccated" image of those he depicted. The backgrounds of his compositions are generally a solid color; he rarely places his figures in interiors or adds accessories. The stark simplicity of these backgrounds highlights the presence of the sitters and invites the viewer to focus on them.

One of the artist's masterpieces, *Madame d'Épinay*, offers an exemplary illustration of his capacity to render in detail not only the delicacy and transparency of embroidered tulle, or the silky sheen of a satin ribbon contrasting with matte black taffeta, but also the intelligence of the gaze and the melancholy of the smile. The touches of gray-green Liotard puts at the temples, near the hairline, suggest a degree of ill health, as do the veins visible under the skin. This portrait admirably conveys both wit and sensibility.

1. Renée Loche, "Jean-Étienne Liotard dans les collections genevoises," *Le Livre du Richemond IV,* 1990, p. 52.
2. Louis Gielly, *L'École genevoise de peinture*, Geneva, 1935, p. 31.
3. François Fosca, *La Vie, les voyages et les œuvres de Liotard, citoyen de Genève, dit le Peintre turc,* Lausanne, Paris, 1956, p. 129.

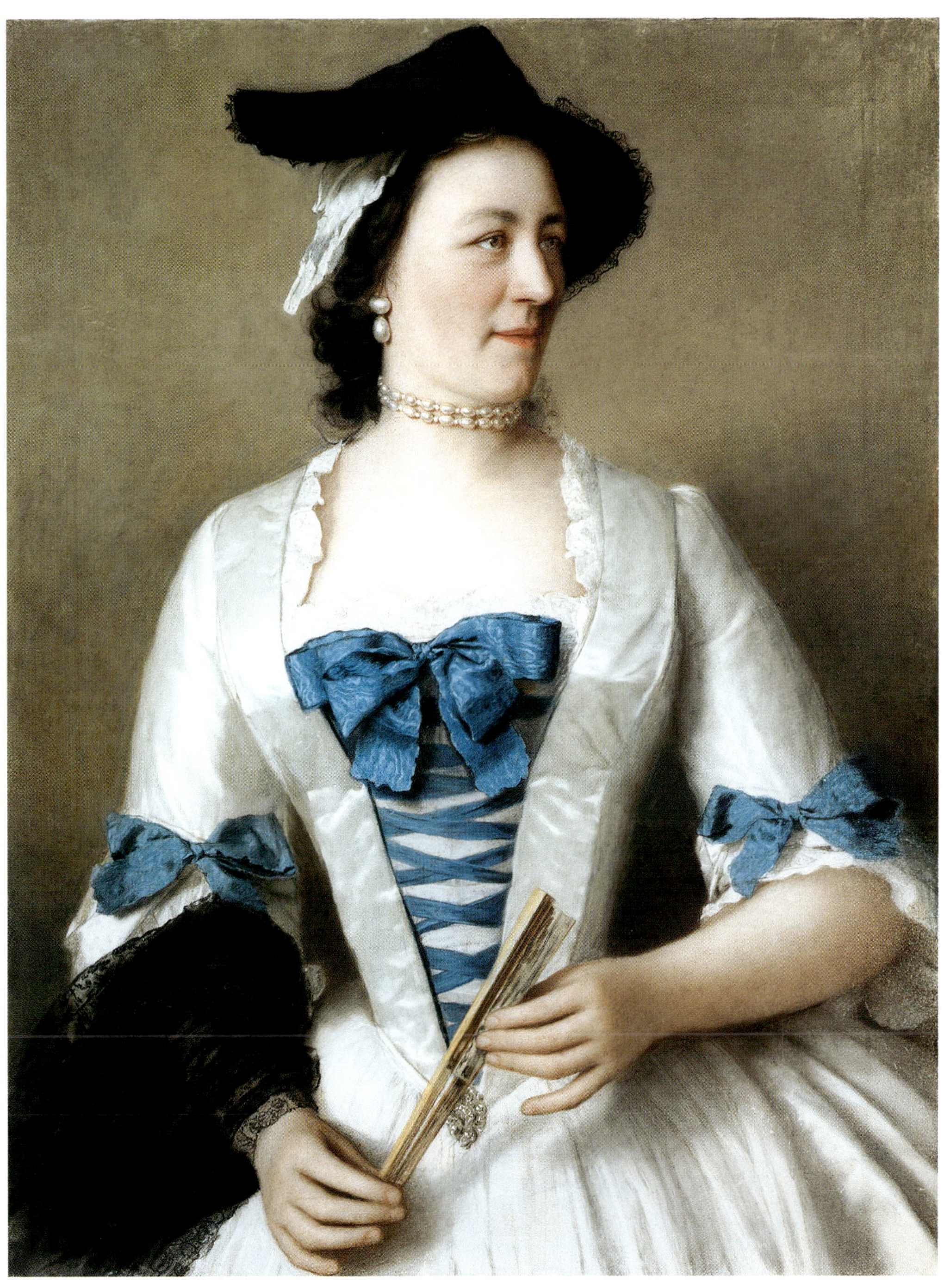

Lady Tyrell, née Jeanne-Élisabeth Sellon (born in 1705)

Circa 1746
Pastel on parchment
62.2 x 46.7 cm
Purchase, 1991
Inv. 1991–14

Lady Tyrell, born Jeanne-Élisabeth Sellon, was the daughter of a merchant from Nîmes, Jean Sellon, who, after the revocation of the Edict of Nantes, had taken refuge in Geneva. That was where she married the baronet Sir Charles Tyrell in 1726. She is shown here in a sumptuous ball gown with a laced bodice holding a fan in her hands. There is a certain contrast between the somewhat robust physique of the model, faithfully captured by Liotard, and the refinement of her clothes. Liotard made a copy of this pastel and kept it in his own collection for the rest of his life (Rijksmuseum, Amsterdam).

This work was owned by the Sellon family and then went, by way of kinship, to the Maurice family (Geneva).

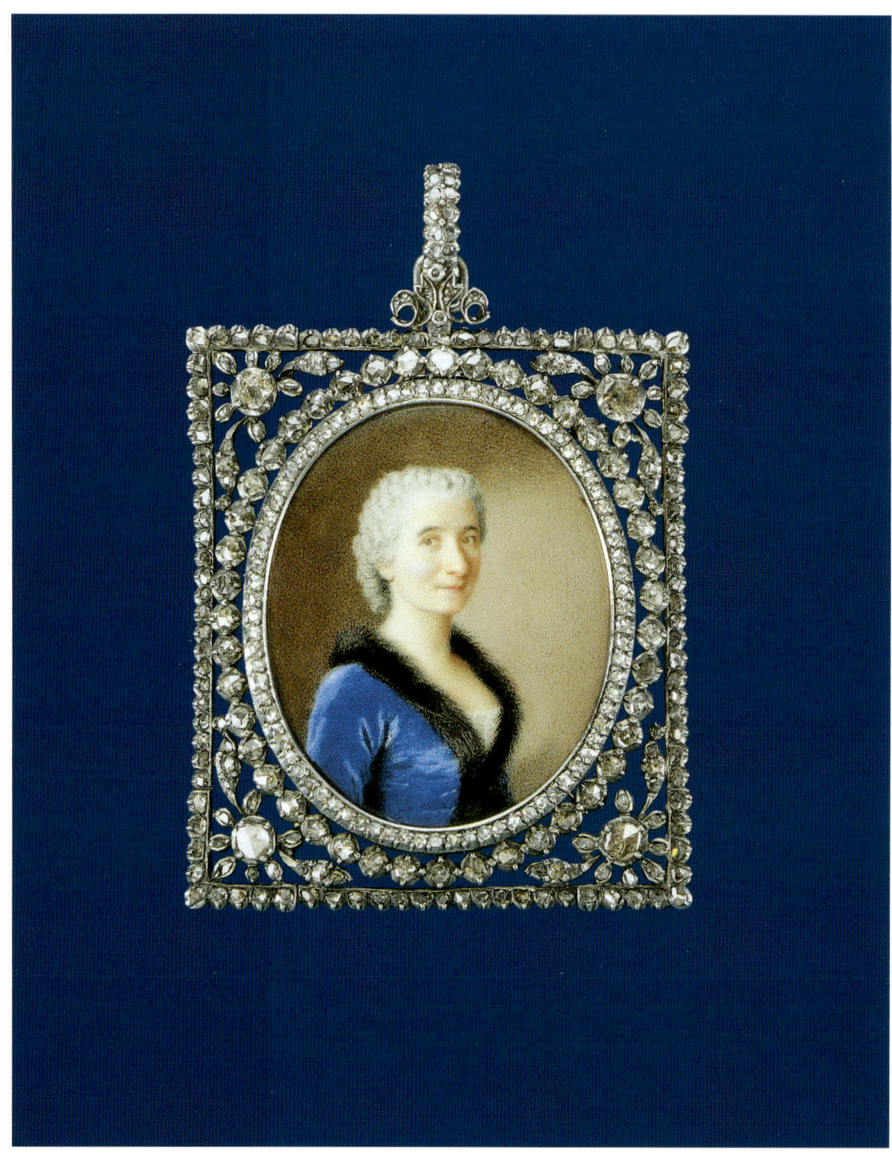

1746
Enamel on copper
5.2 x 4.2 cm
Gift of Madame and Monsieur
Grégoire Salmanowitz, 1988
Inv. AD 6787

When visiting with his cousins, the Lavergnes, in Lyons, Liotard took the opportunity to do some painting on enamels. In addition to the portrait of Maria Theresa of Austria (p. 68), he executed this portrait of Andrienne Cannac. Born into a rich Genevan family, she had married the banker Pierre-Philippe Cannac, who settled in Lyons to run his coach company, Les Coches du Rhône. Thirteen years earlier, Liotard had painted two individual portraits of the banker and his wife in oil on canvas (Hans Boeckh, *Genava*, 1989, pp. 129–30).

This enamel was in private collections in Paris, Geneva, and Zurich.

It was stolen from the Musée de l'Horlogerie et de l'Émaillerie in 2002.

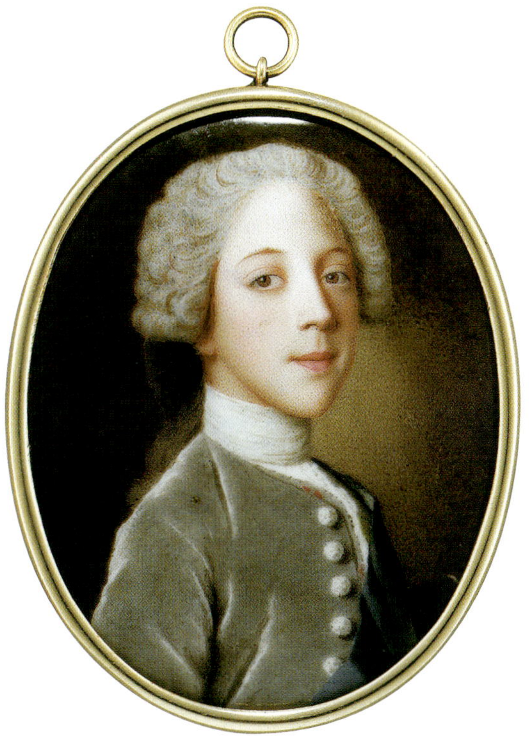 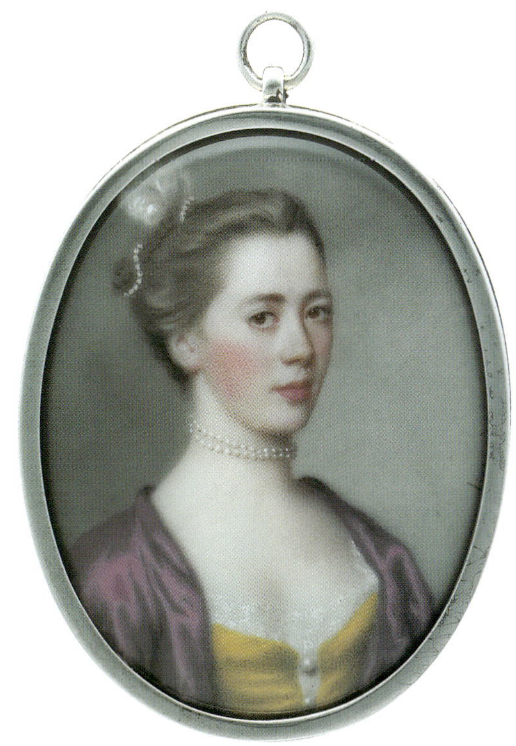

Henry Benedict Marie Clement Stuart (1725–1807)

1737–38
Enamel on copper
5.34 x 4.3 cm
Gift of Madame and Monsieur
Grégoire Salmanowitz, 1993
Inv. AD 8211

Henry Benedict Marie Clement Stuart, the future cardinal of York (1747), was the nominal archbishop of Corinth (1759) and bishop of Tusculum. He is shown here at the age of twelve with powdered hair, wearing a white cravat and a gray velvet jacket. This miniature was painted in Rome in the winter of 1737–38, when the young prince was there with his father, James Francis Edward Stuart, known as "the

Old Pretender," with his mother, Maria Clementina Sobieski, and his older brother, Charles Edward (1720–88), whose portrait Liotard also painted (Hans Boeckh, *Genava*, 1993, pp. 148–49).
This enamel was stolen from the Musée de l'Horlogerie et de l'Émaillerie in 2002.

Georgina Poyntz, Countess Spencer (1736–1814)

1754
Signed and dated
Enamel on copper
4.6 x 3.9 x 0.3 cm
Purchase, 1979
Inv. AD 3721

When Liotard went to London in 1753 he was welcomed by the Earl of Bessborough, whom he had befriended in Rome and with whom he had traveled in Asia Minor. Bessborough introduced him to high society in London and thus enabled him to win many commissions. Among these were a number of miniatures on enamel, including those executed at the

time of the betrothal of Georgina Poyntz to John, first Earl Spencer, who married in 1755. These are some of the artist's finest enamels. This one was previously in the collection of Earl Spencer, F.S.A. (Northamptonshire).
This enamel was stolen from the Musée de l'Horlogerie et de l'Émaillerie in 2002.

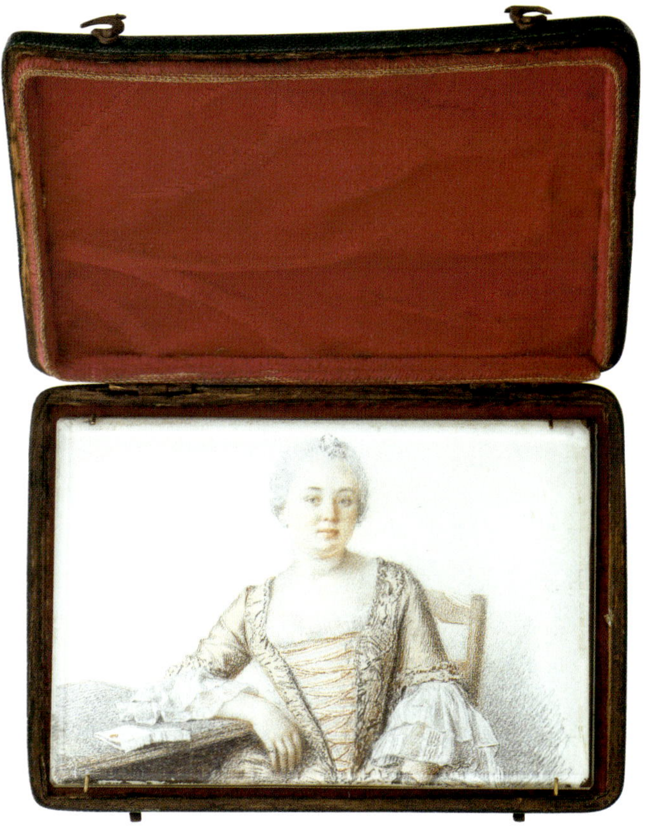

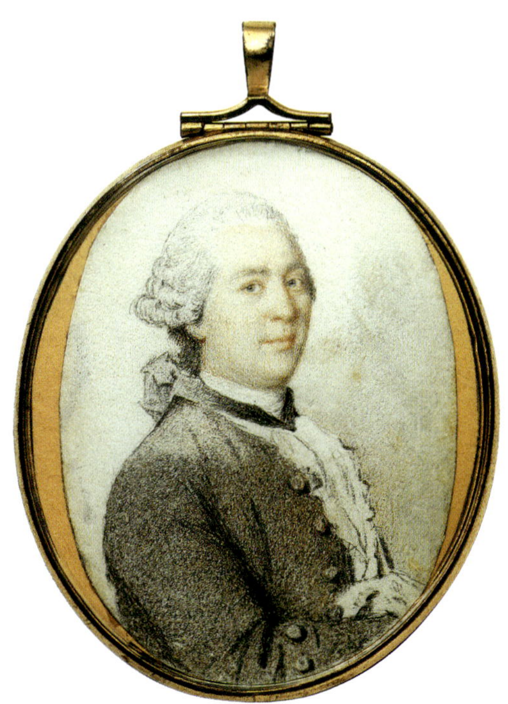

Young Woman with a Letter

1746–50
Wax crayon, black lead,
and red chalk on board
5.83 x 8.7 cm
Purchase, 1948
Inv. AD 337

Portrait of a Man of Quality

1750–60
Graphite and red chalk on
paper glued onto board
6.3 x 4.7 cm
Purchase, 1971
Inv. AD 2209

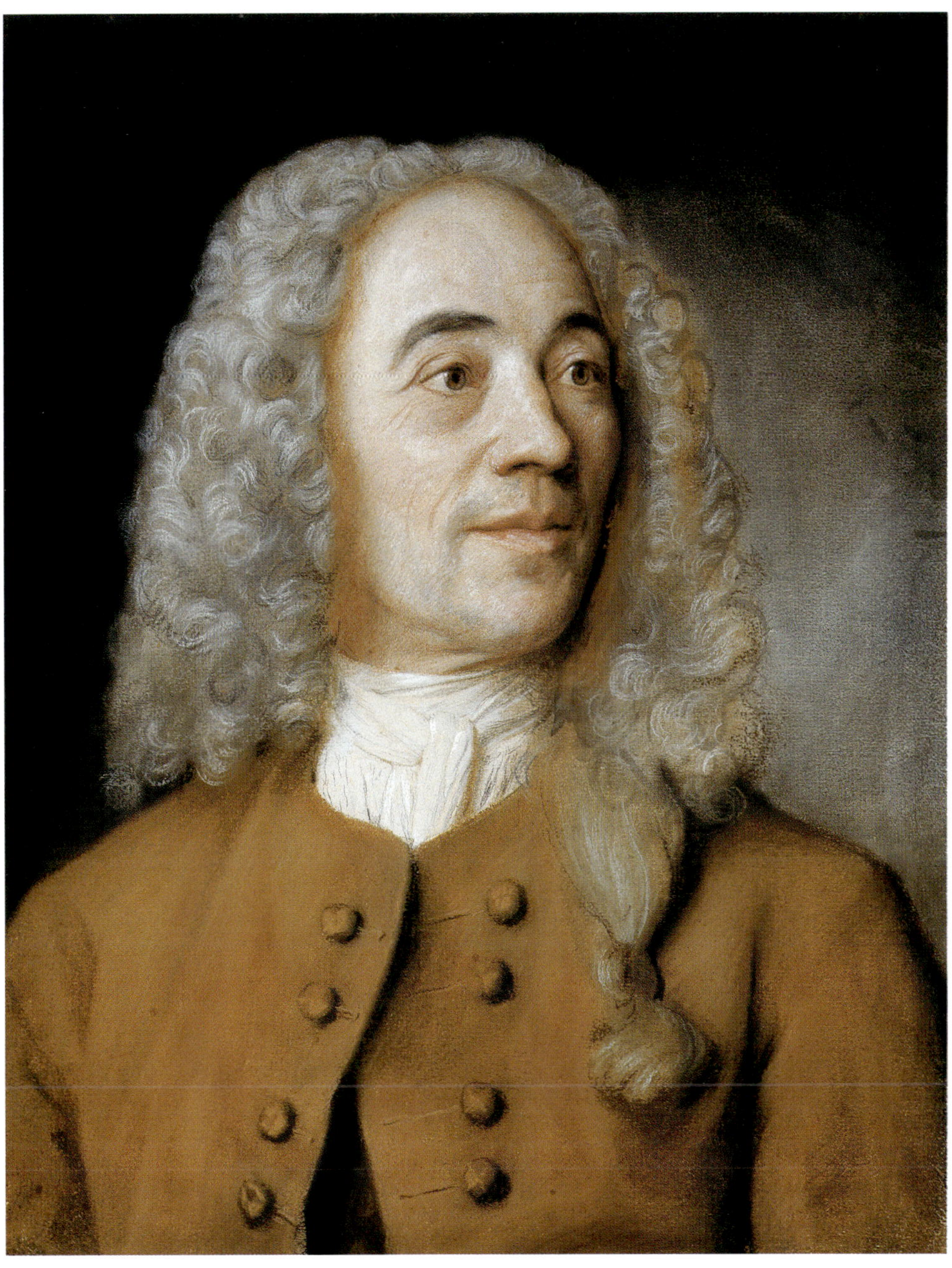

Jean Dassier (1676–1763)

Circa 1726–30
Pastel and watercolor on paper
55 x 44 cm
Purchase, 1998
Inv. D 1998–502

The talented artist Jean Dassier is the only medalist of the eighteenth century whose name appears, together with that of his son Jacques-Antoine (1715–59), in the *Encyclopédie* of Diderot and d'Alembert. Appointed engraver of the Geneva Mint in 1719, he produced several immensely successful series of medals, such as *Les Hommes illustres du siècle de Louis XIV* (1723), *Les Rois d'Angleterre* (1731), and *L'Histoire de la République romaine* (1740–50), executed in collaboration with Jacques-Antoine. According to contemporary sources, Dassier modeled his beautiful portrait of Maria Theresa of Austria (1744) after a contemporaneous portrait of the empress by Liotard (William Eisler, 2005, vol. II, cat. III, 17 and p. 137).

The liveliness of the face, the simplicity of the composition, the unity of the color, the quick, vigorous execution of the wig, and the presence of an underdrawing all support the attribution of this pastel to Liotard. With its echoes of the art of Carriera and Watteau, this piece occupies a singular position in the artist's early work, as the first brilliant demonstration of the mastery he had acquired in Paris. He no doubt painted it between 1726 and 1730, during one of his sojourns back in Geneva.

Depicting an intelligent and vivacious man in his fifties, the pastel was sent to Zurich in 1771 by two of Jean Dassier's sons (Antoine and Jean II) to serve as the model for the frontispiece of their father's biography published in the *Geschichte der besten Künstler in der Schweitz* by Johann Caspar Füssli (vol. IV, 1774 ; see Eisler 2005, p. 14, fig. 1). Afterward it belonged to the Ador family from Geneva, direct descendants of the medalist. [WE-MR]

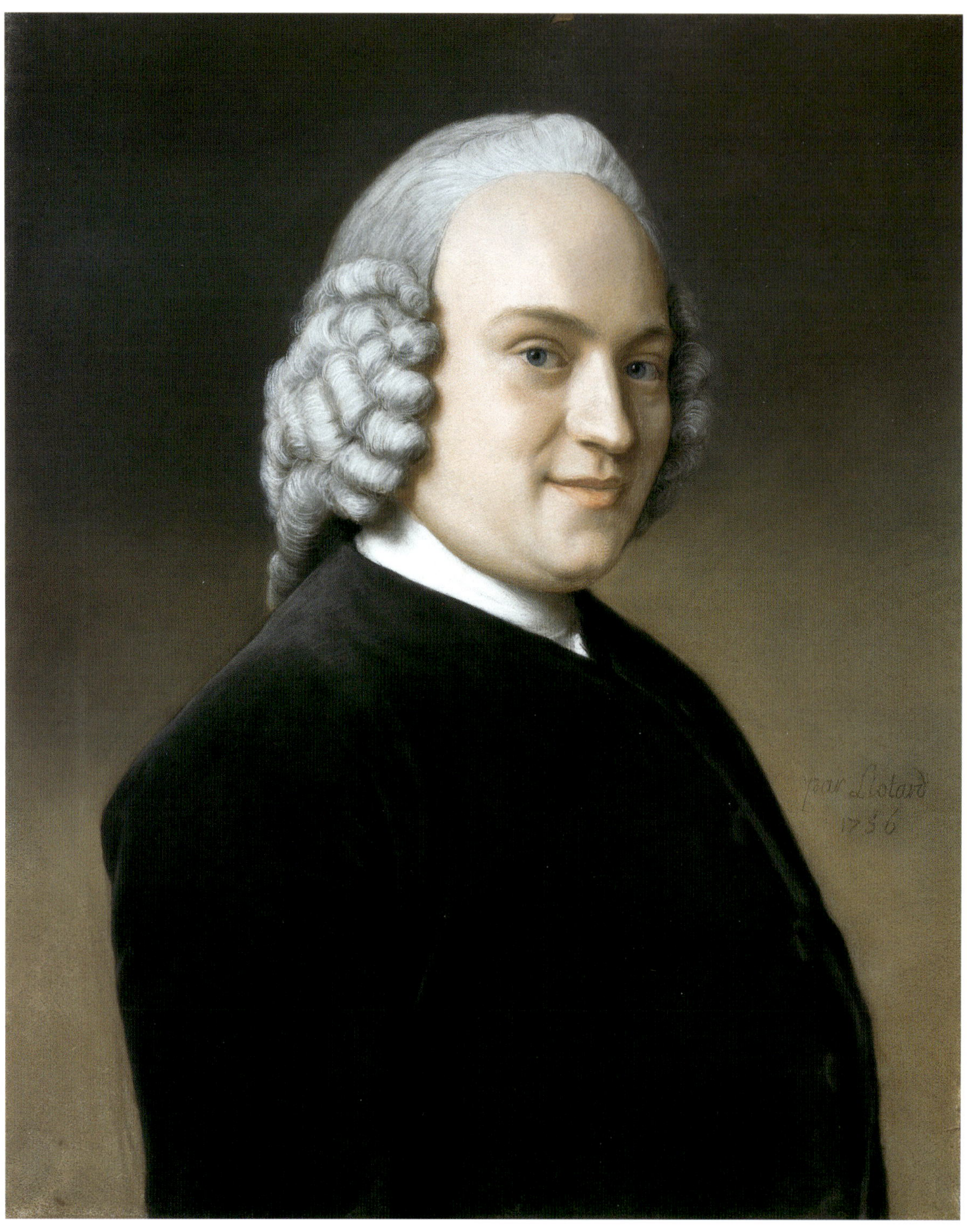

Pieter van Bleiswijk (1724–1790)

1756
Signed and dated
Pastel on parchment
60 x 50 cm
Purchase, 1911
Inv. 1911–33

During his first sojourn in the Netherlands, Liotard executed pendant portraits of Pieter van Bleiswijk and his wife. At the time, Van Bleiswijk was secretary of the city of Delft. In 1772 he obtained the position of pension adviser of the states of Holland and western Friesland and moved to The Hague. He retained this post until his death in 1790 (Frans Grijzenhout, *Genava*, 1985, p. 87). Despite the austerity of its composition and colors, this portrait exudes a certain warmth owing to the sitter's intelligent expression.

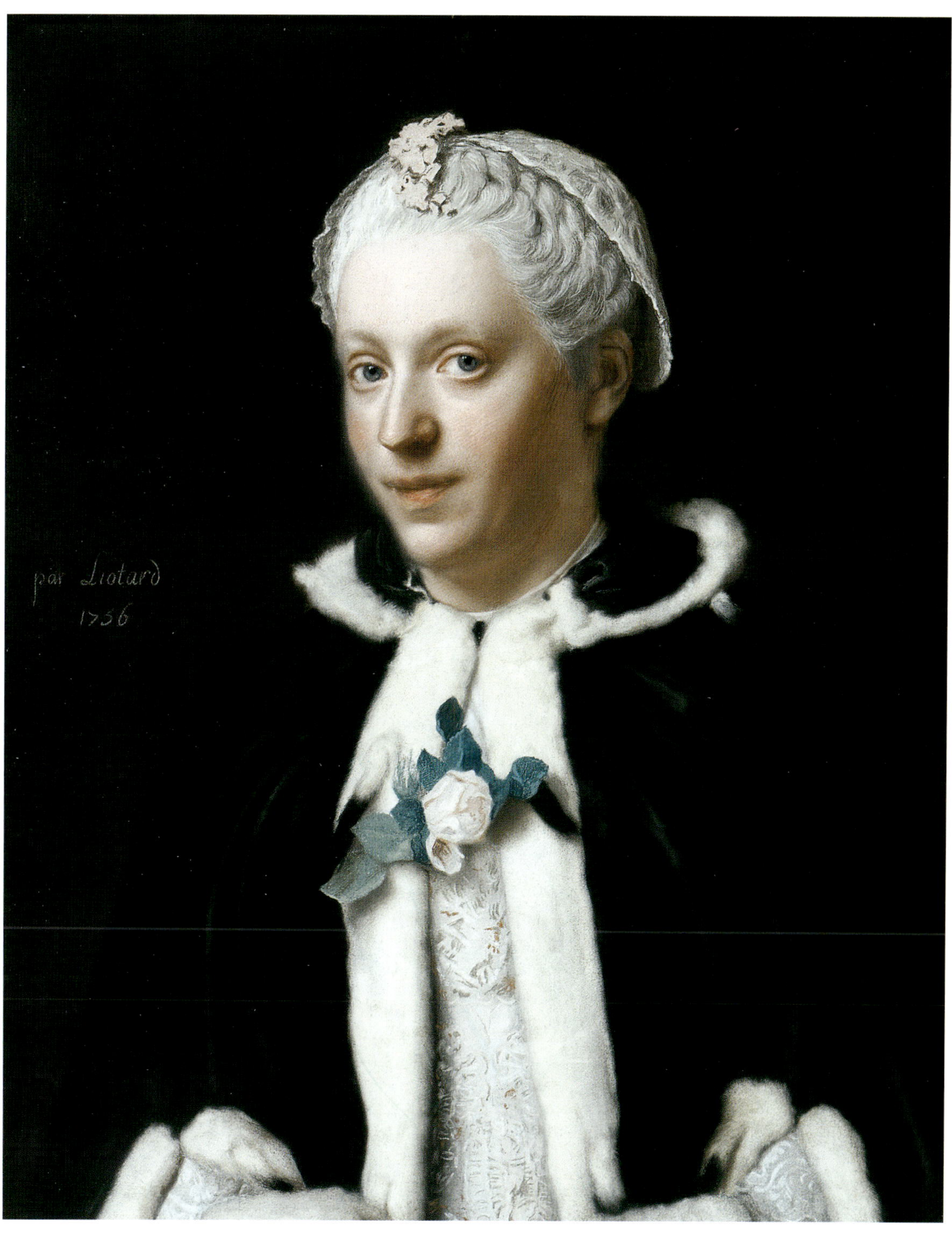

Madame Pieter van Bleiswijk, née Geertruida Antonia (1728–1790)

1756
Signed and dated
Pastel on parchment
59 x 47 cm
Purchase, 1911
Inv. 1911–32

Geertruida Antonia van Bleiswijk wears a black coat on a similarly dark background, from which the white notes of her outfit stand out with particular intensity. The contrast between the dark colors and the delicacy of the light tones (the ermine trim of her coat, the rose pinned to her bodice decorated with lace embroidery, the whiteness of her wig), as well as the gentle, very reticent expression of her face make for a portrait that is both restrained and full of grace. The inventory carried out after her death in her home in The Hague on May 23, 1791, mentions the presence in the "small green cabinet" of these two portraits "in gilded frames" (Frans Grijzenhout, *Genava*, 1985, p. 87). From the collection of Pieter van Bleiswijk the works passed into other private collections in the Netherlands.

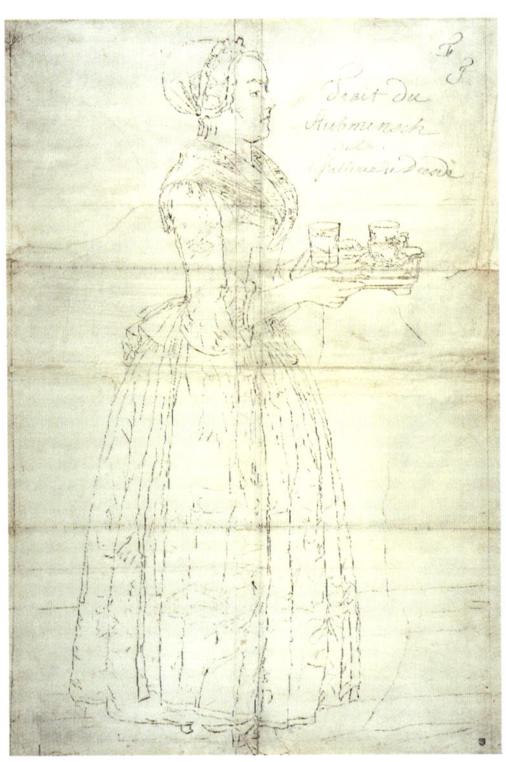

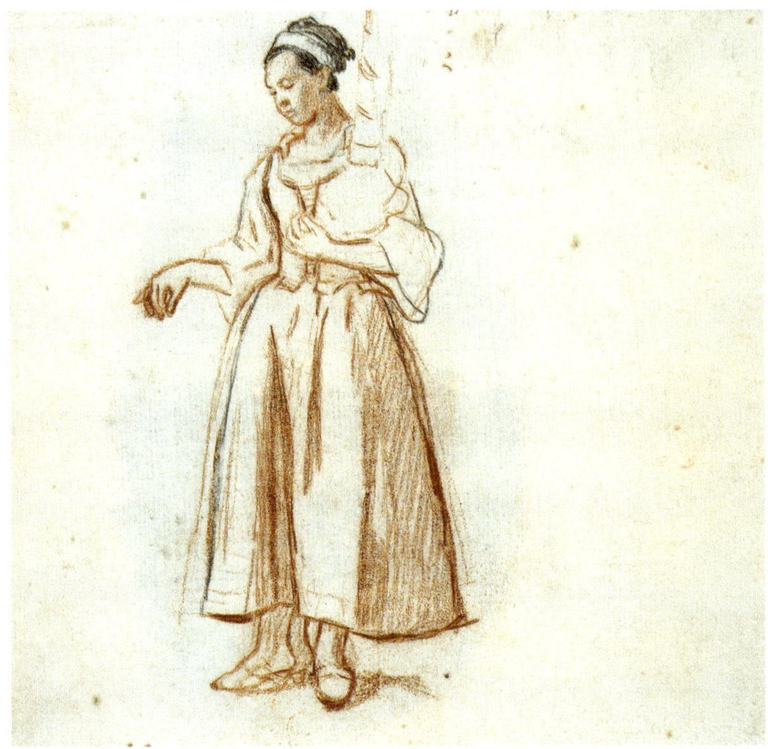

La Belle Chocolatière

1744–45
Pouncing and brown ink
on paper
85 x 59 cm
Gift of the Société Auxiliaire
du Musée, 1934
Inv. 1935–8

The pastel portrait known as *La Belle Chocolatière* (Gemäldegalerie, Dresden) is Liotard's most famous and most frequently reproduced work. Count Algarotti, who bought it from the artist in 1745 for the king of Poland, described it as a "Holbein in pastel." Writing to Pierre-Jean Mariette, he said that it "represents a young German chambermaid in profile carrying a tray with a glass of water and a cup of chocolate." This pounced drawing was used by Liotard to prepare his pastel.

This work remained in the collection of the Liotard family in Amsterdam until 1934.

Shepherdess Spinning

Circa 1757–60
Red chalk and graphite pencil
on paper, heightened with red
chalk on the verso
17.6 x 18 cm
Gift of the Société Auxiliaire
du Musée, 1934
Inv. 1934–37

Its theme makes this red chalk drawing of a shepherdess unique in Liotard's œuvre. It is a preparatory sketch for the pastel copy that Liotard made of a painting by the Dutch animal painter Paulus Potter in 1758–60 (Rijksmuseum, Amsterdam). To this work, which represented two oxen, a cow, and a goat in a landscape, Liotard added the figure of a young shepherdess spinning, engrossed in her work. This drawing must have been important to him, for he kept it in his personal collection. The pastel at the Rijksmuseum in Amsterdam was also among the works that the artist took with him to his house in the country at Confignon for safekeeping during the disturbances in Geneva in 1782. He made an enamel version of it which was exhibited in Paris in 1771, and which reappeared at the sale of the Bessborough Collection in 1801 with the caption "A shepherdess with her herd, well finished and very curious enamel after Paulus Potter and K. du Jardin" (J. W. R. Tilanus, 1897, p. 209. Quoted by Anne de Herdt, 1992, p. 182).

This drawing was kept by the artist and remained in the Liotard family collection in Amsterdam until 1934.

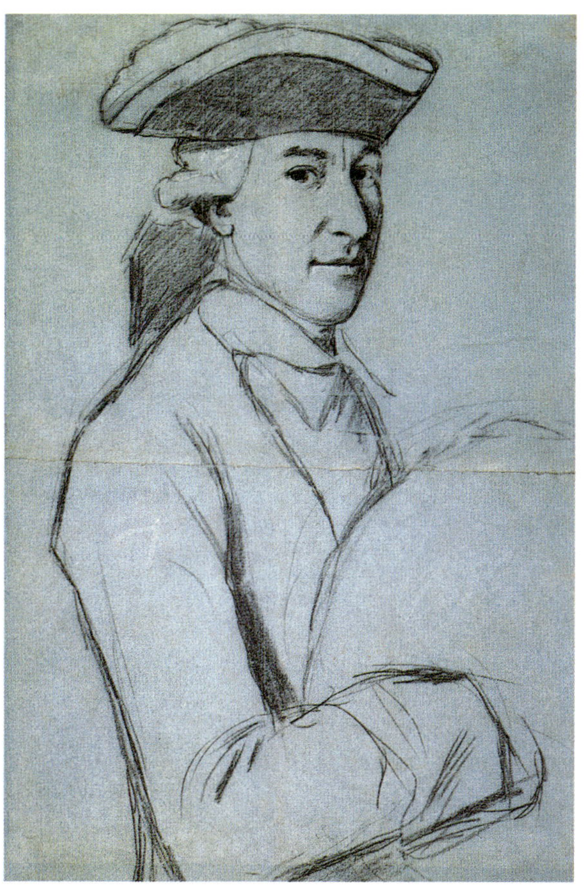 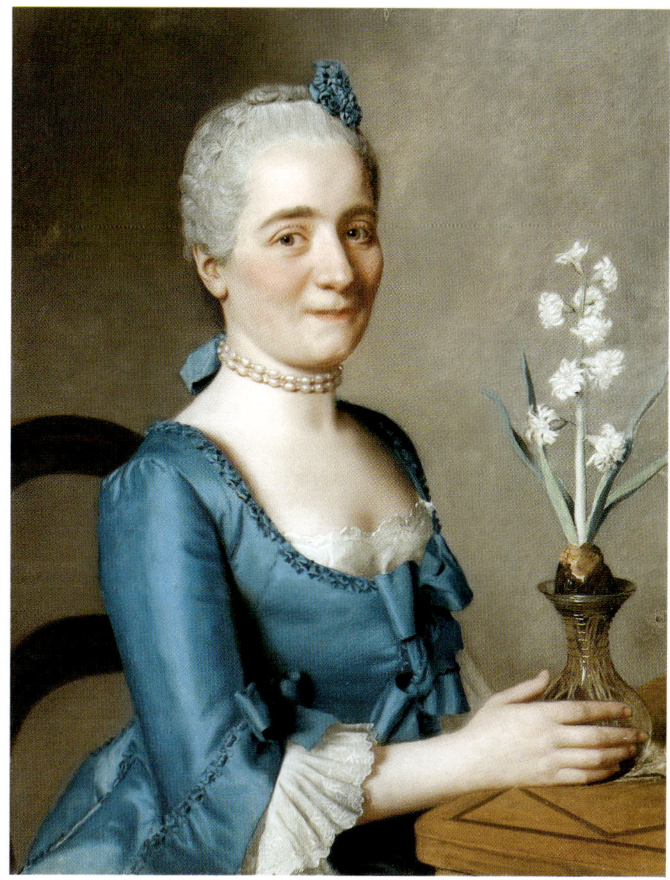

Jean-Jacques Cottin de La Thuilerie

1757 **Black chalk heightened with white chalk on blue paper, heightened on the verso** 71.8 x 48.8 cm **Gift of the Société Auxiliaire du Musée, 1934** Inv. 1934–26	Long known as *Man with a Muff*, this sketch for a pastel (private collection) was identified in 1986 as the portrait of Jean-Jacques Cottin de La Thuilerie, a cavalry captain of the Royal-Cravates regiment. This regiment was created in 1643 under the regency of Anne of Austria. The captain is in uniform, with a tricorn hat, and his hands are in a huge muff, a very fashionable accessory in those days. Liotard's swift, assertive line in this drawing is highly expressive. The piece has the same provenance as Inv. 1934–37.

Woman with a Hyacinth

1757 **Pastel on parchment** 63.5 x 51 cm **Bequest of Gustave Revilliod, Geneva, 1890** Inv. CR 88	In this portrait with its fine, intense colors, Liotard represents an unidentified young woman sitting at a table, her right hand on a vase containing a hyacinth, her face turned toward the viewer. This pastel with its very smooth rendering is handled with tremendous finesse and reveals Liotard's talents as a colorist. The blue of the dress, echoed in the ornament in the young woman's wig, stands out powerfully against the solid ground and combines felicitously with the warm tones of the table, chair, and hyacinth bulb. The luminous areas of white add a note of brightness to the ensemble. This is one of the few portraits by Liotard that include a still life, such as *Marie-Jeanne, known as Mariette, de Bassompierre* (p. 43) and *La Belle Chocolatière* (Gemäldegalerie, Dresden, p. 90). The perfect illusionism with which Liotard captures the transparency of the vase reflects the painterly concerns expounded in règle XX of his treatise on painting. This pastel entered the Gustave Revilliod Collection (Geneva) in 1860.

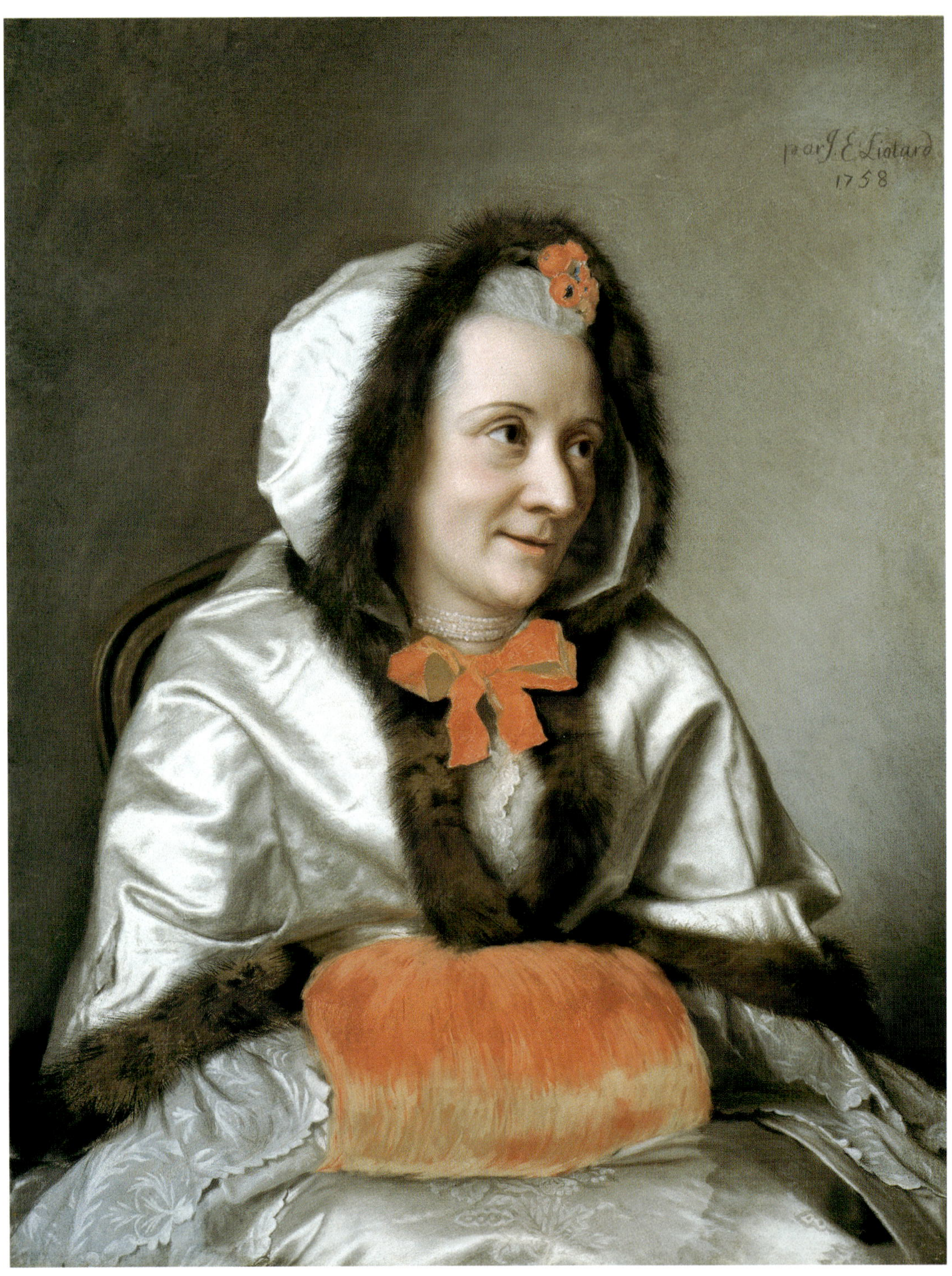

Madame François Tronchin, née Anne-Marie Fromaget (1713?–1788), "Dressed for the Cold"

1758
Signed and dated
Pastel on parchment
68 x 55 cm
On permanent loan from the
Fondation Jean-Louis Prevost,
1985
Inv. 1985–42

Anne-Marie Fromaget, represented, in Liotard's own words, "dressed for the cold," was born in Saint-Quentin.
The daughter of Vincent-Pierre Fromaget, director of the French East India Company, she met François Tronchin (1704–98), counselor and future syndic of Geneva, in Paris in 1736. After their wedding, the couple went back to Geneva. A financial and real estate administrator, François Tronchin was also a man of letters, a great art lover, and a discerning collector of mainly Dutch and Flemish paintings. This is the aspect emphasized in Liotard's portrait of him in his office, looking at a Rembrandt painting (Cleveland Museum of Art).

This portrait was part of François Tronchin's collection and, after his death, stayed in his family until 1957, when it entered a private collection in New York.

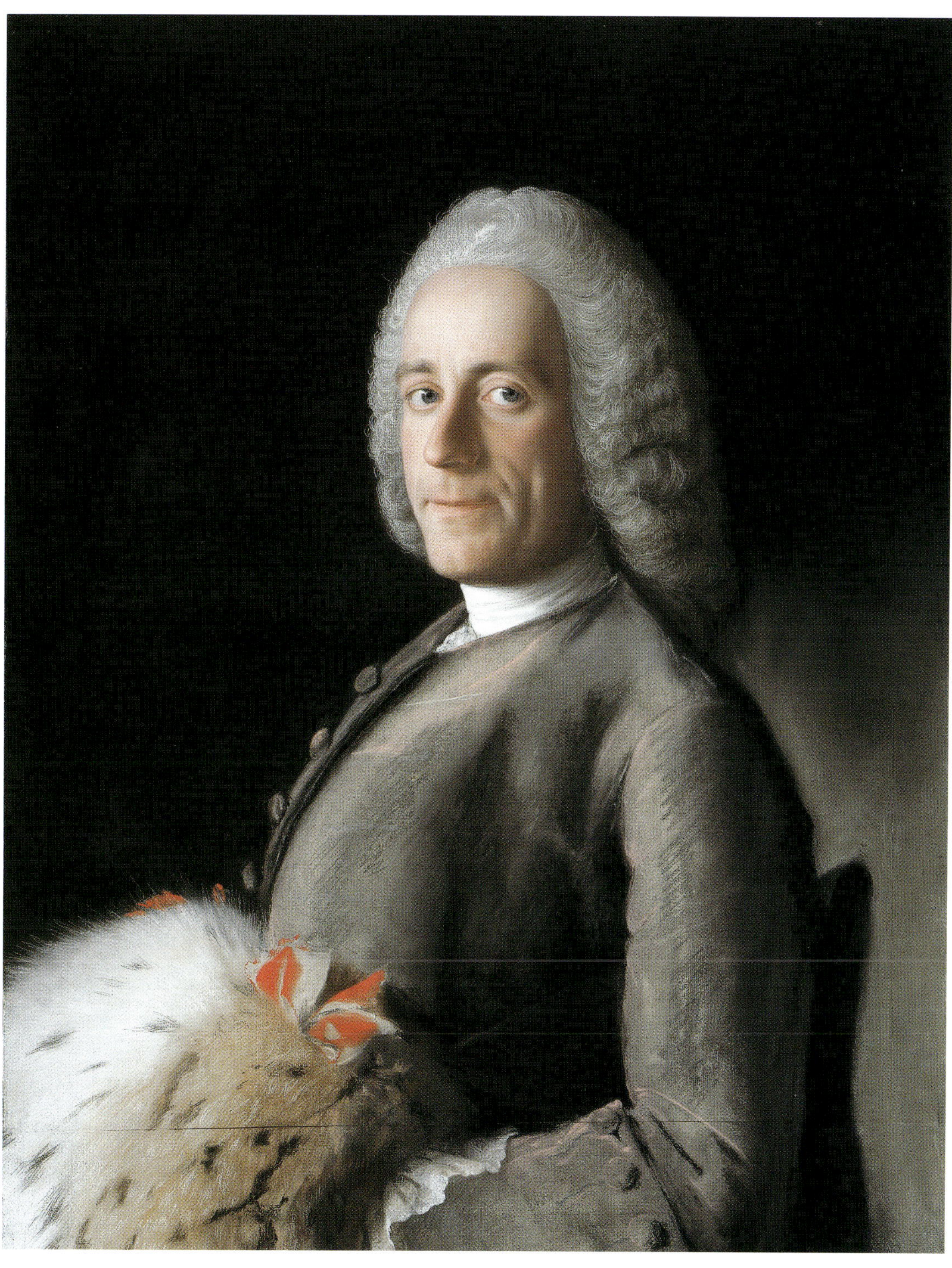

Ami-Jean De la Rive (1725–1800)

1758
**Pastel on paper glued onto
canvas**
82 x 64.5 cm
**Gift of the De la Rive family,
1936**
Inv. 1936–9

Ami-Jean De la Rive, the husband of Jeanne-Élisabeth Sellon, was a magistrate and counselor. While the composition and dark tones of this work are in the tradition of the official portraits executed by Liotard (*Pierre Mussard*, p. 48, *Jean Sarasin*, p. 46), the artist has also enhanced it with touches of warm colors in the background and in the coat, and with the extraordinary red ribbons decorating the lynx fur muff (Danielle Buyssens, 1988, p. 103). This

accessory imparts a singular tone to this pastel and allows Liotard to display his talent with real verve. He had already used this item in his 1757 portrait of *Jean-Jacques Cottin de La Thuilerie* (p. 91).
Probably commissioned from the artist by Ami-Jean De la Rive in 1758, this pastel remained in the sitter's family until 1936.

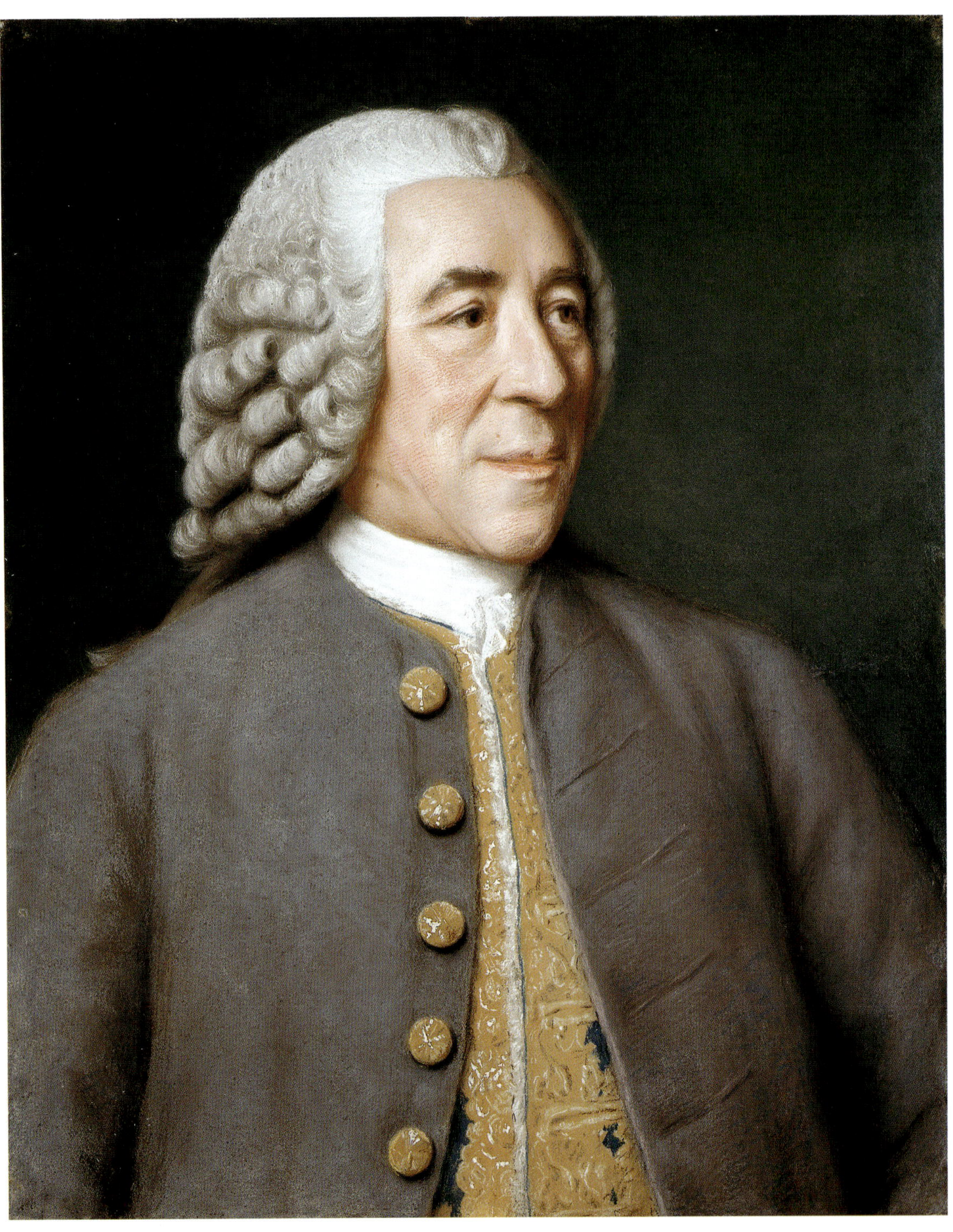

Jean-Jacques Horngacher, Seigneur de Plonjon (1695–1778)

1757–60
Pastel heightened with
gouache on parchment
58.5 x 48 cm
Purchase, 1995
Inv. 1995–1

This portrait, which the painter described as "highly finished," represents the Genevan financier Jean-Jacques Horngacher, a merchant and banker based in Amsterdam. Liotard painted him shortly after his return to Geneva, where he bought the seigneury of Plonjon and Bellerive. This pastel is among the artist's most accomplished works in the rendering of "expression," "relief," "projection," and "effect," painterly values Liotard recommended in his treatise and that are achieved by the harmonious use of "shadow" and "light" (Anne de Herdt, *Genava*, 1996, p. 189).

The work was kept in the sitter's family in Geneva until 1995.

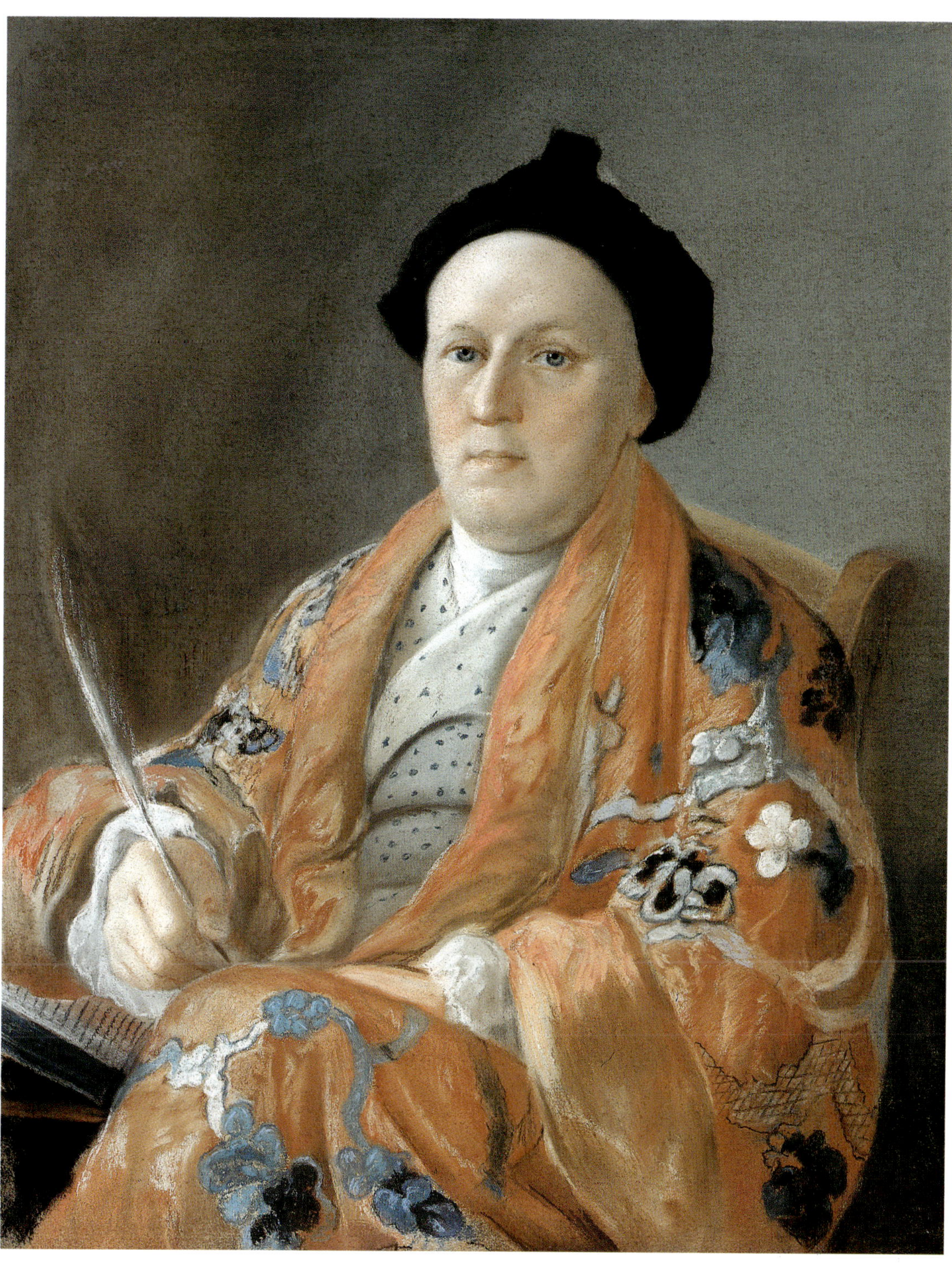

Jean-Antoine Guainier-Gautier (1716–1801)

1758–65
Pastel on paper glued
onto canvas
64.5 x 53 cm
Purchase, 1941
Inv. 1941–10

Counselor Jean-Antoine Guainier-Gautier, future syndic (1772, 1776, and 1780), is shown informally, sitting comfortably, pen in hand. The pattern and bright colors of his robe attest to the Orientalist taste prevalent among the upper bourgeoisie of Geneva, and indeed throughout Europe (Danielle Buyssens, 1988, p. 104). Liotard's handling of the clothes is highly suggestive, and the vague rendering of the dots on the counselor's shirt and of the shades of color, while surprising, also demonstrates his talent.

This pastel went from the sitter's collection (Geneva) to that of his son-in-law, Jacques-Claude Claparède, and remained with his family until 1940.

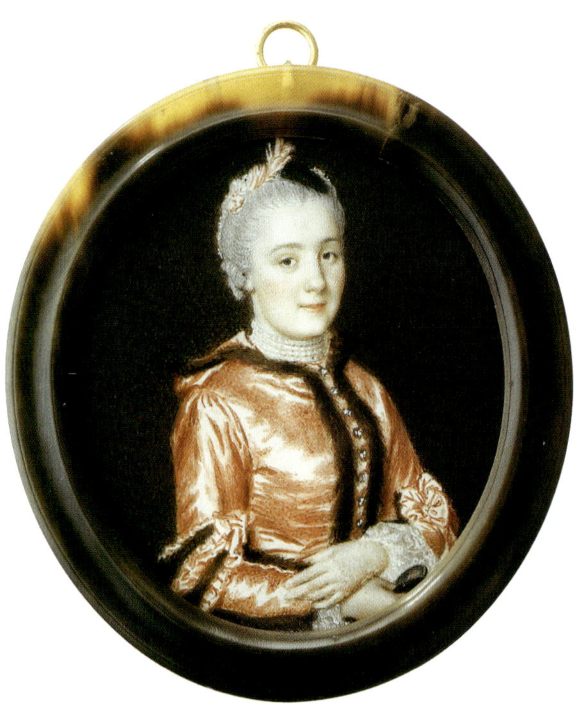

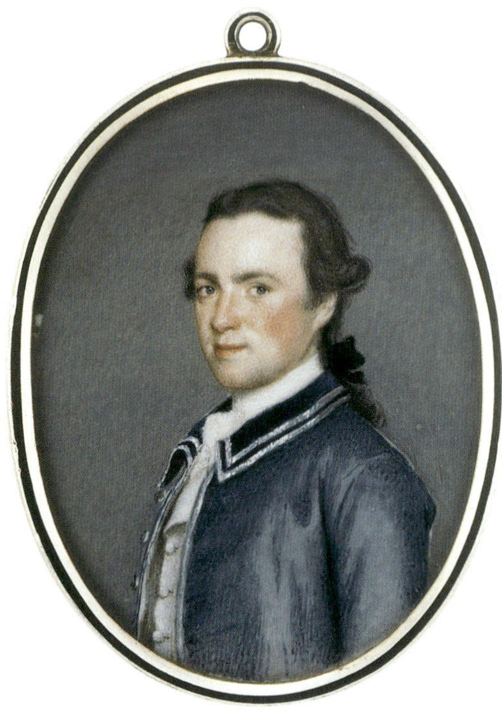

Madame Charles Bonnet (1728–1796), née Jeanne-Marie De la Rive-Franconis

Circa 1760
Watercolor on vellum
5.9 x 5.4 cm
**Bequest of Gustave Revilliod,
1890**
Inv. AD 2302

Jeanne-Marie De la Rive-Franconis married the Genevan philosopher and naturalist Charles Bonnet (1720–98), a friend of the Liotards. The Genevan scientist was delighted with this exceedingly fine portrait of his wife, as can be seen from this letter to Messieurs Dufour and Mallet, dated June 10, 1761: "Forgive this indiscretion, on account of the tenderness of a husband who cannot resist the pleasure of having in his pocket the portrait of a beloved and truly estimable wife. This portrait was painted in miniature by our famous Liotard. It is a very good piece. It now needs to be set in a snuff box."

Ami Rilliet-Chapeaurouge (1730–1796)

Circa 1760
Watercolor on vellum
6.23 x 4.8 cm
**Bequest of Gustave Revilliod,
1890**
Inv. AD 2293

Born into a long-established family of the Geneva bourgeoisie, Ami Rilliet-Chapeaurouge was the son of Pierre Rilliet by his second wife, Jeanne Chapeaurouge, and the great grandfather of Gustave Revilliod, who bequeathed this miniature to the museum. A banker, he served an apprenticeship in Marseilles with the merchant Jean-Louis Ployard and worked for a while in the family banking business, then traveled to London to join his brother, Jacques Rilliet-Plantamour. Returning to Geneva in 1762, he sat on the Council of Two Hundred (1764) and devoted his time to the magistrature. He died in Begnins in 1796, at the age of sixty-six (Fabienne Xavière Sturm, *L'Âge d'or du petit portrait*, 1995). Liotard depicts the young man in three-quarter view against a gray background, which delicately matches the color of his coat.

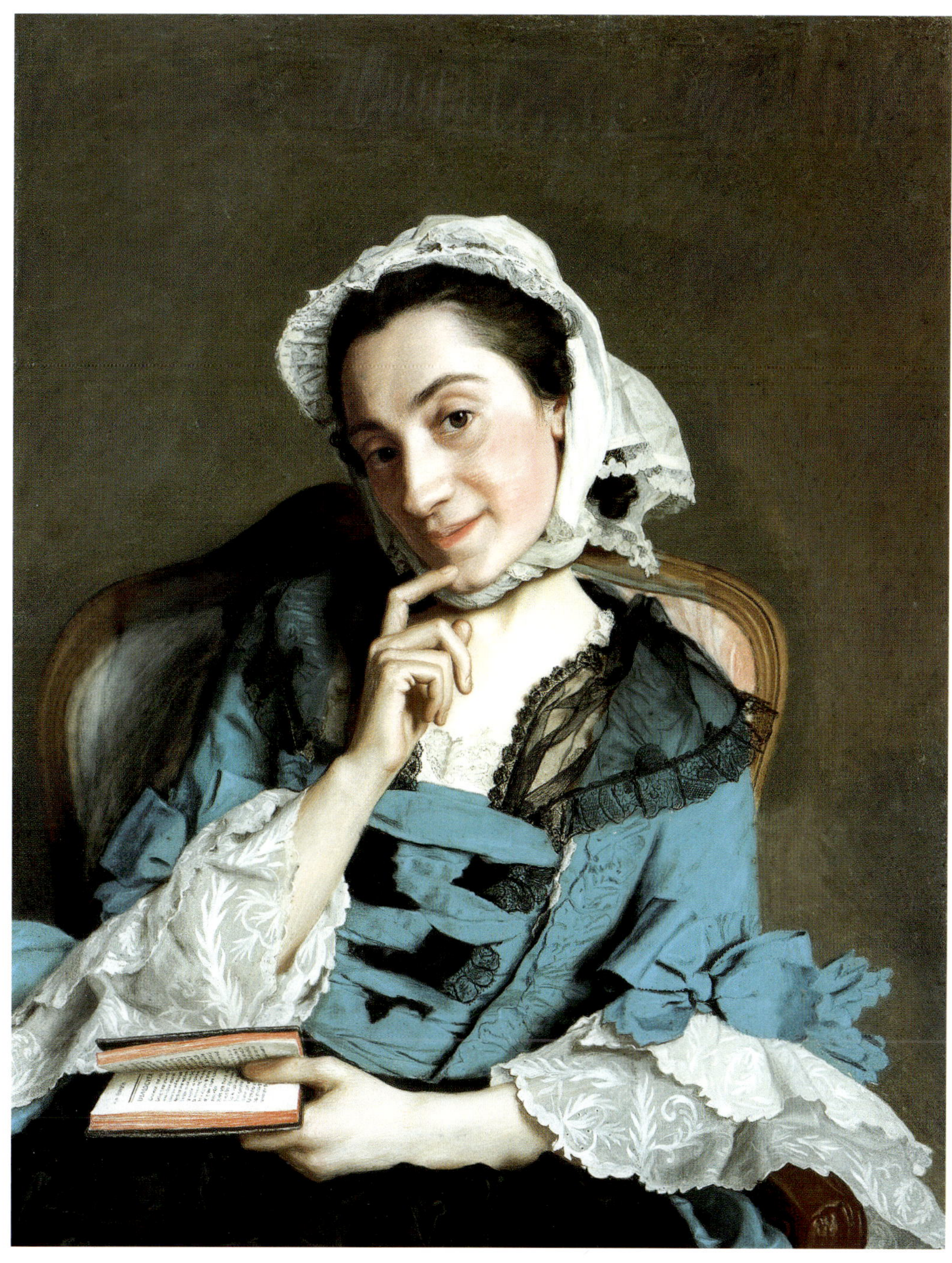

Madame Denis-Joseph La Live d'Épinay, née Louise-Florence Pétronille Tardieu d'Esclavelles (1726–1783), known as Madame d'Épinay

Circa 1759
Pastel on parchment
69 x 55 cm
Donated by Monsieur
Charles-Richard Tronchin-
Bernard, 1826
Inv. 1826–7

Like Madame de Vermenoux and other notables, Louise d'Épinay, who had stomach cancer, traveled to Geneva to consult the famous Doctor Théodore Tronchin. Seen today as a precursor of alternative medicine, he was official doctor to the Duc d'Orléans and one of the first to inoculate against smallpox. Madame d'Épinay stayed in Geneva from 1757 to 1759 and offered Tronchin this portrait to thank him for his care. An eminent woman of letters and protector of Rousseau, she wrote a treatise on women's education entitled *Les Conversations d'Émilie*, whose ideas were thoroughly antithetical to those of her protégé's Rousseau's

Émile (Danielle Buyssens, 1988, p. 93), as well as various essays and a volume of *Mémoires*. On visiting the Musée Rath, Flaubert wrote the following of this, one of Liotard's most famous portraits: "Mme de l'Épinay [*sic*], thin face, black hair, black eye, long jaw, homely, but a woman one notices and that one would surely love greatly if one loved (she must have smelled either rank or sweet)" (*Notes de voyages. Voyage en famille, avril-mai 1845*, Paris, 1910, p. 56). This pastel from Dr. Tronchin's collection stayed in his family until 1826.

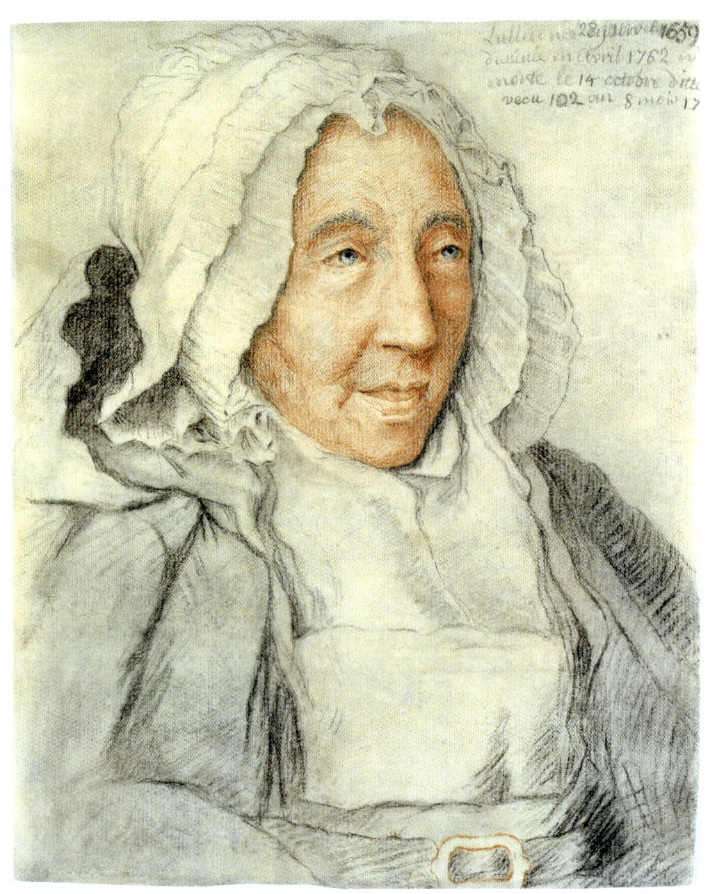

Madame Alexandrine Lullin-Fatio (1659–1762), Widow of the Syndic Pierre Lullin, at the Age of a Hundred and Two

1762
**Black and red chalk with
stumping on paper, heightened
on the verso**
21.5 x 17.2 cm
**On permanent loan from the
Fondation Jean-Louis Prevost,
1985**
Inv. 1985–43

Alexandrine Lullin-Fatio, daughter of Jean-Baptiste Fatio, seigneur of Duillier in the canton of Vaud, was the widowed second wife of the counselor and then syndic Pierre Lullin (1646–1717). As a handwritten annotation by the artist in the top right-hand corner tells us, she had only six months to live when Liotard did her portrait: "Lullin born January 28, 1659 / drawn in April 1762 / died October 14 the same year / lived 102 years 8 months 17 [*sic*]." Liotard offers a very acute portrait of this woman to whom Voltaire dedicated the following quatrain on the occasion of her hundredth birthday: "Our forefathers knew you as a belle /

At a hundred, 'tis your wit that does shine / Truly, you deserve to marry Fontenelle / And to be his widow for a long, long time." The artist emphasizes the sitter's expression. Rendered in red chalk, in contrast with the black chalk of her clothes, her face conveys a woman who, for all her years, has real presence, even if her gaze does express a certain weariness.

This drawing was the property of the Maillart-Gosse family in Geneva, then went to the collection of a relative in the Baud-Bony family (Geneva).

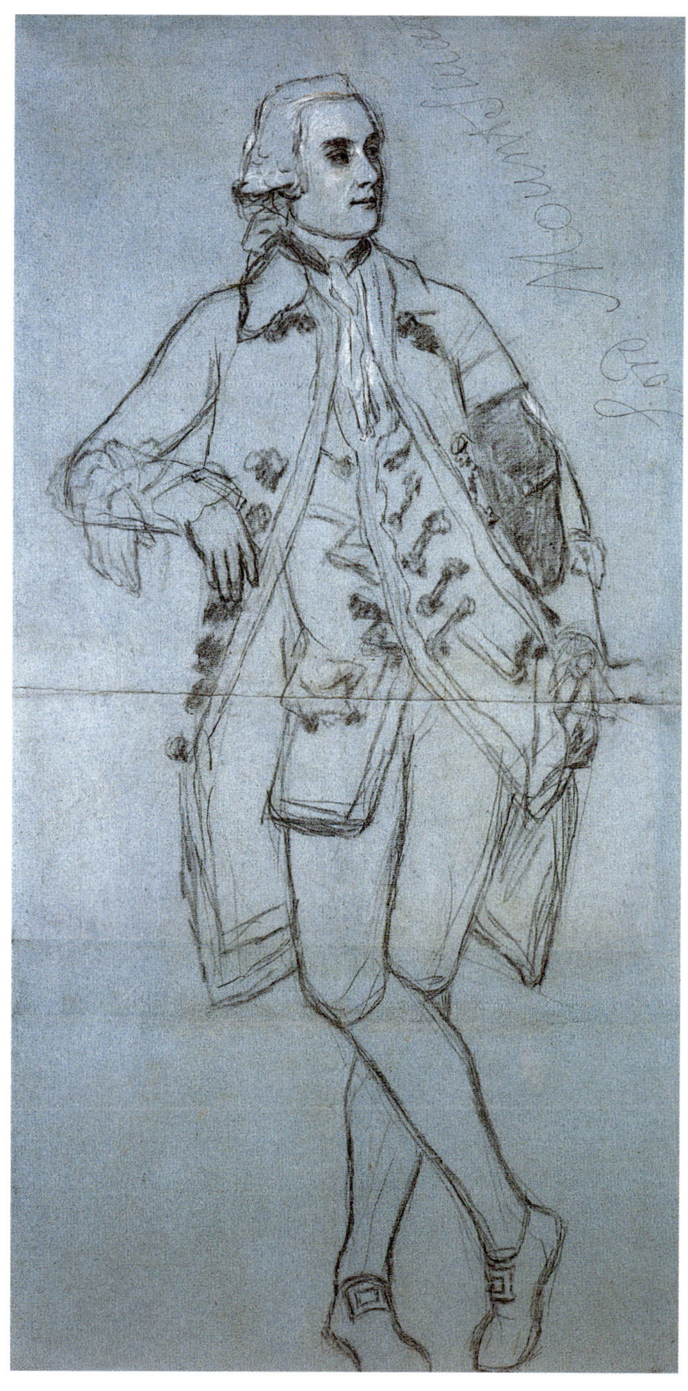

Portrait of Lord Mount Stuart (1744–1814), Future First Marquess of Bute

---

1763
Black and white chalk,
heightened with red chalk
on blue paper
90.7 x 48.1 cm
Gift of the Société Auxiliaire
du Musée, 1934
Inv. 1934–27

Lord Mount Stuart was the British ambassador to Spain and was the oldest son of Lord Bute, future prime minister to George III, and grandson of the British ambassador in Constantinople (1716–18) and Lady Mary Wortley Montagu, author of a famous volume of *Letters*. This drawing is the preparatory study for the pastel portrait of his son that Lord Bute commissioned from Liotard (Getty Museum), and which the artist executed in Geneva. The emphatic line here is both lithe and rigorous, and the result is very expressive.

The white chalk highlights indicating the play of light, as used in other sketches (*Jean-Jacques Cottin de La Thuilerie*, p. 91; *Gaspard Joly*, p. 100), give this study a considerable degree of finish. John Mount Stuart inherited his father's title in 1792 and became a marquess in 1796. He died in Geneva in 1814.
This drawing remained in the artist's family in Amsterdam until 1934.

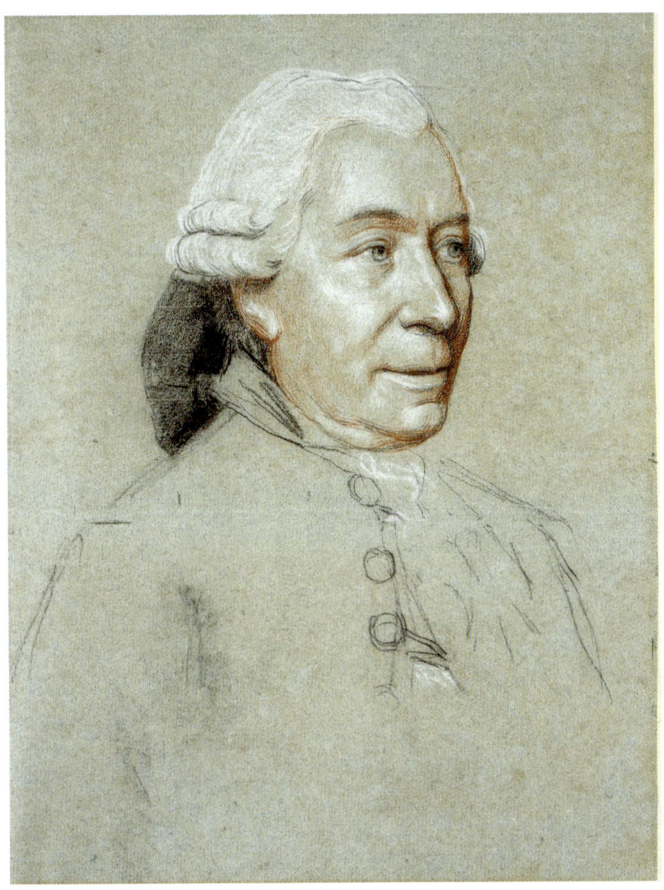

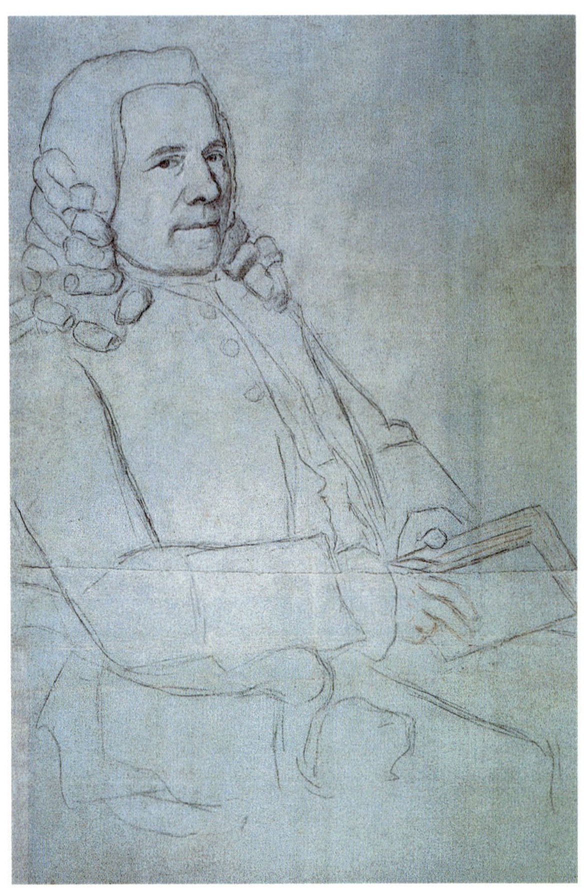

Portrait of a Man, known as "The Magistrate"

Circa 1763–65
Black and white chalk,
heightened with red chalk on
faded blue paper
56.5 x 44.5 cm
Gift of the Société Auxiliaire
du Musée, 1934
Inv. 1935–5

This drawing, which has great psychological intensity, is one
of a number of portraits by Liotard of Genevan figures
(*Pierre Mussard*, p. 48, *Ami-Jean De la Rive*, p. 93).
The drawing has the same provenance as below.

Portrait of the Doctor Gaspard Joly (born 1718)

Circa 1768–75
Black and white chalk,
heightened with red chalk on
blue paper, heightened on the
verso
87.1 x 58.9 cm
Gift of the Société Auxiliaire
du Musée, 1934
Inv. 1934–29

Wishing to become a doctor, Gaspard Joly went to study in
Montpellier since Geneva did not as yet have a medical
school. Back in his home town, in 1751 he and his colleague
Cramer published a "Letter on Inoculation Against
Smallpox," which showed him to be a real precursor. He sat
on the Council of Two Hundred in 1752 and was a
counselor of state in 1768, then obtained the position of
syndic in 1780 and 1784. In this preparatory drawing for an
oil painting, Liotard reveals the personality of his sitter with
great vivacity and the immediacy that so characterizes
his drawings.
The artist kept this drawing in his own collection, and it
later entered the collection of his family in Amsterdam.

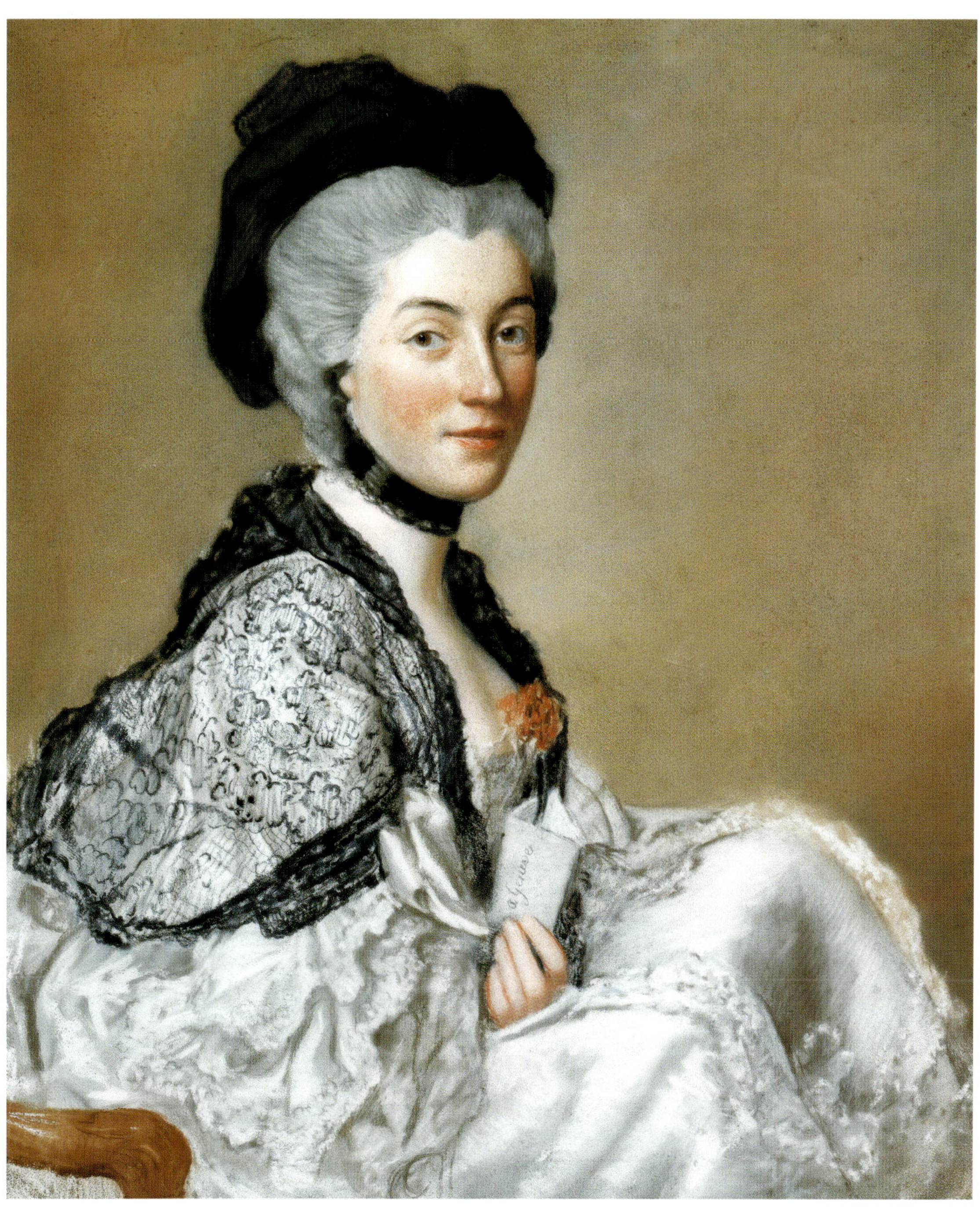

Madame Paul Girardot de Vermenoux, née Anne-Germaine Larrivée (1739–1783)

1772
Pastel on parchment
61 x 51.5 cm
Purchase, 1984
Inv. 1984–107

Anne-Germaine Larrivée was the daughter of a master draper in Sedan and grew up in a very wealthy bourgeois family. She married Paul Girardot de Vermenoux at a very young age, but was soon widowed. Her own fragile health took her to Geneva to consult Dr. Tronchin in 1758. There she resided at Place de la Taconnerie, in the Cayla household. Other residents included Paul Moultou, a correspondent of Rousseau's, who developed a passionate attachment to her, and Suzanne Curchod, later to become Madame Necker, whom she hired in 1759 to look after her son. Elegant and full of charm, as the light touch of Liotard's pastel attests, Anne-Germaine Larrivée de Vermenoux was nicknamed "the Enchantress." As a relative of the Thellussons, she became acquainted with Geneva's most eminent families. She met Liotard at the home of the Tronchins. In 1764, the year of her return to Paris, she commissioned a second, allegorical portrait (Geneva, collection of X. Givaudan) which she gave to Dr. Tronchin. Jean-François Marmontel said that her face "shone with that air of goodness, sweetness, with that serenity, that naïve and seemly gaiety that embellishes reason and makes wisdom lovable" (Renée Loche, *Genava*, 1985, p. 241). This portrait no doubt dates from Madame Vermenoux's second stay in Geneva, in 1772. After belonging to the Moultou Collection (Geneva), it was acquired by a private collection in the city, and then entered the collection of Ernest Odier (also in Geneva).

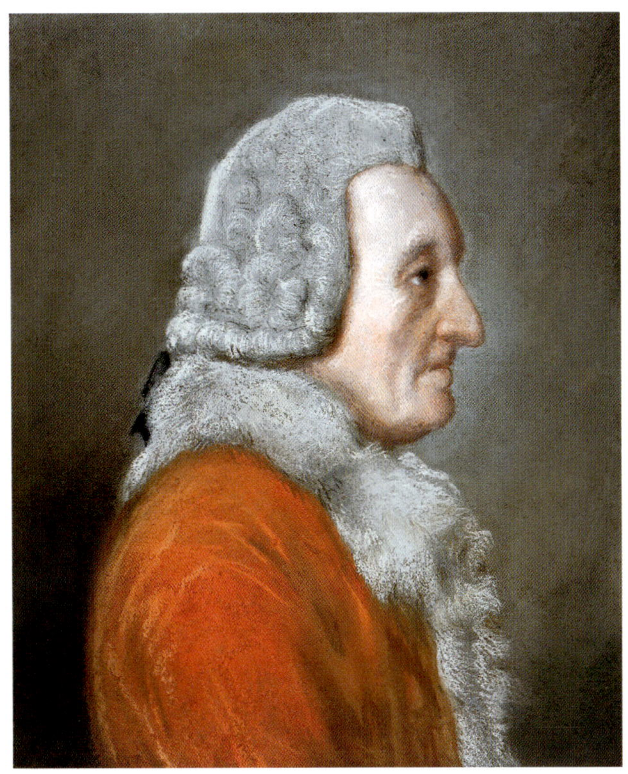

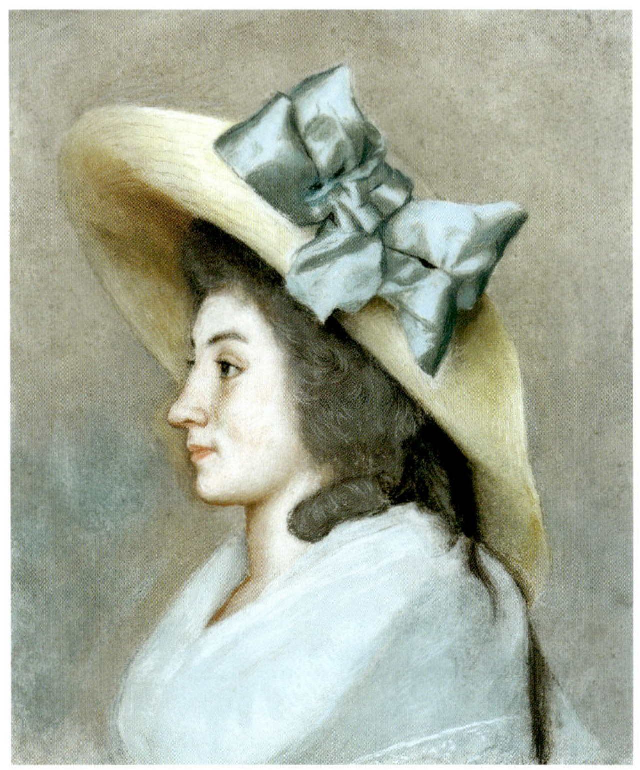

Pierre Favre (1695–1788)

1780
Pastel on paper
23 x 19 cm
Bequest of William Favre to
the city of Geneva in 1918, on
permanent loan to the museum
since 1929
Inv. LG 4920

Pierre Favre was one of the Liotard's neighbors in Geneva, and the painter made this portrait of him for his own pleasure. It is mentioned in a letter from Madame Liotard to her eldest son dated March 17, 1780: "Today [Liotard] started a small, profile portrait of Monsieur de Tournes Rilliet and one of our good neighbor Monsieur Favre, who at the age of eighty-four is as healthy in body and mind as a man of forty. It is one of those 2-louis portraits, but it amuses your father" (Public and University Geneva Library (BPU), ms. Fr. 355. Quoted by Renée Loche and Marcel Roethlisberger, 1978, p. 327). Portraits in profile are fairly rare in Liotard's œuvre, as are works in small formats. This very sober pastel is executed in shades of gray brightened by the red of the sitter's garment.

This work stayed in the Favre family until 1918, when Pierre Favre's great grandson, William Favre (1843–1918), donated the Villa la Grange, its grounds, and all the collections within, to the city of Geneva.

Louise-Marguerite Marcet, Future Madame Pierre Prevost (1764–1788)

1785
Pastel on parchment
37 x 32 cm
On permanent loan from the
Fondation Jean-Louis Prevost,
1975
Inv. 1975–73

In 1788 Louise-Marguerite Marcet married Pierre Prevost (1751–1839), who was successively a barrister, a tutor in Holland and Paris, a member of the National Assembly (in 1792), and a teacher of physics and philosophy in Geneva (Renée Loche, *Mille objets pour Genève. La Fondation Jean-Louis Prevost*, 1989, p. 68). She died of a malignant fever at the age of twenty-four, less than a year after their wedding. Seven years later, in 1795, Pierre Prevost married again, this time to the sister of his first wife, Jeanne-Louise Marcet. This pastel is among the last known portraits by Liotard, along with the one of Rodolphe Coteau (p. 103). Depicted in profile, the young woman wears a straw hat, one edge of which is turned up and held in place by a blue bow. The soft tones of this delicate, lightly executed work set off the delicacy of her face.

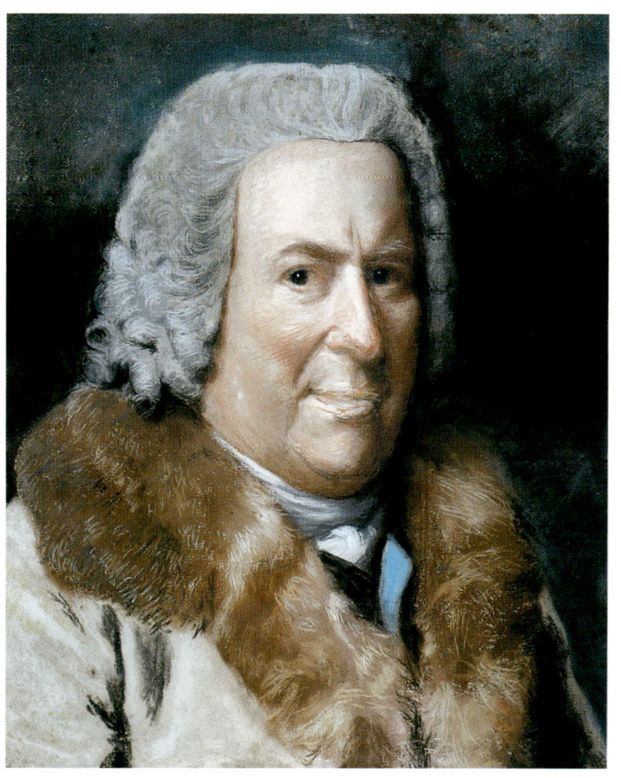

1788
Signed and dated
Pastel on paper glued
onto canvas
41.8 x 35.5 cm
Purchase, 1974
Inv. 1974–13

This, the last known portrait by Liotard, surprises by the very free and suggestive treatment of the face, clothes, and even the pastel ground, which prefigures the painting of the following century. Originally a ship owner in Marseilles, Rodolphe Coteau settled in Geneva in 1750 after his marriage to the Genevan Anne Vignier in 1741. There he worked as a merchant.

Commissioned by the sitter in 1788, this pastel remained in the collection of the Coteau family (Geneva) and then entered the collection of the Filliol family (Geneva).

4. Anne de Herdt, *Dessins de Liotard*, ex. cat., Paris, Geneva, 1992, no. 111, p. 186.
5. Jean-Étienne Liotard, *Traité des principes et des règles de la peinture, par M. J.-É. Liotard, peintre, citoyen de Genève*, Geneva, 1781, p. 58.

Madame François Tronchin, née Anne-Marie Fromaget (1713?–1788), "Dressed for the Cold," was, along with the portrait of her husband, the counselor François Tronchin, the first commission received by the painter on his return to Geneva after a thirty-two-year absence.[4] Represented, as the artist put it, as "the Shivering One," she offers another quiveringly alive demonstration of Liotard's mastery of pastel. He was, indeed, highly satisfied with both this portrait and that of Monsieur Tronchin. "This painting and the one of his lady wife," wrote Liotard in his treatise, "have, I believe, a finish, a brilliance, an effect and a truth that are extraordinary."[5] With two or three delicately harmonized touches of gray, the artist manages to convey the sheen and highlights of the satin coat. With economy of means and mastery of contrasts, he adds dynamism to the composition with a few accents of red. The subtle play of light, the delicate highlights in the shadows, and the very precise, delicate tonal relationships all make this portrait a true masterpiece.

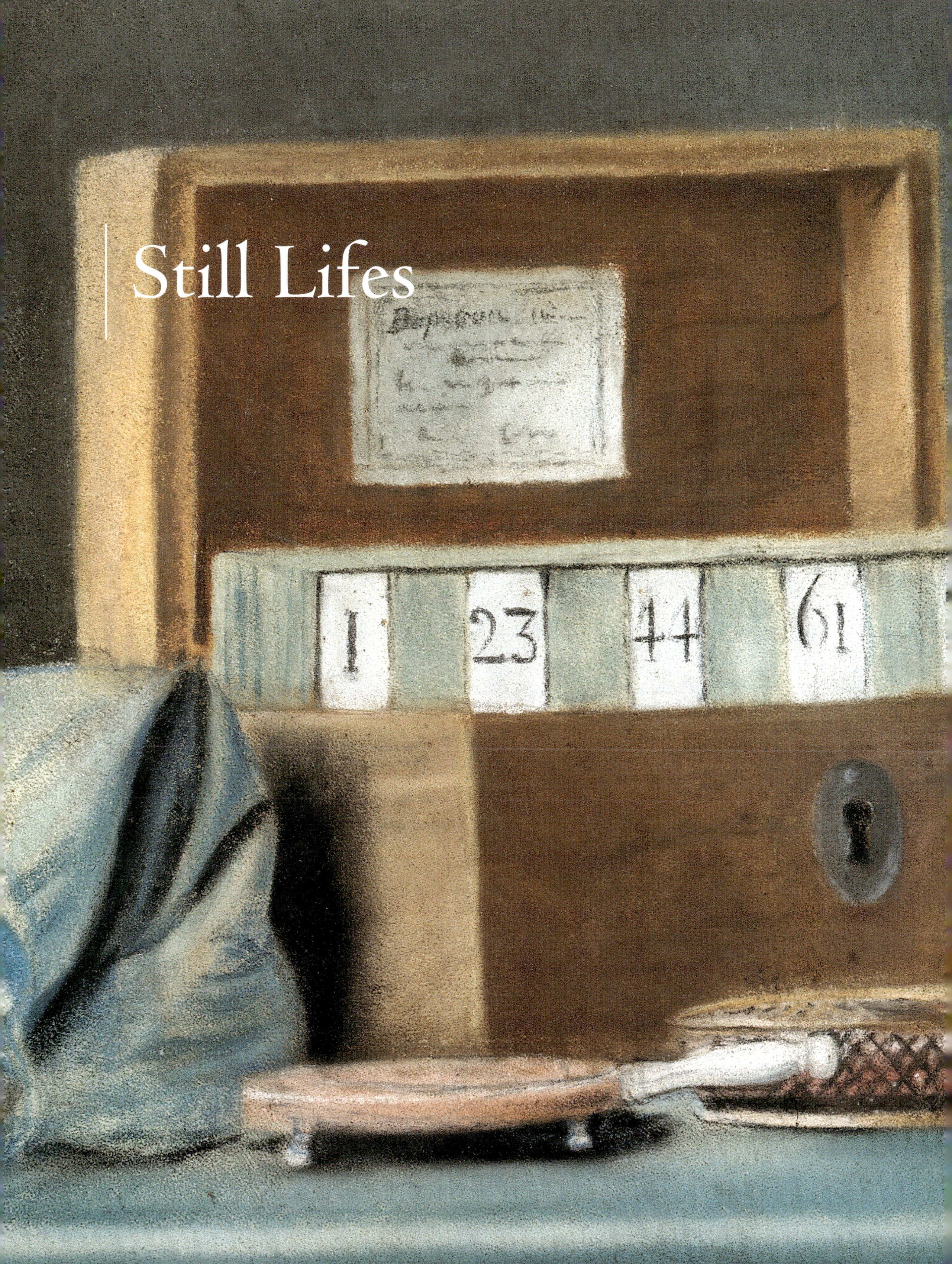
Still Lifes

Cäsar Menz

1. "Over the past month and a half I have painted four pictures of fruit [...] these four pictures are fresher and more vivid, and the objects are more detached, stand out in greater relief and are more realistic than those by Van Huysum, but they are not as accomplished. When I was only thirty I would not have painted them as well. Being more sophisticated than my work at that age, everyone has found them so fine that I have been obliged to sign them and indicate my age of eighty years [...]."
2. Renée Loche and Marcel Roethlisberger, *L'opera completa di Jean-Étienne Liotard*, Milan 1978: Classici dell'Arte 96, no. 336.
3. Ibid., no. 281.
4. Horace Walpole, *Anecdotes of Painting in England*, London 1888.
5. *Chardin, 1699–1779*, ex. cat., Galeries Nationales du Grand Palais, Paris 1979, no. 136; Pierre Rosenberg, *Chardin*, Geneva 1963, pp. 104–5.
6. Loche and Roethlisberger 1978, no. 284.
7. See Marcel Roethlisberger, "Jean-Étienne Liotard as a Painter of Still Lifes," in *The J. Paul Getty Museum Journal*, 13, 1985, pp. 109–20, particularly p. 112.
8. Loche and Roethlisberger 1978, no. 283.
9. Ibid., no. 286.

"J'ay peint depuis un mois et demi 4 tableaux de fruits [...] ces 4 tableaux ont plus de fraîcheur de vivacité et les objets sont plus détachez, plus sortants et plus de relief et plus vrais que ceux de Vanhuysum mais ils ne sont pas aussi finis quand je n'avois que 30 ans je ne les aurois pas fait aussi bien ayant plus d'art que je n'en avois alors, on les a trouvé si beaux qu'on ma obligé d'y mettre mon nom et mon age de 80 ans [...]."[1]

This excerpt from a letter from Liotard to his eldest son, Jean-Étienne, dated September 24, 1782, describes a still life depicting pears, figs, plums, a bread roll, and a knife on a table (p. 109).[2] The still life is executed in pastel and characterized by extreme simplicity, even sparseness. The fruit is carefully arranged in rows on a folded napkin. A silk ribbon protrudes from the drawer of the little table, which bears the signature "peint par J.-E. Liotard agé de 80 ans." The tabletop, the contours of which are cut off by the edges of the picture, appears to have been tilted. The signature and the passage from the letter quoted above reveal the elderly artist's pride in his virtuosity, even in advanced years.

Liotard, the cosmopolitan Genevan artist who traveled over half of Europe and to the Near East, acquired a fine reputation as portrait painter to the aristocracy and the *haute bourgeoisie*. He returned to Geneva in 1778, where he wrote *Traité des principes et des règles de la peinture*—his treatise on painting, which was published in Lyons in 1781. In his later work, Liotard explored his immediate surroundings, creating still lifes of great simplicity, portraits of his family and friends, and astonishingly realistic self-portraits. His late work is heralded, as it were, by an impressive self-portrait of the aging artist (p. 32),[3] created in Geneva in 1770 and admired by Horace Walpole, who saw the work at the Royal Academy in 1773 and described it as "very bold."[4] The artist pitilessly exposes the ravages of time: thinning hair, a deeply lined brow, his face bare, denuded of the usual beard, his expression pensive. Everything in this portrait is reduced to essentials; little is concealed. The realism of this picture is even more pronounced than that of Chardin's 1775 self-portrait "à l'abat-jour," which moved Marcel Proust to pronounce: "Eh bien oui, je suis vieux!"[5]

This period also features three trompe l'œil pictures and one still life. The palette and composition of the pastel entitled *Still Life with Lotto Set*,[6] acquired by the Fondation Prevost for Geneva's Musées d'Art et d'Histoire in 1997, reflects the spirit of Chardin.[7] On the one hand, the game of lotto is a representation of reality; and at the same time, as a well-known *vanitas* symbol, it refers to the fickleness of human destiny.

With its two classically inspired depictions of Venus and Cupid— contrasted with the drawings of two women's heads referred to as "coeffure Turque" and "coeffure de Ulm"—the *Trompe l'œil (deceptio visus)* in The Frick Collection in New York[8] is interesting from an iconographical perspective, and indicates that contemporary art, which Liotard also considered to be documentary, is just as valuable as the art of antiquity. The bas-reliefs reveal very clearly the connection with the work of Chardin, who cultivated the trompe l'œil genre in particular.

In his *Traité* (règle XX, p. 93), Liotard mentions the pastel drawing of two bunches of grapes on a grained wooden board[9] that is now in Vienna's Kunsthistorisches Museum. Alluding to Pliny's anecdote about the Greek painter Zeuxis, whose paintings of grapes were so naturalistic that even birds were deceived by them, Liotard mentions a girl who thought the painting was real.

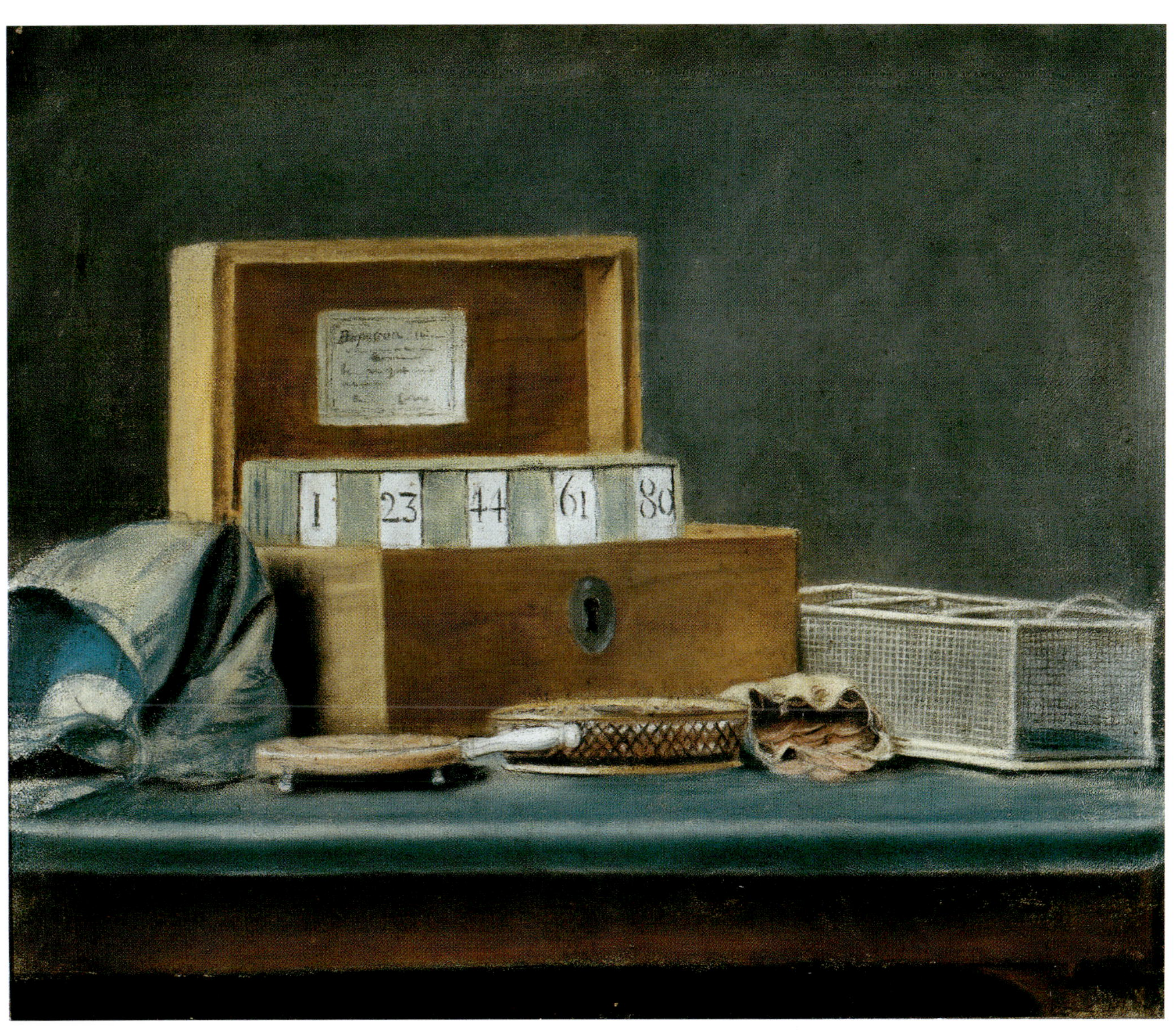

Still Life with Lotto Set

1773–75
Pastel on paper
36.8 x 44.5 cm
On permanent loan from the
Fondation Jean-Louis Prevost,
1997
Inv. D 1997–12

This work belonged to the collections of Jean Cailleux
(Paris) and Vitale Bloch (Paris), and then to a private
collection in Caracas.

10. Roethlisberger 1985,
p. 111.
11. Loche and Roethlisberger
1978, no. 244.
12. Ibid., no. 277.
13. *Chardin 1699–1779*, Paris,
1979, no. 73.
14. See Anne de Herdt, *Dessins
de Liotard*, ex. cat., Paris,
Geneva, 1992, nos. 135 and
136; *Chardin 1699–1779*, Paris,
1979, no. 75.
15. Roethlisberger 1985, pp.
109–20.
16. Numa S. Trivas, "Les
natures mortes de Liotard," in
Gazette des Beaux-Arts XV, 1936,
pp. 307–10.
17. Michel Faré, *La Nature morte
en France*, vol. 1, Geneva 1962,
p. 172.
18. Loche and Roethlisberger
1978, no. 336.
19. See *Chardin 1699–1779*,
pp. 52–53, 70.
20. Roethlisberger 1985,
p. 117.
21. "[…] je suis décidé
d'envoyer deux à l'Imperatrice
de Russie, et je lui manderai
que j'ay les 2 plus beaux
Tableaux de Vanhuysum"
(letter to his son, Jean-Étienne
Liotard, dated September 24,
1782). "I've decided to send
two to the empress of Russia,
and I will tell her that I have
the two finest paintings by Van
Huysum."
22. Loche and Roethlisberger
1978, no. 340.
23. Ibid., no. 336.
24. Ibid., no. 338.
25. Ibid., no. 337.
26. "[…] Over the past month
and a half I have painted four
pictures of fruit. One of them
is of apricots; the second of
pears, figs and plums; the third
of peaches, Bon Chrétien pears,
red pears, a torch and a key;
and the fourth of three
nectarines on a little plate with
a melon and a knife. I intend
to paint one of grapes, another
of apples […]."
27. Loche and Roethlisberger
1978, no. 336.
28. Ibid., no. 341.
29. Ibid., no. 343.
30. Ibid., no. 344.

As Marcel Roethlisberger[10] notes in his important article on the subject, still lifes also played a significant role in Liotard's portraits. In this connection, the 1761 portrait of Madame Necker is worthy of mention.[11] On the little table on which the woman is leaning stands a basket of fruit—a genre-like attribute and an expression of domestic intimacy. The 1770[12] portrait of Liotard's eldest son, Jean-Étienne, who is spreading butter on a slice of bread at a table with an open drawer, is similarly atmospheric. The butter, towering like a pyramid on the plate, undoubtedly has the character of a still life. The composition of the picture is reminiscent of Chardin's famous *House of Cards*[13] and *Boy with a Top*.[14]

Twelve still lifes dating from Liotard's creative period between 1782 and 1786 have survived, revealing an astonishing development and expressing a new artistic attitude. Marcel Roethlisberger[15]—like Numa S. Trivas[16] and Michel Faré[17] before him—has drawn attention to the extraordinary character, even "modernity" of this work, which already appears to anticipate artistic tendencies that were to emerge at the end of the nineteenth century.

The still life with fruit of 1782 mentioned above,[18] which the artist created at eighty years of age, is ostensibly oriented toward Chardin, who arranges his objects in a composition on a tabletop, reminiscent of a stage. The motif of the half-open drawer from which an object protrudes,[19] encountered frequently in Chardin's œuvre, also occurs in Liotard's work. However, this is the only reference to the work of Chardin, whom Liotard, incidentally, does not mention at all in his writings, but with whose œuvre he appears to have been very familiar. By contrast with Chardin's work, the tabletop is shown from above and slightly tilted into the space. Deliberate asymmetry dominates the composition of the picture, further emphasized by the position of the napkin. The fruit is lined up in a row along the edges of the napkin, rather than being artistically arranged, as would have been customary in the eighteenth century.

The comparison with Jan van Huysum mentioned in Liotard's letter to his son, quoted at the beginning of this article, shows that Liotard was concerned with "fraîcheur" (freshness), "vivacité" (vividness), and "authenticity," and not, as in Van Huysum's case, with perfection. According to the artist, his friends and acquaintances found these works beautiful, and insisted that he add his signature and indicate his age. Liotard was evidently aware that he had created a work that marked a departure from his earlier creations. Marcel Roethlisberger has also rightly pointed out that the principles of Liotard's *Traité*, published the previous year in Lyons, are no longer respected in these paintings.[20] Liotard was not dependent on commissions, but wanted to sell two of these still lifes to Catherine the Great of Russia; at the same time, he let her know that he had two fine works by Van Huysum available.[21] In his letter to his son, he mentions a series of still lifes he has painted over the previous one-and-a-half months, and others that he still intends to paint: "[…] j'ay peint depuis 1 mois et demi 4 tableaux de fruits l'un sont des abricots,[22] le 2e poires figues et prunes,[23] le 3e des peches des poires bon cretien un rousselet une torche et une clef le 4e,[24] 3 brugnons sur une petite assiette plate un Melon et un couteau, je conte d'en faire un de raisins,[25] un autre de pommes […]."[26] It would appear that the artist intended to realize an entire series.

The analysis of those still lifes that have survived will reveal that they are all composed similarly to the still life with fruit[27] and are far more radical than this work in terms of the deliberately simple devices employed. Note the way Liotard conspicuously depicts the wooden board or tabletop on which the objects are displayed as tilted or with a considerable upward slant, his simple arrangement of the fruit in a row or in a pile, and his treatment of the ground as an undefined surface. The artist also refrains from excessively *impasto* brushwork or an overly sophisticated palette. This is particularly apparent in his *Still Life with Apricots* of 1783,[28] signed "par J.-E. Liotard à 80 1/2, 1783," or in the still lifes with fruit now in Geneva's Musées d'Art et d'Histoire[29] and at the Oskar Reinhart Museum at Winterthur,[30] both of which indicate the artist's age (eighty and eighty and a half) and are dated 1783. This reference to the artist's age, which is rather unusual for the eighteenth century, suggests that he was especially proud of creating such important works at so great an age; on the other hand, it can be interpreted as an indication of his awareness that time was running out. The *vanitas* theme has a dual meaning here: on the one hand the artist refers to his own mortality; on the other, it reminds us that the beauty of the painting's subject itself—the fruit—is perishable. All the still lifes mentioned in Liotard's letter to his son are characterized by the artist's endeavors to depict the objects with the greatest frugality

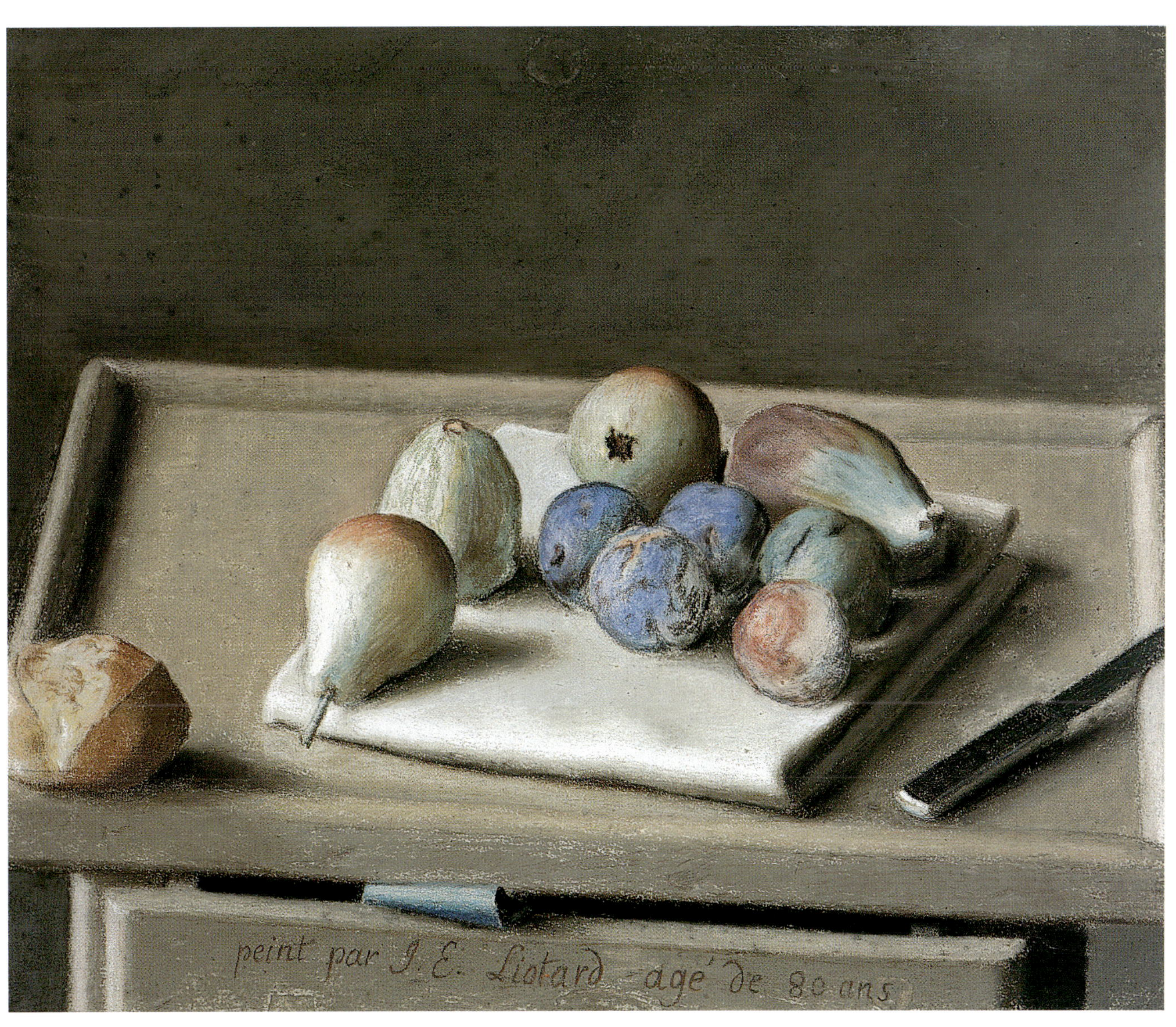

Still Life: Pears, Figs, Plums, Bread Roll, and Knife on a Table

1782
Signed and dated
Pastel on canvas
33 x 38 cm
Purchase, 1897
Inv. 1897–10

Kept in the artist's personal collection, this still life could
be one of the two inherited by his daughter, Marie-Jeanne
de Bassompierre (Geneva) in 1790. It entered the collection
of Charles de Lor (Geneva) in 1886.

31. Faré 1962, p. 172. "Of all the painters of still lifes in the eighteenth century, Liotard is the most restrained. Beside him, Chardin almost seems conventional to us. Liotard surpasses all the artists of his time in terms of the preoccupation with sculptural qualities with which, a century later, the name of Cézanne is associated."

32. Trivas 1936, p. 309. "In all the art of the eighteenth century, we find nothing comparable; even Chardin is more declamatory in his still lifes than the provincial Liotard. The modesty of the devices he employs, the simplicity of the arrangement, and the sincerity of his expression remind us of the still lifes of another provincial who lived one hundred years later: Paul Cézanne."

33. Roethlisberger 1985, p. 117.

34. Cited in Trivas 1936, p. 308. "For some time now he has been painting four pictures of fruit that really are a masterpiece. [...] They are admired by everyone. We are extremely glad about this because it will make him give up printmaking, which was very harmful for his eyes, very expensive to make and not at all profitable."

35. Loche and Roethlisberger 1978, no. 351.

36. Louise Lippincott, "Liotard's 'China Painting,'" in *The J. Paul Getty Museum Journal*, 13, 1985, pp. 121–30.

37. Roethlisberger 1985, pp. 119–20.

38. Loche and Roethlisberger 1978, no. 365.

39. Ibid., no. 363.

40. Cited after Michel and Fabrice Faré, *La vie silencieuse en France. La nature morte au XVIIIe siècle*, Fribourg 1976, p. 208. "[...] One of the two colors was very useful for a daffodil and the speckles on a lily that I painted in a picture showing the daffodil and some jasmine blossom in a glass of water placed on a pinewood board. There is a pansy on the edge of it. Roux was delighted with it, particularly with the lily, the water glass and the pansy."

and simplicity in terms of form and composition. Michel Faré writes in his book on the still-life genre in France: "De tous les peintres de nature morte du XVIIIe siècle, Liotard est le plus sobre. Chardin, à ses côtés, nous paraît presque conventionnel. Il dépasse tous les peintres de son temps par des préoccupations plastiques auxquelles, un siècle plus tard, le nom de Cézanne est associé."[31] Full of admiration, Numa S. Trivas, the first to refer to the significance of this late work by the Genevan artist, wrote: "Dans tout l'art du XVIIIe siècle nous ne trouvons rien de pareil; Chardin même est plus déclamatoire dans ses natures mortes que ce provincial de Liotard. La modestie de ses moyens, la simplicité de l'arrangement et la sincérité de l'expression nous font penser aux natures mortes d'un autre provincial, qui vécut cent ans plus tard: Paul Cézanne."[32]

For Marcel Roethlisberger, these works remain ambivalent: "In part, one has the impression that it was simply beyond the artist's range to invent more complex images; in part one feels that his great age—which he spells out in at least three signatures ('peint par J.-E. Liotard agé de 80 ans')—accounts for some apparent awkwardnesses of execution and design, such as the irregular perspective of the tables; and in part, one senses in these unparalleled images, which are so much *sui generis*, the wisdom and the serenity of an aged master who expresses himself with a greater freedom and candor than ever before."[33]

It is by all means possible that Liotard's great age slightly impaired his technical aptitude. His daughter Marie-Thérèse also mentions her father's work and physical state in a letter addressed to her elder brother, dated September 10, 1782: "Il fait depuis quelque temps 4 tableaux de fruits qui sont en vérité un chef-d'œuvre [...]. Ils sont admirés de tout le monde. Nous sommes extrêmement contents de cela parce que ça lui a fait quitter la gravure qui lui faisait beaucoup de mal aux yeux, beaucoup de dépence et point de profit."[34] The strain on his eyes to which Marie-Thérèse refers presupposes that the artist's eyesight had somewhat deteriorated; although this is apparent in some works, it in no way detracts from their quality. As the letter from Liotard's daughter shows, they were admired, and certainly not dismissed as the weak and bizarre products of an aging, frail artist. It is also astonishing that Marie-Thérèse should refer to the four still lifes as "un chef-d'œuvre," implying that she considers them to be a single entity.

The extraordinary *Still Life with Tea Service* in the Getty Museum in Malibu[35] proves that Liotard had lost none of his technical skill. Liotard shows the fine painted Chinese porcelain service on a tray, arranging the pieces in a manner that is very unusual for his time. Once again, the pronounced upward slant is conspicuous, but also the way in which the individual pieces of the service and the spoons are presented. The objects seem to be arranged as if someone has helpfully, though rather hastily, put them aside to be tidied away into the kitchen. The remains of a cake are scattered on the tray, and some of the cups are turned upside down beside the spoons on their saucers, or in a bowl. The artist is interested in the apparently haphazard, emphasizing the careless treatment of these fragile objects. This depiction focuses on the everyday, unpretentious aspects of the scene as well as simultaneously referring to the transience of its beauty in this precarious state. The artist's withdrawal into the privacy of his household and his love of the objects that surround him and become the subject of his works are manifest. As Louise Lippincott has rightly observed, the principles of Liotard's *Traité* are most accurately applied in the painterly execution of the work.[36] Yet the structure of the composition also reveals Liotard's admiration for the still-life painting of the seventeenth century, which Roethlisberger proves with reference to a still life by Pieter van Roestraeten.[37]

However, the still life of Chinese porcelain in the Getty Museum also heralds a more radical development: the motifs become even more sparse, barer, and plainer. A fine example of this is the still life of four peaches on an ordinary plate, placed on a tabletop.[38] It is dated 1786 by the artist—the year he settled in the Vaudois village of Begnins with his daughter Marie-Jeanne and his son-in-law, the printer François de Bassompierre. The floral still life entitled *The Lily*,[39] signed "J.-E. Liotard à 84 ans," was painted the same year. In a letter to his son, dated June 21, 1786, the artist reports: "[...] l'une des deux couleurs m'a très bien servi pour une fleur jonquille et pour les mouchets d'une fleur de lis que j'ay peinte dans un tableau où il y a cette fleur Jonquille et du Jasmin dans un verre d'eau posé sur une planche de sapin. Sur le bord est une pensée. Roux en a été enchanté, surtout du lis, du verre d'eau et de la pensée."[40]

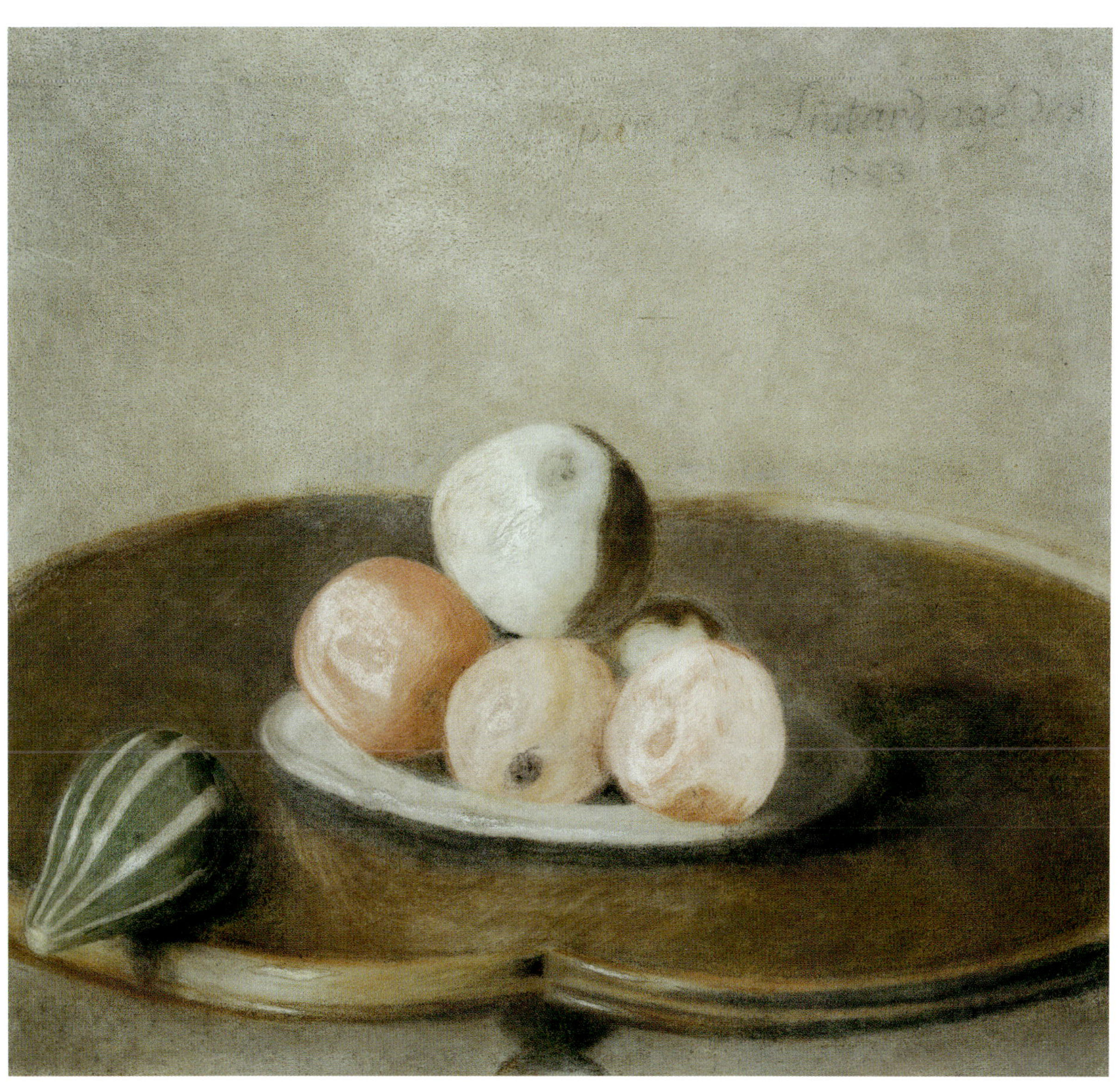

Still Life: Apples and Colocynth

1783
Signed and dated
Pastel on parchment
33 x 37 cm
Purchase, 1897
Inv. 1897–9

The pendant to *Still Life: Peaches and a Small Melon* (Oskar Reinhart Museum at Winterthur), this pastel was kept in the artist's collection and entered the collection of Charles de Lor (Geneva) in 1886.

A lily, an as yet unopened daffodil, and jasmine blooms are arranged in a simple water glass standing on a grained pinewood board; a pansy bloom lies on the board. This work is one of a series of four floral still lifes[41] of which two no longer survive. The fourth, a similar composition, depicts a water glass, containing one rose in bloom and one rosebud, a poppy and a blue cornflower, on a wooden board.[42] The leaves of the four flowers create a naturalistic pattern in the water, calling to mind the inscription of a seventeenth-century engraving: "Flos speculum vitae modo vernat et interit aura" (The flower mirrors life; although it is still in bloom, it fades away like a breath of air).[43]

In these two late still lifes, the subject is rendered with the greatest possible simplicity. No décor is needed to aggrandize it. The entire spectrum of the picture consists of a wooden board, flowers in a glass, and an indeterminate, *impasto* background. Here, the "imitatio sapiens"—the wise imitation of nature—is authentic, and expresses the artist's own immediate experience. For the painter, mimesis, the pure imitation of nature, is sufficient; he condenses his subject, which he finds in the immediate surroundings of his own garden, to the extreme. Liotard invents for himself a new visual world; this can also be interpreted as the artist coming to terms with his own mortality, of which—at his great age—he is constantly aware.

Liotard's late portraits are also characterized by a similar notion, which is expressed very strikingly in the (possibly) unfinished portrait of the Marseilles ship owner Rodolphe Coteau, dated 1788.[44] The pastel is the artist's last dated work, and bears witness not only to great human depth and serenity, but also—despite some weaknesses in terms of form—to a brilliant handling of both painterly technique and draftsmanship.

A high-point of Liotard's late work is the portrait of his daughter Marie-Jeanne de Bassompierre (p. 43).[45] The artist portrays her in a delicate blue Louis XVI dress, richly decorated with lace and ribbons. A blue ribbon ornamented with a carnation and a rose is wound around her wig. In graceful, elegant pose, a gentle, alert gaze, and a pretty smile on her face, she presents a plate of peaches in her right hand. Liotard again takes up the theme of the portrait with still life. He admires his daughter's youthful beauty; there is something fragile about her appearance, almost as if he were afraid of losing her. The background of the picture is divided into simple planes representing indeterminate architectural elements. The question arises as to whether the artist is consciously working with the "non-finito" technique to contrast with his daughter's face, which is both perfect and complete.

Most of Liotard's late still lifes and portraits remained in his family. The artist could not—or would not—sell them. Perhaps they are too personal; they certainly did not reflect the prevailing taste of the time. All these works express an idiosyncratic, very personal artistic credo. In terms of their rigid formal expression, they are far ahead of the eighteenth century, and evince a spirit of astonishing modernity. Liotard, the artist celebrated at the courts of the eighteenth century, who was to live almost a century, reorients himself as an old man, leaving behind him the courtly sophistication of his earlier work and turning toward new visual worlds and subjects.

Most of these works went unnoticed by contemporary art critics. They owe their rediscovery to art historians of the twentieth century, as well as to outstanding collectors such as Jacques and Grégoire Salmanowitz, who were unable to resist these fascinating creations.

N.B. This article was first published in German by the Institut suisse pour l'étude de l'art in 2001.

41. Loche and Roethlisberger 1978, nos. 361–64.
42. Ibid., no. 364.
43. On a print after a painting by Jakob Kempener, which has survived only in the form of an engraving. See *Stilleben in Europa*, ex. cat., Westfälisches Landesmuseum, Münster 1979–80; Kunsthalle Baden-Baden 1980, p. 322.
44. Loche and Roethlisberger 1978, no. 368.
45. Ibid., no. 333. Thanks to the generous bequest of Baron Edmond de Rothschild, the pastel has belonged to Geneva's Musées d'Art et d'Histoire since 1998.

Works in the Exhibition

Dimensions are in centimeters, followed in parentheses by inches; height precedes width.

1. *Jean-Michel Liotard, the Painter's Twin Brother (1702–1796)*, c. 1718–20
Brush and watercolor, Chinese ink, and red chalk heightened with white gouache on paper glued to a board
23 x 16.5 (9 1/16 x 6 1/2)
Musées d'Art et d'Histoire, Cabinet des Dessins

2. *Double Portrait of Prince Henry Benedict Marie Clement Stuart (1725–1807) and Prince Charles Edward Stuart (Bonnie Prince Charlie, 1720–1788)*, 1738
Watercolor and gouache on ivory
5.2 x 7.3 (2 1/16 x 2 7/8)
Private collection

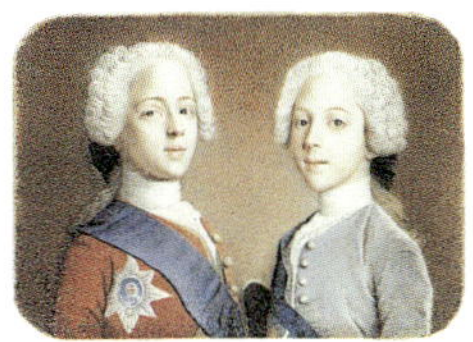

3. *Frankish Woman from Pera Followed by a Little Girl*, 1738–42
Red and black chalk on paper
22.9 x 16.9 (9 x 6 5/8)
Musées d'Art et d'Histoire, Cabinet des Dessins

4. *Greek Dancer*, 1738–42
Red and black chalk on vellum
7.6 x 5.3 (3 x 2 15/16)
Private collection

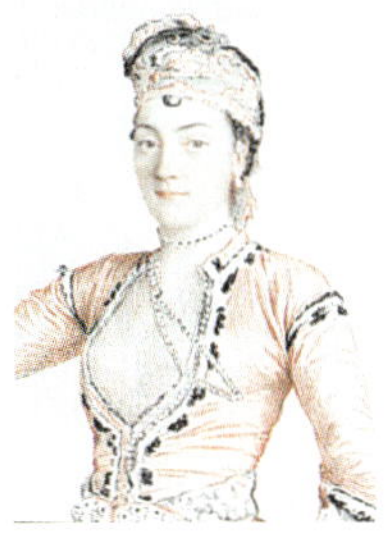

5. *Turkish Woman with a Tambourine*, 1738–43
Pastel, gouache and red chalk on off-white laid paper, adhered to a wooden strainer
61.6 x 47 (24 1/4 x 18 1/2)
Private collection

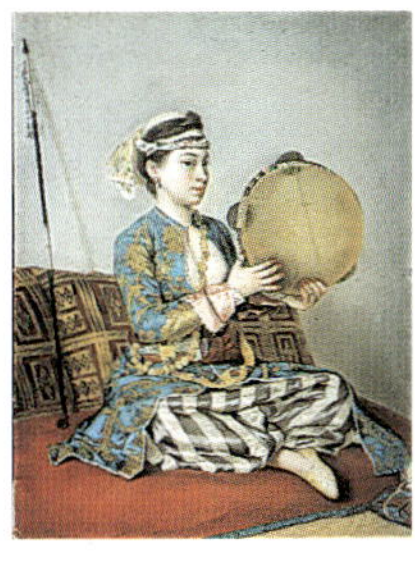

6. *Woman with a Tambourine Dressed in Turkish Costume*, 1738–43
Oil on canvas
63.5 x 48.5 (25 x 19 15/16)
Musées d'Art et d'Histoire, Beaux-Arts Department

7. *The Divan. Liotard's Bedroom in Constantinople*, c. 1742
Red chalk and graphite pencil on paper
18.6 x 22.8 (7 5/16 x 9)
Musées d'Art et d'Histoire, Cabinet des Dessins

8. *Gentleman in a Fur-lined Robe at the Court of Jassy*, 1742–43
Red chalk, graphite pencil, and black chalk on paper
22.9 x 17.8 (9 x 7)
Musées d'Art et d'Histoire, Cabinet des Dessins

9. *Presumed Portrait of Maria Theresa of Austria in Turkish Costume (1717–1780)*, 1743–45
Watercolor and gouache on vellum
7.3 x 5.4 (2 7/8 x 2 1/8)
Musée de l'Horlogerie et de l'Émaillerie

10. *Mademoiselle Lavergne, the Lovely Reader, the Artist's Niece*, 1746
Pastel
37.5 x 30.5 (14 3/4 x 12)
Private collection

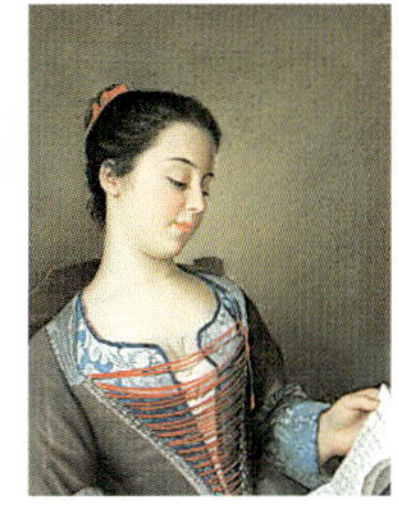

11. *Liotard with a Beard*, 1749
Pastel on brown paper with two borders added on the right and left sides
68.5 x 56.5 (27 x 22 1/4)
Private collection

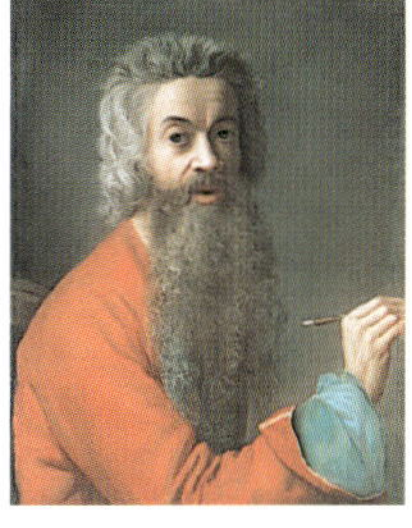

12. *Jean-Jacques Cottin de La Thuilerie*, 1757
Black chalk heightened with white chalk on blue paper, heightened on the verso
71.8 x 48.8
(28 1/4 x 19 1/4)
Musées d'Art et d'Histoire, Cabinet des Dessins

13. *Shepherdess Spinning*, c. 1757–60
Red chalk and graphite pencil on paper, heightened with red chalk on the verso
17.6 x 18
(6 15/16 x 7 1/16)
Musées d'Art et d'Histoire, Cabinet des Dessins

14. *Jean-Étienne Liotard (1758–1822), the Artist's Eldest Son, at Twenty-Two Months*, 1760
Red and black chalk, and graphite pencil on paper
23.5 x 17.1 (9 1/4 x 6 3/4)
Musées d'Art et d'Histoire, Cabinet des Dessins

15. *Madame Charles Bonnet (1728–1796), née Jeanne-Marie De la Rive-Franconis*, c. 1760
Watercolor on vellum
5.9 x 5.4 (2 5/16 x 2 1/8)
Musée de l'Horlogerie et de l'Émaillerie

16. *Ami Rilliet-Chapeaurouge (1730–1796)*, c. 1760
Watercolor on vellum
6.23 x 4.8 (2 7/16 x 1 7/8)
Musée de l'Horlogerie et de l'Émaillerie

17. *Madame Alexandrine Lullin-Fatio (1659–1762), Widow of the Syndic Pierre Lullin, at the Age of a Hundred and Two*, 1762
Black and red chalk with stumping on paper, heightened on the verso
21.5 x 17.2
(8 7/16 x 6 3/4)
Musées d'Art et d'Histoire, Cabinet des Dessins

18. *The Archduchess Maria Anna of Austria (1738–1789)*, 1762
Black and red chalk, graphite pencil, watercolor, white gouache glaze, and red chalk wash on thin paper, heightened with color on the verso
32 x 24 (12 5/8 x 9 7/16)
Musées d'Art et d'Histoire, Cabinet des Dessins

19. *The Archduchess Maria Christina of Austria (1742–1798)*, 1762
Black and red chalk, graphite pencil, and watercolor glaze on thin white paper, heightened with color on the verso
32 x 26 (12 5/8 x 10 1/4)
Musées d'Art et d'Histoire, Cabinet des Dessins

20. *The Archduchess Maria Elisabeth of Austria (1743–1808)*, 1762
Black and red chalk, graphite pencil, watercolor, and watercolor glaze on thin paper, heightened with color on the verso
32.1 x 24.6
(12 5/8 x 9 11/16)
Musées d'Art et d'Histoire, Cabinet des Dessins

21. *The Archduchess Maria Amalia of Austria (1746–1804)*, 1762
Red and black chalk, graphite pencil, and watercolor on thin paper, heightened with color on the verso
31.8 x 25.7
(12 1/2 x 10 1/8)
Musées d'Art et d'Histoire, Cabinet des Dessins

22. *The Archduke Peter Leopold of Austria, Future Emperor Leopold II (1747–1792)*, 1762
Red and black chalk, graphite pencil, and watercolor on thin paper, heightened with color on the verso
32 x 26.5
(12 5/8 x 10 7/16)
Musées d'Art et d'Histoire, Cabinet des Dessins

23. *The Archduchess Johanna Gabriele of Austria (1750–1762)*, 1762
Red and black chalk, graphite pencil, and watercolor glaze on thin paper, heightened with color on the verso
32.3 x 24.8
(12 3/4 x 9 3/4)
Musées d'Art et d'Histoire, Cabinet des Dessins

24. *The Archduchess Maria Josepha of Austria (1751–1767)*, 1762
Red and black chalk, graphite pencil, and watercolor glaze on thin paper, heightened with color on the verso
32.3 x 24.8
(12 3/4 x 9 3/4)
Musées d'Art et d'Histoire, Cabinet des Dessins

25. *The Archduchess Maria Karolina of Austria (1752–1814)*, 1762
Red and black chalk, stumping, watercolor, and pastel on thin paper, heightened with color on the verso
32 x 24.5 (12 5/8 x 9 5/8)
Musées d'Art et d'Histoire, Cabinet des Dessins

26. *The Archduke Ferdinand Karl Anton of Austria (1754–1806)*, 1762
Black and red chalk, graphite pencil, and gray glaze on paper, heightened with color on the verso
32.3 x 24.7
(12 3/4 x 9 3/4)
Musées d'Art et d'Histoire, Cabinet des Dessins

27. *The Archduchess Marie-Antoinette of Austria (1755–1793)*, 1762
Black chalk, graphite pencil, watercolor, and pastel on thin paper, heightened with color on the verso
31.1 x 24.9
(12 1/4 x 9 13/16)
Musées d'Art et d'Histoire, Cabinet des Dessins

28. *The Archduke Maximilian Franz of Austria (1756–1801)*, 1762
Black and red chalk, graphite pencil, pastel, and watercolor glaze on thin paper, heightened with color on the verso
32.2 x 24.8
(12 11/16 x 9 3/4)
Musées d'Art et d'Histoire, Cabinet des Dessins

29. *The Archduchess Maria Christina of Austria (1742–1798)*, c. 1762
Mezzotint with etching and engraving on satin
36 x 24.2 (14 3/16 x 9 1/2), image; 37.3 x 28.2 (14 11/16 x 11 1/8), plate
Musées d'Art et d'Histoire, Cabinet des Estampes

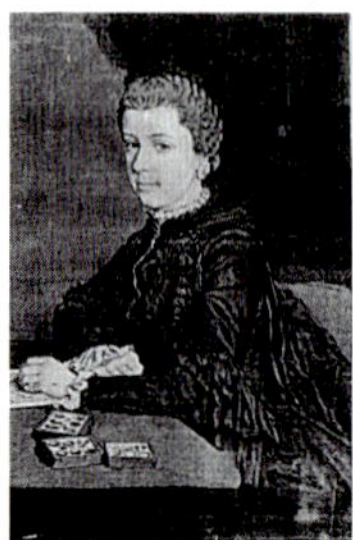

30. *Madame Jean-Étienne Liotard (1728–1782), the Artist's Wife, with Her Eldest Son, Jean-Étienne (1758–1822)*, c. 1762
Black and red chalk and watercolor on paper, heightened with color on the verso
24.5 x 19.6 (9 5/8 x 7 3/4)
Musées d'Art et d'Histoire, Cabinet des Dessins

31. *Portrait of Lord Mount Stuart (1744–1814), Future First Marquess of Bute*, 1763
Black and white chalk, heightened with red chalk on blue paper
90.7 x 48.1
(35 3/4 x 18 15/16)
Musées d'Art et d'Histoire, Cabinet des Dessins

32. *Portrait of a Man, known as "The Magistrate,"* c. 1763–65
Black and white chalk, heightened with red chalk on faded blue paper
56.5 x 44.5 (22 1/4 x 17 1/2)
Musées d'Art et d'Histoire, Cabinet des Dessins

33. *Self-Portrait, known as "in a Red Cap,"* 1765–67
Black chalk, graphite pencil, red chalk, red and blue pencil on vellum
12.1 x 10.2 (4 3/4 x 4)
Musées d'Art et d'Histoire, Cabinet des Dessins

34. *Portrait of the Doctor Gaspard Joly (born 1718)*, c. 1768–75
Black and white chalk, heightened with red chalk on blue paper, heightened on the verso
87.1 x 58.9
(34 1/4 x 23 3/16)
Musées d'Art et d'Histoire, Cabinet des Dessins

35. *Preparatory Drawing for the Portrait of Jean-Étienne Liotard, Eldest Son of the Artist, Buttering a Piece of Bread*, c. 1769–70
Red, black and white chalk on blue paper
46.7 x 57.2
(18 3/8 x 22 1/2)
Private collection

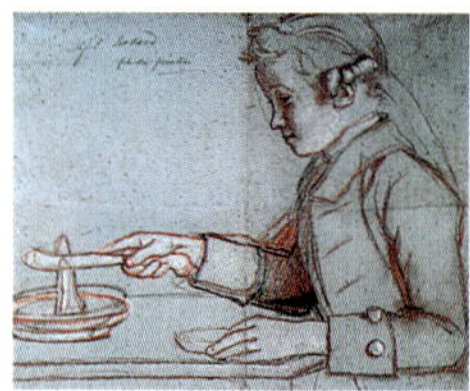

36. *Portrait of Jean-Étienne Liotard, Eldest Son of the Artist, Buttering a Piece of Bread*, c. 1770
Oil on canvas
63 x 70
(24 13/16 x 27 9/16)
Private collection

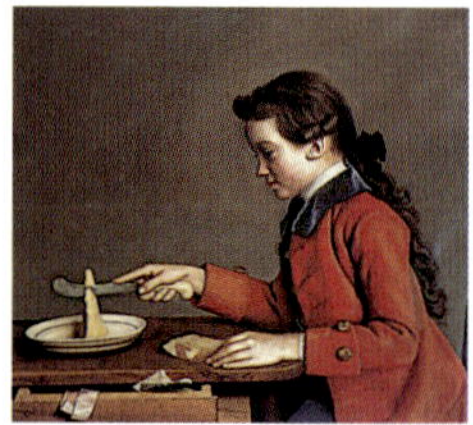

37. *Self-Portrait*, c. 1770
Black and white chalk heightened with red chalk on blue paper glued to cardboard
48.8 x 35.9
(19 1/4 x 14 1/8)
Musées d'Art et d'Histoire, Cabinet des Dessins

38. *Liotard Laughing*, c. 1770
Oil on canvas
84 x 74 (33 1/16 x 29 1/8)
Musées d'Art et d'Histoire, Beaux-Arts Department

39. *Self-Portrait in a Red Cap,*
c. 1770
Pastel on parchment
50 x 41
(19 11/16 x 16 1/8)
Private collection

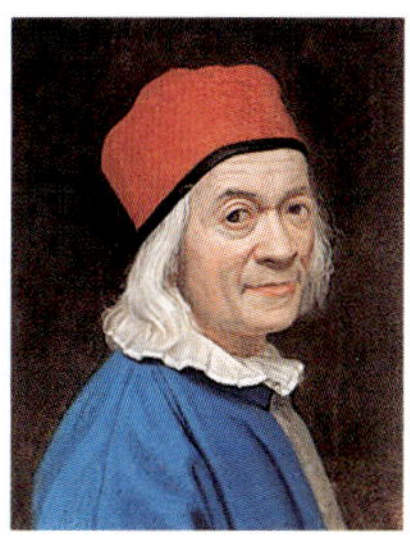

40. *Trompe l'œil,* 1771
Oil on silk transferred to
canvas
23.3 x 32.3
(9 3/8 x 12 3/4)
The Frick Collection,
Bequeathed by Lore
Heinemann in memory of
her husband, Dr. Rudolph
J. Heinemann, 1997

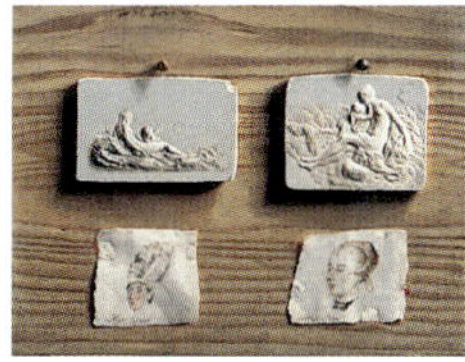

41. *Portrait of Frederika Luise
Wilhelmina of Orange-Nassau at
the Age of Two (1770–1819),*
1772
Black, red, and white chalk
with stumping on blue paper
heightened with color on the
verso
62.5 x 51.7
(24 5/8 x 20 3/8)
Musées d'Art et d'Histoire,
Cabinet des Dessins

42. *James Hamilton, Second Earl
of Clanbrassill,* 1774
Pastel on paper
77 x 59.5
(30 5/16 x 23 7/16)
Private collection

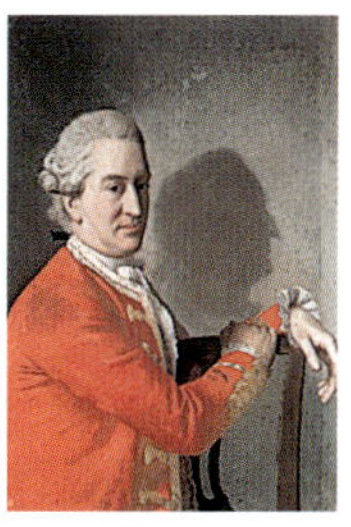

43. *Grace, Countess of
Clanbrassill,* 1774
Pastel on paper
77 x 59.5
(30 5/16 x 23 7/16)
Private collection

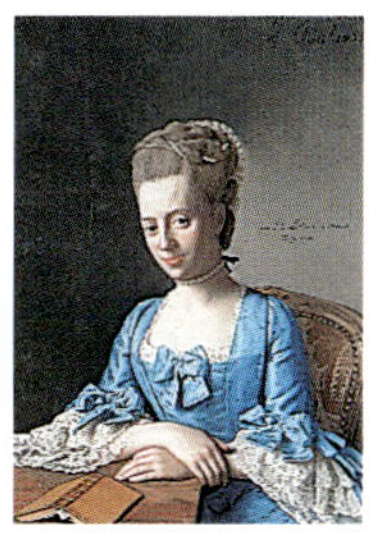

44. *Liotard's Two Daughters
(Marie-Jeanne and Marie-
Thérèse) Dancing the Allemande,*
1777
Black and white chalk on five
joined sheets of blue paper
65 x 44.5
(25 9/16 x 17 1/2)
Jan Krugier and Marie-Anne
Krugier-Poniatowski
Collection

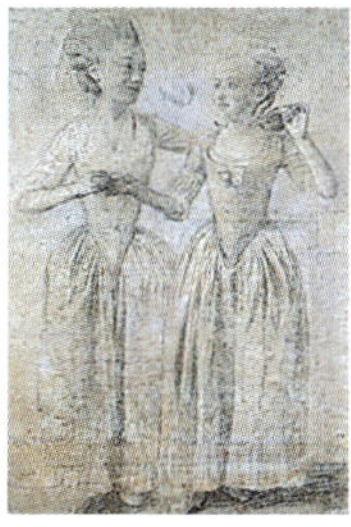

45. *Jean-Étienne Liotard
(1758–1822), the Artist's Eldest
Son, in Court Dress,* 1777
Red and black chalk
heightened with pastel on
canvas prepared with a white
ground
28.1 x 21.4
(11 1/16 x 8 7/16)
Musées d'Art et d'Histoire,
Cabinet des Dessins

46. *The Emperor Joseph II of
Austria (1741–1790),* 1778
Graphite pencil and red
chalk on paper
40 x 25.5 (15 3/4 x 10 3/8)
Musées d'Art et d'Histoire,
Cabinet des Dessins

47. *Marie-Thérèse Liotard
(1763–1793), the Artist's
Daughter, Seen in Left Profile,*
c. 1779
Graphite pencil, black and
red chalk heightened with
faint blue watercolor and
traces of white gouache on
yellowed white paper,
heightened with color on the
verso
24.2 x 18.9
(9 1/2 x 7 7/16)
Musées d'Art et d'Histoire,
Cabinet des Dessins

48. *Marie-Thérèse Liotard
(1763–1793), the Artist's
Daughter, Looking at Her Portrait
in Miniature,* c. 1779–80
Red chalk on paper squared
with graphite pencil
41.3 x 32.6
(16 1/4 x 12 13/16)
Musées d'Art et d'Histoire,
Cabinet des Dessins

49. *Marie-Thérèse Liotard, the
Artist's Daughter,* 1780
Mezzotint and burin
on paper
48.1 x 39.9
(18 15/16 x 15 3/4),
image; 60.6 x 45.8
(23 7/8 x 18), plate
Musées d'Art et d'Histoire,
Cabinet des Estampes

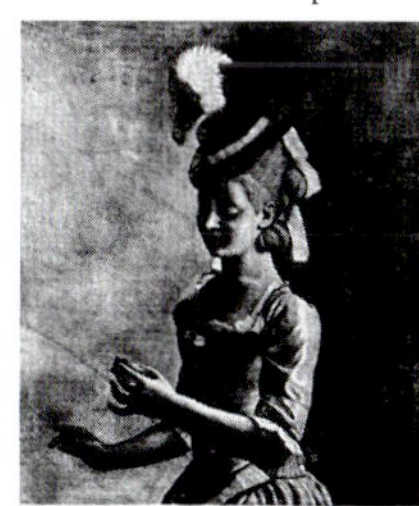

50. *Venus with a Beautiful
Bottom,* 1780
Mezzotint with etching on
paper
40.9 x 26.3
(16 1/8 x 10 3/8), image;
55.8 x 37.3
(22 x 14 11/16), plate
Musées d'Art et d'Histoire,
Cabinet des Estampes

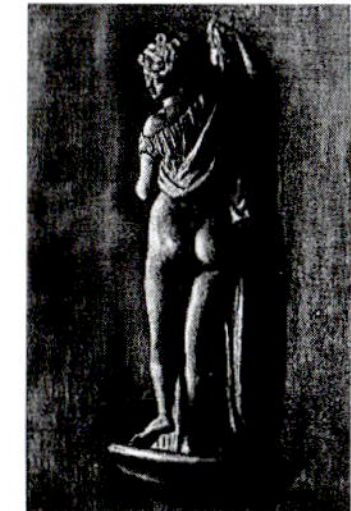

51. *Self-Portrait,* c. 1780
Engraving and roulette over
mezzotint on paper
43.4 x 37.8
(17 1/16 x 14 7/8), image;
61 x 46 (24 x 18 1/8), plate
Musées d'Art et d'Histoire,
Cabinet des Estampes

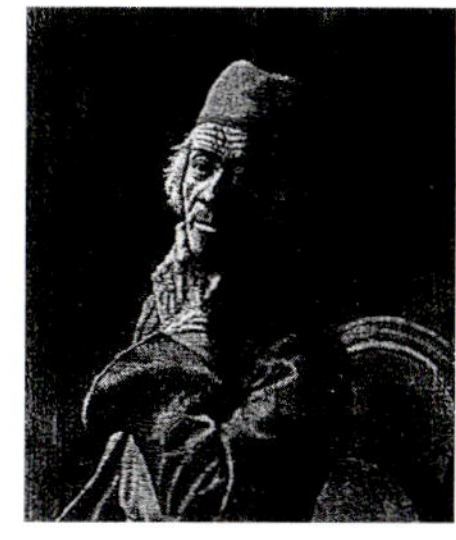

52. *Self-Portrait, known as
"with a New Beard,"* 1782
Graphite pencil and black
chalk, stumping and
heightened with white chalk
on faded blue paper
54 x 43 (21 1/4 x 16
15/16)
Musées d'Art et d'Histoire,
Cabinet des Dessins

N.B. The painting *Woman
with a Tambourine Dressed in
Turkish Costume* (no. 6) was
restored in 2006 by Victor
Lopes with the support
of The Frick Collection
of New York.

Biography

1702   December 22: birth in Geneva of the twins Jean-Étienne and Jean-Michel Liotard, sons of Antoine Liotard and Anne Sauvage, Protestants from Montélimar, in the province of Dauphiné (France), who had taken refuge in the Calvinist city after the revocation of the Edict of Nantes (1685). Jean-Étienne Liotard spends his childhood and adolescence in his native city. At nineteen, he serves an apprenticeship of four months in the workshop of the miniaturist Daniel Gardelle (1679–1753).

1723–35   The young Liotard makes his first trip to Paris where, for three years, he is the apprentice of Jean-Baptiste Massé (1687–1767), a portraitist, miniaturist, and engraver. By 1726 he is working independently, painting miniatures and portraits.

1735   After two short sojourns in Geneva he travels with the comte de Puisieux to Naples, where the count has been made ambassador of the French court.

1736–37   From Naples he travels to Rome and then Florence. In the Eternal City he meets William Ponsonby, the future Earl of Bessborough, who is taking the Grand Tour with friends, and is invited to travel with them to Asia Minor.

1738   From Naples, the painter sails to Constantinople via Capri, Messina, Syracuse, Malta, Milos, Paros, Chios, and Smyrna. At each port of call, Liotard draws his surroundings and paints some portraits (*Madame James Fremeaux*, circa 1738, p. 57).

1738–42   He stays in Constantinople, where he executes some portraits of the local English community (*Richard Pococke*, 1740, p. 55), diplomats, and some locals.

1742–43   Liotard is invited by Prince Mavrocordato of Moldavia to the court at Jassy (present-day Romania). He stays there ten months, painting members of the aristocracy (*Gentleman in a Fur-lined Robe at the Court of Jassy*, 1742–43, p. 62). He takes to wearing the costume of the local nobility, including the fur hat, and grows a beard, earning himself the sobriquet of "Turkish Painter." The alluring exoticism of this nickname contributes to his success in Europe.

1743–45   Liotard arrives in Vienna in September 1743 and stays there for two years. He enjoys an amicable relationship with Empress Maria Theresa and her husband, Francis Stephen of Lorraine, the future Holy Roman Emperor Francis I, and becomes painter to the Austrian court. Helped by Joseph Cameratta, he produces engravings from the drawings brought back from Turkey. These are available in Paris well before his return and make him famous in France while he is still away.

Liotard travels to Venice, where his brother Jean-Michel lives. He visits the pastelist Rosalba Carriera and Count Francesco Algarotti, whose portrait he paints. He stays in Milan and then Frankfurt, for the coronation of Emperor Francis I, whom he follows to Darmstadt. He becomes the drawing teacher of Princess Caroline of Hesse-Darmstadt, the future Margrave of Baden.   **1745**

Stays in Basel and Geneva, where the members of the Petit Conseil (Council of State) come to his home to pay their respects. He then travels to the home of the Lavergne branch of his family in Lyons, and continues on to Paris.   **1746-48**

In spite of the objections of the Royal Academy of Painting, which is shocked by his taste for realism, Liotard enjoys real success at the French court (*Madame Sophie de France*, 1750–53, p. 79) and among the bourgeoisie and intelligentsia of Paris. From 1751 to 1753 he exhibits at the Salon de l'Académie de Saint-Luc of which he is the "conseiller" with the title of "peintre ordinaire du Roy." Liotard's Parisian sojourn is interspersed with trips to Geneva and Lyons.   **1748–53**

In 1753 he leaves Paris for London, where he meets again with William Ponsonby, now the Earl of Bessborough. Through him he gains numerous patrons, including members of the family of the Prince of Wales.   **1753–55**

He travels to the United Provinces, stopping in Delft, home of his nephew Jean-Louis Maisonnet (*Jean-Louis Maisonnet, a Pastor in Delft*, 1755, p. 44), The Hague, and Amsterdam. In August 1756 he marries Marie Fargues, the daughter of a French merchant who emigrated to Amsterdam. He receives portrait commissions from merchants and aristocrats (pendant portraits of Pieter van Bleiswijk and his wife, 1756, pp. 88–89). During this sojourn, Liotard acquires works by seventeenth-century Dutch artists.   **1755–56**

After another stay in Paris, he settles in Geneva. Wealthy and famous, he is sought out by all the city's eminent figures (*Ami-Jean De la Rive*, 1758, p. 93; *Madame Alexandrine Lullin-Fatio*, 1762, p. 98) and by visiting foreigners (*Madame d'Épinay*, circa 1759, p. 97). He befriends François Tronchin, who commissions portraits of members of his family (*Madame François Tronchin, née Anne-Marie Fromaget, "Dressed for the Cold,"* 1758, p. 92).   **1757**

Liotard buys a house in rue Saint-Antoine, Aubigné, and another in rue des Chaudronniers. His son Jean-Étienne is born in November.   **1758**

The painter is visited by Count Reiffenstein. Birth of Marie-Jeanne Liotard.   **1761**

In spring he sets out for Vienna, where he executes portraits of the imperial couple (*Maria Theresa of Austria*, 1762, p. 67) and of eleven of their children (pp. 70–77).   **1762**

Marie-Thérèse Liotard is born in January. Maria Theresa of Austria agrees to be her godmother. In August, Liotard buys a country house in Confignon and moves there.   **1763**

Birth of a son, Jean-Daniel.   **1764**

Liotard passes through Turin.   **1766**

1767   Birth of his third daughter, Marie-Anne-Françoise.

1770   While in Lyons, Liotard produces a portrait of Jean-Jacques Rousseau, who refuses it.

1771–72   In early 1771 Liotard travels to Paris to paint the portrait of the dauphin and dauphine (Maria Theresa's daughter, Marie-Antoinette, p. 76). There he organizes an exhibition of his works and of his collection of paintings.

1771–73   Another sojourn in the United Provinces, where he finds that his fame has waned.

1773–74   During a stay in London, Liotard exhibits at the Royal Academy and enjoys a notable success. He organizes two sales of his works, the second of which (1774) is managed by Christie's. Liotard starts writing his treatise on painting.

October 1774   Back in Geneva, he buys the Buisson gardens at Plainpalais in order to build a house there.

1775   Visit from Charles Frederick, Margrave of Baden.

1777   In July, Emperor Joseph II pays a visit to Liotard under the name of Count Falkenstein, and in October Liotard sets off for Vienna with his eldest son. Stopping in Zurich, he meets the thinker and theologian Johann Caspar Lavater, author of the famous *Physiognomy*, and the poet Salomon Gessner. The painter and his son reach the Austrian capital in November.

June 1778   He returns to Geneva.

1779   With the number of commissions decreasing, Liotard devotes himself to printmaking and writing his treatise on painting. Short stay in Vevey.

1781   Geneva undergoes a period of political instability. For his safety, the artist travels to Lyons, where he lives from May to September, and where his *Traité des principes et des règles de la peinture* is printed and published. The imprint is nevertheless Geneva.

1782   Fearing arrest, Liotard takes refuge in Confignon. Death of his wife. He paints still lifes.

1784   Liotard is made a deputy member of the Council of Two Hundred. He sells his property in Confignon and is visited by Prince Heinrich of Prussia.

1786   Liotard moves in with his daughter Marie-Jeanne and son-in-law the printer François de Bassompierre at Begnins-sur-Nyon.

1787   Liotard stays in Nyon.

1788   He returns to Geneva.

1789   Liotard dies on June 12.

Select Bibliography

Buyssens, Danielle, *Peintures et pastels de l'ancienne école genevoise, XVIIe-début XIXe siècles*, Musées d'Art et d'Histoire, Geneva, 1988.

Eisler, William, *The Dassiers of Geneva: 18th Century European Medallists*, vol. II: *Dassier and Sons: an Artistic Enterprise in Geneva, Switzerland and Europe, 1733–1759*, Lausanne, 2005.

Fosca, François, *Les grands siècles de la peinture. Le XVIIIe siècle de Watteau à Tiepolo*, Geneva: Skira, 1952.

———, *La Vie, les voyages et les œuvres de Liotard, citoyen de Genève, dit le Peintre turc*, Lausanne/Paris: La Bibliothèque des Arts, 1956.

Humbert, Édouard, Alphonse Revilliod, and J. W. R. Tilanus, *La Vie et les œuvres de Jean-Étienne Liotard 1702–1789*, Amsterdam: C. M. Van Gogh and Geneva: Georg, 1897.

Leymarie, Jean, Geneviève Monnier, and Bernice Rose, *Le Dessin*, Geneva: Skira, 1979.

Liotard, Jean-Étienne, *Traité des principes et des règles de la peinture, par M. J.-É. Liotard, peintre, citoyen de Genève*, Geneva: 1781 and 1945: Pierre Cailler.

Loche, Renée, "Jean-Étienne Liotard dans les collections genevoises," *Le Livre du Richemond IV*, Geneva: Franco Maria Ricci, 1990.

Loche, Renée, and Marcel Roethlisberger, *L'opera completa di Jean-Étienne Liotard*, Milan: Rizzoli, 1978.

Menz, Cäsar, " 'Flos speculum vitae modo vernat et interit aura,' Zu Jean-Étienne Liotards Alterswerk," *Horizons Essays on Art and Art Research: 50 Years Swiss Institute for Art Research*, Zurich, Institut suisse pour l'étude de l'art, 2001, pp. 73–80.

Monnier, Geneviève, *Le Pastel*, Geneva: Skira, 1983.

Trivas, Numa S., "Jean-Étienne Liotard, peintures, pastels et dessins," manuscript, Archives of the Musées d'Art et d'Histoire, Geneva, 1936.

See also the articles published in *Genava*, the journal of the Musées d'Art et d'Histoire, Geneva.

Exhibitions

1773, London, *Catalogue of a Collection of Pictures to be Seen at Mr. Liotard's…*

1885, Amsterdam, *J.-É. Liotard, et Genève.*

1886, Geneva, Société des Arts, *Liotard.*

1925, Geneva, Musée d'Art et d'Histoire, "Catalogue des œuvres de Jean-Étienne Liotard exposées au Musée d'Art et d'Histoire," *Pages d'art*, pp. 103–120.

1944, Geneva, Musée Rath, *Le dessin. Rétrospective de l'école genevoise, de Liotard à Hodler.*

1948, Paris, Musée de l'Orangerie; and Geneva, Musées d'Art et d'Histoire, *Jean-Étienne Liotard (1702–1789), Johann Heinrich Füssli (1741–1825).*

1978, Zurich, Kunsthaus, *Jean-Étienne Liotard, Genf 1702–1789, Sammlung des Musées d'art et d'histoire, Genf.*

1984, Geneva, Musée Rath, and Dijon, Musée des Beaux-Arts, *Dessins genevois de Liotard à Hodler.*

1985, Utrecht, *Liotard in Nederland.*

1992, Paris, Musée du Louvre; and Geneva, Musées d'Art et d'Histoire, *Dessins de Liotard.*

2002, Geneva, Musées d'Art et d'Histoire, *Liotard dans les collections des Musées d'art et d'histoire.*

Index of Works from the Musées d'Art et d'Histoire of Geneva

Photograph Credits